Field Guide to

Wildflowers of Nebraska
and the Great Plains

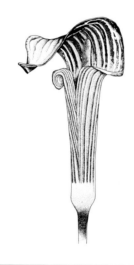

Jon Farrar

NEBRASKAland Magazine
Nebraska Game and Parks Commission
Lincoln, Nebraska

Library of Congress Cataloging-in-Publication
Farrar, Jon, 1947-
    Field guide to wildflowers of Nebraska and the Great Plains / Jon Farrar.
        p.   cm.
    Includes bibliographical references and index.
    ISBN 0-9625959-1-8
    ISBN 0-9625959-0-X (pbk.)
    1. Wild flowers—Nebraska—Identification. 2. Wild flowers—Great
Plains—Identification. 3. Wild flowers—Nebraska—Pictorial works.
4. Wild flowers—Great Plains—Pictorial works. I. Title.
QK172.F37 1990
582.13'0978—dc20   90-6524
                                                                  CIP

For additional copies of this book write:
Field Guide, NEBRASKAland Magazine, P.O. Box 30370, Lincoln, NE 68503.

Cover photograph: Prairie gentian *(Eustoma grandiflorum)*

Foreword

    This field guide is designed to help wildflower enthusiasts identify the common wildflowers encountered in Nebraska and across the Great Plains, and help them to learn a bit more about each in the process. It is a visual identification guide to some of the region's showiest and most interesting wildflowers as well as to some which are becoming increasingly uncommon or even rare. While "keying out" a plant is certainly the most reliable method of determining a flower's identity, it requires a depth of knowledge and mastery of technical terminology most of us lack. Instead, those of us without formal training in botany more often identify wildflowers by comparing the plant before us with illustrations in field guides, regardless of how the guides are organized.

    Accepting this premise, and following the lead of several other wildflower identification books, this field guide is organized by flower color. Within each color chapter, flowers are arranged roughly by their flowering time, from the earliest of spring to the last of autumn. Occasionally, this chronology has been compromised so that species which might be easily confused or are found in a particular region or habitat could be grouped together. Admittedly, this artificial system has drawbacks. While one color may be typical of a species, there is often considerable variation. Color is one of the least reliable identification characteristics for wildflowers. The only unequivocal organizational scheme is taxonomical; that is, ordering the species by family. But to find a plant quickly, taxonomical organization requires the user to know the name of the flower, or at least the family to which it belongs, or, to look at every photo and make a visual identification. In spite of their shortcomings, wildflower guides organized by color seem to be the easiest and quickest for most people to use. Because knowledge of a wildflower's distribution, preferred habitat, time of flowering and a description of the plant can aid or confirm identification, the photograph and description of each wildflower in this guide appear together.

    Technical language has been minimized. With the use of minimal technical terminology comes the need to generalize more than if precise botanical language were used. In some cases, this generalization may make it difficult to distinguish between similar species. Again, we have chosen to run that risk in order to produce a convenient guide for the person with little or no botanical training. Many wildflower enthusiasts will want to move on to more comprehensive and detailed reference texts. Some are listed as additional references on page 209.

Acknowledgements

This field guide represents the time, knowledge and cooperation of many people. While most of the photographs were taken on public land, we wish to acknowledge the hospitality of those private landowners whose grasslands and woodlands we visited. Timely telephone calls from several "wildflower spotters" were especially helpful in locating many of the species. Each wildflower illustrated was identified from pressed specimens and/or photographs by at least one of the following botanists: Mike Fritz and Curtis Twedt, Nebraska Game and Parks Commission; Hal Nagel, Kearney State College; Ronald Weedon, Chadron State College; and David Sutherland, University of Nebraska-Omaha. Additional identifications were provided by James Stubbendieck and Steve Rolfsmeier, University of Nebraska-Lincoln. The species descriptions were reviewed by David Sutherland, Mike Fritz, Curtis Twedt and Hal Nagel. In several cases, when pressed specimens were not available, identification from photographs was somewhat speculative. Any errors in identification or text, and potential loss of accuracy resulting from the decision to limit technical terminology, are solely the responsibility of the author.

Field Guide to Wildflowers of Nebraska and the Great Plains was designed by Duane Westerholt. Design production was by Dan Curran with assistance from Steve O'Hare. The text was edited by Lowell Johnson and Don Cunningham. Pen-and-ink illustrations are the work of Tim Reigert. Sonja Aerni and Jim Weitzel assisted in maintaining a semblance of order for the thousands of wildflower photographs taken during this project.

Permission to reproduce the vegetation map on page 8 was graciously extended by A.W. Küchler, University of Kansas. It was first published by the American Geographical Society in 1964.

Finally, I wish to acknowledge the support of the Nebraska Game and Parks Commission administration which made this publication possible: Rex Amack, Director; Jim MacAllister, Chief, Information and Education Division; and the Board of Commissioners.

Contents

Nebraska's Wildflower Regions

The Great Plains is an enormous area (see map on page 216) where grasses are the dominant vegetation. Even before settlers began to control wildfires—a natural element of grasslands which discouraged the establishment of trees—there were wooded areas on the Great Plains, though they were much less extensive than today. But it was the seemingly endless expanse of grassland which defined the region's character and dictated its animal life.

Nebraska is roughly in the center of the Great Plains region and the North American continent. Because of its location and size, it is a crossroads where floral associations meet and merge. Within its boundaries are found not only plants expected in mid-continental grasslands but also those venturing tentatively onto the Great Plains from the Rocky Mountains to the west or the deciduous forests to the east. Plants pay scant attention to man-made boundaries.

Even to the untrained eye it is soon evident that grasslands are not homogeneous environments. Different plant associations dominate in different regions of the Great Plains. A.W. Küchler, of the University of Kansas, recognized 11 major plant associations in Nebraska, eight of which are grasslands. Just as the characteristic species of grasses differ from one type of grassland to another, so, too, do the type of wildflowers. Each species evolved in an environment with a particular mix of soil types, moisture, exposure to sun and length of growing season.

While some wildflowers, particularly those not native to North America, seem to thrive in a variety of habitats, others are exacting in their requirements. To find these natives you must know where they live, and so it is necessary to know something of Nebraska's plant associations. The following descriptions and the accompanying map are based on **Potential Natural Vegetation of the Conterminous United States** by A.W. Küchler.

The western edge of the **eastern deciduous forest** reaches Nebraska's Missouri River Valley and the lower portions of its major tributaries. Its dominant species are broadleaf trees, including several species of hickory and oak, basswood, black walnut and, formerly, American elm. It is here, too, where eastern woodland flowers reach their westernmost distribution: showy orchis, large yellow lady's-slipper, May-apple, Virginia spring beauty, sweet cicely, bloodroot, Jack-in-the-pulpit, waterleaf and wild columbine. Here, the wildflower season is compressed, from late April into June, as they rush to complete their annual affairs before towering trees leaf out and shade the forest floor. By early summer, wildflowers have become few and far between. Public lands where this plant association can be found include Indian Cave State Park in Richardson and Nemaha counties, Fontenelle Forest in Sarpy County, and Ponca State Park in Dixon County. Platte River and Mahoney state parks on the lower Platte River also have some of the same wildflowers found in the Missouri Valley.

Northern floodplain forest extends west across Nebraska along the major river valleys and their tributaries. Once, rivers such as the central Platte were nearly treeless except on islands and peninsulas or in canyons protected from prairie fires. Today, most are at least partially wooded with willow, cottonwood, hackberry, ash, box elder and, formerly, American elm. Here, wildflowers such as American bellflower, which appreciate a bit of shade and protection from the wind, range westward from the Missouri Valley. These floodplains are the preferred sites for wildflowers which thrive on periodic disturbance caused by spring floods, a natural element of river ecology prior to the construction of impoundments. On the sandbars are gatherings of Alleghany monkey-flower and beggar-ticks, and in the rich, moist soils where cottonwoods merge with big bluestem and Indiangrass, New England aster, purple meadow rue and Joe-Pye weeds. Examples of this plant association can be found on many of the state's wildlife management areas along the Platte, Elkhorn and Loup rivers.

On the Pine Ridge escarpment in the northern Panhandle, the Wildcat Hills escarpment south of the North Platte River, and along the north canyon walls of the central Niobrara River is **eastern ponderosa forest**, dominated by ponderosa pine, southeasterly outliers of the same plant community found in the Black Hills of South Dakota. Here, northwestern wildflowers venture onto the plains—pasque flower, prairie buckbean and harebell. Public lands where this plant association can be found include Fort Robinson and Chadron state parks, Metcalf and Ponderosa wildlife management areas, and Nebraska National Forest lands between Chadron and Crawford.

These three plant associations, representing less than three percent of the state's total area, comprise Nebraska's indigenous woodlands. The remainder of the state was once the domain of grasses.

Before it was plowed and converted to cropland, the eastern quarter of Nebraska was **tallgrass prairie**, dominated by the tall, sod-forming grasses which grew head high and taller—big bluestem, switchgrass and Indiangrass, with little bluestem (a bunchgrass) on the higher and drier slopes. Less than three percent of Nebraska's original tallgrass prairie remains. Pristine remnants, though, still provide a showy procession of wildflowers through the growing season—the low-growing prairie violets and ground-plums of early spring, followed by wild indigos, milkweeds and silphiums of midsummer, and the early autumn rush of sunflowers and asters. Public lands where this plant association can be found include many of the wildlife management areas in southeastern Nebraska, and Rock Creek Station State Historical Park in Jefferson County. The tallgrass prairie association also is found in wet meadows of the Sandhills and along portions of river valleys in central Nebraska.

West of the tallgrass region, once covering much of central Nebraska, was a band of **mixed-grass prairie**, a broad transition zone between tallgrass prairie to the east and the Sandhills and shortgrass plains to the west. With declining precipitation and shallower soils than those which support tallgrass prairie, the vegetation of mixed-grass prairie is shorter and more open. Here, forbs (non-grass plants which die back to the ground each year, a category including most of our wildflowers) become a more conspicuous constituent of the grassland community. Today, much of this land is farmed, but pastureland is still abundant in areas with rolling terrain and moderate slopes. Unfortunately, most pastures are chronically overgrazed, encouraging the dominance of plants thriving on disturbance. Characteristic wildflowers of this plant association include purple poppy mallow, sensitive brier, Flodman's thistle, false sunflower, dotted gayfeather, white aster and prairie coneflower. High-quality mixed-grass prairie is difficult to find, but several wildlife management areas having at least some native mixed-grass prairie are Pressey in Custer County, Arcadia in Valley County, Sherman Reservoir in Sherman County, Red Willow Reservoir in Frontier County and Grove Lake in Antelope County.

Bluestem-grama prairie is a distinctive form of mixed-grass prairie found in the south half of the southern tier of counties in south-central Nebraska, extending south through central Kansas into Oklahoma. It is characterized by little bluestem, blue and side-oats gramas, and an abundance of showy wildflowers. Some of the association's representative wildflowers, such as Dakota vervain, alkali milk-vetch and purple locoweed, are found elsewhere in the state but seem particularly abundant on this grassland type. Others, species often closely associated with limestone outcrops or formations near the surface, such as Fremont's clematis, Fendler's aster and rock sandwort, are found in Nebraska only here. Willa Cather Memorial Prairie in Webster County is the only extensive tract of public land where this plant association can be found, although with a bit of searching for both landowners and grasslands, equally good sites can be found on private land. County roadsides are also worth searching.

In southwestern Nebraska and extending into northeastern Colorado, is **sandsage prairie**. Its dominant plant species are little bluestem, sand bluestem, sand sagebrush and hairy grama. Characteristic wildflowers are soapweed, woolly locoweed, prairie sunflower, bractless mentzelia and broom snakeweed. During the last two decades, much of this grassland has been converted to crop production under center-pivot irrigation. The plant composition

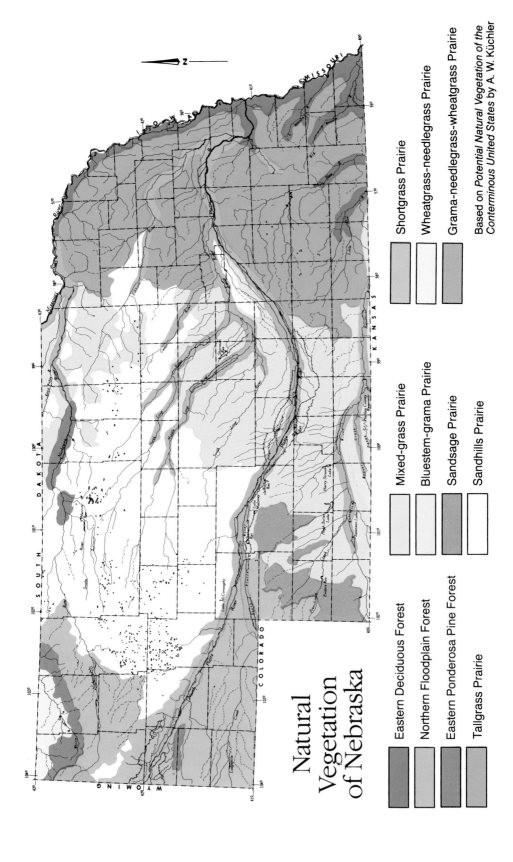

Natural Vegetation of Nebraska

Eastern Deciduous Forest

Northern Floodplain Forest

Eastern Ponderosa Pine Forest

Tallgrass Prairie

Mixed-grass Prairie

Bluestem-grama Prairie

Sandsage Prairie

Sandhills Prairie

Shortgrass Prairie

Wheatgrass-needlegrass Prairie

Grama-needlegrass-wheatgrass Prairie

Based on *Potential Natural Vegetation of the Conterminous United States* by A. W. Küchler

of remaining remnants has been drastically altered by heavy grazing, which increases the abundance of sand sagebrush at the expense of grasses and forbs, or by the use of herbicides, which spares the grasses but reduce or eliminate sand sagebrush and forbs. Finding sandsage prairie with the natural balance of sand sagebrush, grasses and forbs is difficult. Public lands where remnants of this plant association can be found include Enders Wildlife Management Area in Chase County and Rock Creek State Recreation Area in Dundy County.

Sandhills prairie, an association of plants essentially unique to Nebraska, extending only a short distance into South Dakota, covers some 19,000 square miles in north-central Nebraska. Most of it remains in pasture and so, of all grassland associations found in the state, it has fared the best. A tallgrass prairie community is found in the wet meadows and some river valleys, but the uplands are dominated by an open gathering of shorter grasses, forbs and small shrubs. Characteristic grasses include prairie sandreed, needle-and-thread grass, and big, sand, and little bluestems. Among the uncommon wildflowers are western red lily, prairie fringed orchis and Hayden's penstemon. More common representative wildflowers include gilia, silky prairie clover, hoary vetchling, wild begonia and hairy puccoon. Public lands where this plant association can be found include two divisions of the Nebraska National Forest, McKelvie in Cherry County and Bessey in Thomas County, and two national wildlife refuges, Valentine in Cherry County and Crescent Lake in Garden County.

Shortgrass prairie, covering most of Nebraska's Panhandle and extending south into the Texas Panhandle, is a nearly flat plain dissected by drainages. Its vegetation is characterized by buffalo grass, blue grama and other low-growing plants. Here, most of the showy wildflowers bloom in the spring, before the onset of the hot, dry summers. Representative wildflowers include standing milk-vetch, scarlet gaura, cutleaf ironplant, plains phlox, miner's candle, narrow beardtongue and plains prickly pear. Rock outcrops are particularly good sites to find such low-growing species as sandwort and the townsendias. Perhaps the best public lands for wildflowers in this region are Agate Fossil Beds National Monument in Sioux County, Buffalo Creek Wildlife Management Area in Banner County, and Scotts Bluff National Monument in Scotts Bluff County.

North of the Pine Ridge escarpment in northwest Nebraska is a band of **wheatgrass-needlegrass prairie**, the dominant plant association of the western Dakotas. Typical of northern Great Plains grasslands, it is dominated by cool-season grasses which initiate growth early, and complete their life cycles before the onset of summer. Dominant grasses include western wheatgrass, needle-and-thread grass, green needlegrass and blue grama. Here, as on shortgrass prairie, the showiest wildflowers bloom in the spring, and rocky outcrops and eroded banks are good sites to search for them. Representative wildflowers include sego and mountain lilies, several milk-vetches, leafy musineon, and penstemons not found farther east. Public lands where this plant association can be found include Oglala National Grasslands and Toadstool Park in northern Sioux County.

Along Nebraska's western border, south of the Pine Ridge, a relatively small area of **grama-needlegrass-wheatgrass prairie** enters the state, a plant association more widespread across Wyoming and Montana. It is similar to grasslands found north of the Pine Ridge, typically with rather short, open to fairly densely spaced grasses. Dominant grasses are western wheatgrass, blue grama and needle-and-thread grass. Many of the wildflowers found on the grasslands north of the Pine Ridge will also be found here: sandwort and townsendia on rock outcrops, narrow beardtongue, occasional lupines, plains phlox and miner's candle. There is no public land in this area, and few roads.

How to Use This Field Guide

Many wildflowers are distinctive. Others are more difficult to identify, and are beyond the scope of this guide. Because wildflowers are so colorful, it is easy to only *see* the flower, to not look beyond our first general impression. It is essential, though, if plants are to be identified, to train our eyes to look closely at details. The following steps are suggested to make an identification using this guide.

First, match the flower's color to one of the color chapters. Select the photo or photos most like the plant before you. If only one photo looks like the plant, compare the plant, point by point, with the description in the text to confirm your identification. If several photos look like the plant, narrow the options, detail by detail. Is that plant found in the region where you are? Does the site match the habitat where the plant usually grows? Is it flowering within the time period given in the text? If, at this point, you still have not narrowed the options to one species, compare the description of the plant to the plant before you. Consider the plant one part at a time. How tall is it? Does it branch? If so, where: low on the stem or near the top? How are the leaves arranged on the stem? What is the leaf shape and size? Are any parts of the plant covered with hairs or prickles, and if so, what parts? How are the flowers arranged on the plant? What is their size and shape? How many petals or petal-like structures does the flower have?

This procedure will usually make it possible to identify the wildflowers illustrated in this guide. There are, however, hundreds of other flowering plants found in our region, often several of which are closely related to those illustrated. In many of these cases, the guide will take you to the right family and often to a closely related species.

The species accounts are concisely written so that as many wildflowers as possible could be included, accompanied by photographs large enough to be useful for identification. The following explanations of how to interpret information given in the species accounts will make the guide easier to use and identifications more accurate.

Plant Names

Names are no more than abbreviations for a collection of information. The names death camass or *Zigadenus venenosus* are shorthand for: "a not-too-tall, grass-like plant with creamy-white flowers, growing from a bulb resembling that of a wild onion, blooming in June in grasslands in northwest Nebraska, which could kill livestock if they ate too much of it but they seldom do when the range is in good condition." Common names such as death camass are often colorful and easier for us to remember than the scientific names used by botanists. The difficulty with using common names, though, is that one wildflower may have many, and different species may share the same common name. Some have no common name at all.

In the mid-18th century, the Swedish botanist Linnaeus devised a system in which every living thing was given a two part Latin name. Latin, frequently borrowing from Greek, was chosen because it was a "dead," fixed language. The first word in a scientific name, the first letter of which is always capitalized, is that of the *genus,* a closely related group of plants. The second word is the *species,* the name applied to plants which are all alike except for individual variation. Usually a genus contains more than one species. The species name *canadense*, for example, tells us this plant is a specific *Desmodium*—not just any tickclover but Canada tickclover. Learning scientific names is intimidating, but provides much useful information about plant relationships. Common names for wildflowers vary from region to region and from one reference to another. Scientific names are infrequently changed. Often, only by comparing scientific names can you be sure a plant found in one region or reference book is the same as one found in another. Once mastered, the use of scientific names avoids the confusion accompanying the use of common names.

Scientific names, like common names, are often descriptive, at least if you are well versed in Latin. *Desmodium*, for example, is from a Greek word meaning "like a chain," a reference to the plant's jointed fruit pods. Names may also give an indication of where the plant occurs, as *canadense* implies that the plant was first collected and described from Canada, or they may be descriptive, such as *hirsuta*, meaning the plant is hairy. Other times, though, a name honors some noted botanist, such as the scientific name for spring beauty, *Claytonia virginica*, which was given to recognize John Clayton, an early American botanist. Genera (more than one genus) are organized into families which share broader characteristics than plants within a genus. These, too, are given in the text because they indicate relationships which will make identification easier.

For the most part, the common names used in this guide are from **Flora of the Great Plains**, published by University Press of Kansas in 1986. In a number of cases, though, the common names used here deviate from those in the **Flora**. In those cases we chose to use older common names which are widely accepted and more descriptive of the plant. When no common name was given in the **Flora**, or when several species shared the same common name, we also chose to use older names so that each wildflower in this guide has its own unique common name. For example, in the **Flora**, white dog's-tooth violet is the common name given for both *Erythronium albidum* and *Erythronium mesochoreum*. They are not violets, and dog's-tooth is a reference to a European member of the genus whose root is said to resemble a dog's tooth, which the North American plants do not. Instead, we chose to use the older common name white fawn lily for *Erythronium albidum*, a white-flowered woodland lily with leaves dappled like a fawn, and the common name prairie fawn lily for the very similar species *Erythronium mesochoreum*, a prairie wildflower. In every case, though, deviations from names used in the **Flora** are made only to ensure that each plant has a distinctive, and when possible a descriptive, common name.

Flowering Period

The flowering dates given in the text should not be interpreted to mean that wildflower species will never be found in blossom earlier or later. Many factors affect the time a particular plant blooms—where within its range the plant is found, the site where it is growing, moisture availability and seasonal weather fluctuations, just to name a few. A plant which is mowed or browsed may flower long after others of its kind.

Wildflowers found statewide, such as ground-plum, may bloom two to four weeks earlier in southeast Nebraska than in the northwest The time of flowering for a plant with a wide distribution across the Great Plains may vary even more. There are wildflower species, though, which bloom in Nebraska's far northwest just as early as the first spring wildflowers in the extreme southeast. Pasque flower is flowering in the Pine Ridge as early as Virginia spring beauty along the Missouri River. As a general rule, the peak of flowering for a species will fall in the first half of the range given in the text, with late-flowering individuals stringing out for some time thereafter.

Distribution

In the species accounts, a plant's distribution is given first for Nebraska, second for the Great Plains. The Great Plains distribution often provides an indication of where in Nebraska a wildflower will most likely be found. For example, a species with a range principally to the north is most likely common in northern Nebraska. The distribution listed implies only that the flower may be found in appropriate habitat within the area. It does not imply that it will never be found outside the area described, nor that it will be found everywhere within the area.

Terms such as eastern third or western half, and regional terms such as Panhandle, Pine Ridge, Missouri Valley and Sandhills, are self-explanatory. It should be noted, though, that the western portion of the Sandhills extends into the Panhandle with outliers into the northeast. "Central," in a general sense, denotes the middle of the state. Other regional terms, such as northeast or southwest, are somewhat more ambiguous and overlap.

Description

For the most part, technical botanical language has been avoided. However, if avoiding technical terms required repeated, lengthy and awkward descriptions, we chose to use the precise botanical term. Those terms are defined in the glossary and illustrated at the end of the guide. The roots of annual wildflowers are not described in the species accounts unless they are unusual. Unless otherwise noted, all annual plants may be assumed to have fibrous root systems.

There is infinite variation in the leaf shape of plants and even variation within a species and on an individual plant. Those illustrated in the back of this guide represent some common, generalized shapes found on wildflowers. Occasionally, a leaf shape falls somewhere between two common shapes. Oblong-lanceolate, for example, describes a leaf shape somewhat between oblong and lanceolate. The term *stalkless*, as used in this guide, indicates that the leaf lacks a stem, or to use the precise botanical term, a petiole.

Wildflowers are occasionally encountered which to the layman have "leaves" that technically are *leaflets*. Examples of such *compound leaves* are found in the milk-vetches, lead plant, showy partridge pea and the lupines. Such leaf arrangements are always noted in the species accounts. If the term leaflet does not appear in the text, what looks like a leaf is technically a leaf.

Unless otherwise noted, it should be assumed the plant's herbage is not pubescent or hairy, or at least not noticeably so. Botanists employ dozens of terms to describe the degree or type of hairiness. The distinctions are often minute, require at least a hand lens to see, and are somewhat subjective. In this guide, such distinctions are not made. Pubescent is used in its most general sense, meaning "covered with fine, soft hairs." Bristly or stiff hairs are generally noted. The pubescence of some plants or plant parts described in the text may not be evident without magnification but is noted as it is an important identification feature.

Important identification characteristics appear in *italics*.

Flower Color

Color terminology is highly subjective and often imprecise. The color classification and the color terms used in this field guide are, for the most part, based on spectrum colors; the measurable colors produced when light is separated by passing through a prism. While spectrum colors are constant, they are a continuum with no hard lines separating one from another.

Some color terms are readily understood. Green, yellow and red need no further explanation. Colors falling in the violet range are the most troublesome. Violet covers a range of hues between red and blue. In this guide we have drawn an imaginary line midway between the spectrum colors red and blue, through the middle of the violet range. On one side of that line are the blue-violet to blue flowers, on the other side the pink to red-violet flowers. Pink is a pale or diluted red-violet. To the human eye, red is a "warm color," and blue is a "cool color." A violet flower which is reddish in hue, a "warm violet," will be in the pink to red-violet chapter, a flower bluish in hue, a "cool violet," will be in the blue-violet to blue chapter. With a bit of experience, the value of using a system for organizing color which avoids subjective color names will become increasingly evident and useful. Occasionally, though, where it seems useful, commonly understood color terms, such as lavender, are used.

Most wildflower species (particularly those with red, orange, violet or blue flowers) have a range of color varying with soil chemistry, where they are found within their range, and genetics. Some may show marked variation. Shell-leaf penstemon is typically pink to lavender, but crimson, blue-violet and even white blossomed plants are not uncommon. Most species were placed in the chapter we felt was, on the average, the most typical color for that flower, even if the particular flower illustrated deviated from that color. There are several instances, however, where a violet-colored flower might well have been placed in a different violet chapter, but was grouped with others to which it is closely related or with which it might be confused. In those cases it seemed more important to aid the user of the guide in making an identification than to quibble over where that flower color fell on the violet spectrum range. The choice between blue-violet and red-violet was often difficult.

If you do not find a photo which matches the plant before you, look in the next most likely color chapter. This is particularly true for flowers in the violet range and those which are basically white with only a slight color tint. The flowers of white-eyed grass, for example, may have a light tint of pink or blue. An individual flower could have justifiably been placed in either the white, pink or blue chapters. Additionally, some blossoms undergo dramatic color changes as they mature. Some evening primroses begin as pure white but quickly age to pink.

Additionally, the "warmth" of light falling on a flower can shift its color from one range to another. For example, the blossom of blue lobelia appears blue-violet or even blue on overcast days or in midday light, but red-violet (as in the photo on page 197) early and late on sunny days. Most photographs reproduced in this guide were taken in the warm light of early morning or late in the day and so may appear warmer in tone than if they had been photographed at midday. Also, the type of film used to make the photograph, and the printing process used to reproduce photographs can significantly affect the color.

Applying one name to the color of a flower blossom that is actually a blending of colors, colors which may vary from plant to plant, will always be imperfect, it can be no more than a generalization, an attempt to make the complex simple.

General Information

Notes about the edibility or medicinal uses of plants are provided only as points of interest. They should not be considered a guide to edible wild plants or an endorsement of their use. Numerous plants found on the Great Plains are toxic, and some could be readily confused with edible species. But just because a plant is potentially poisonous does not mean it should be feared or eradicated. They are rightful constituents of the plant community. Livestock avoid these plants when more desirable forage is available, and most must be consumed in significant quantities to cause illness or death.

Historically, the medicinal use of plants was not conducted casually, but rather represented the accumulation of hundreds of years of first-hand experience. Even so, the value of most of these medicinal applications is suspect. Often, potentially toxic plants were used medicinally, but in minute quantities. Many edible or medicinal plants are now considered uncommon or even rare and should not be sacrificed out of curiosity. The best way to sample edible wild plants is with someone experienced in plant lore and knowledgeable about identification and preparation. Many of the edible species can be grown in the home garden for kitchen use, where they are attractive as well as edible, without diminishing the native supply. This also precludes the possibility of collecting plants in the wild which may have been recently treated with pesticides.

Conservation of Wildflowers

Half a century ago, ranch children in the northern Sandhills could pick a bouquet of western red lilies for their mother to put in a vase in the kitchen window. Farm children along the Missouri River in southeastern Nebraska might have done the same with yellow lady's-slippers. Today, these showy wildflowers are so uncommon or even rare, that picking a bouquet would be difficult, and certainly should not be done even if they are found.

In the last century we have reshaped the landscape of Nebraska and the Great Plains. Even areas of natural vegetation which escaped the plow have been significantly altered by the widespread use of herbicides and decades of pasturing regimes much different than the natural grazing under which these environments evolved.

Only in recent decades have we begun to make an accounting of what remains of the native flora. The tallgrass prairie of eastern Nebraska has been reduced to scattered remnants. Mixed-grass prairie in central Nebraska has fared slightly better in the battle with the plow but its vigor and variety of plants have declined markedly under chronic overgrazing until today it is difficult to find a site where the full complement of plants native to the region is represented. Since the development of center-pivot irrigation in the late 1960s, much of the state's sandsage prairie in southwest Nebraska has disappeared, and what remains has been degraded by the use of herbicides. Irrigation development in the eastern and southern Sandhills has likewise led to the plowing of soil too fragile to be farmed. Horizon-to-horizon wheat fields now cover much of the shortgrass plains, and the wet meadows of the state's river valleys have been almost entirely converted to corn.

Under this unrelenting assault, our native flora has been reduced both in quantity and quality, until today many species are uncommon, and others rare. Hayden's or blowout penstemon, a wildflower not known to grow anywhere outside Nebraska, is listed as endangered under the federal Endangered Species Act. Prairie fringed orchis is considered threatened under the same act. Many others are becoming increasingly difficult to find, including several of the lady's-tresses, western red and Turk's cap lilies, large yellow and small white lady's-slippers and showy orchis. Once, each of these wildflowers was apparently quite common in its appropriate habitat. In the coming decades, other wildflower species will certainly join their ranks.

Each of these uncommon or rare wildflowers suffered a similar fate—destruction of native habitat. The widespread and indiscriminate use of herbicides and chronic overgrazing contribute to their decreasing numbers even where appropriate habitat still exists.

We can slow the loss of what natural vegetation remains. An obvious start is to enjoy wildflowers where they grow, particularly those which are not abundant. The fleeting joy of picking wildflowers eliminates that plant's opportunity to proliferate. Regulations prohibit the taking of any plants on most public lands, and it is illegal to pick or dig any wildflowers listed as threatened or endangered. Transplanting most wildflowers is seldom successful. Each plant is highly selective about its growing site—the chemistry of the soil, amount of sun, shade and moisture. Wildflowers in the home garden can be a special pleasure, and require little care or watering once established. A handful of seeds collected in the wild and properly introduced to the garden is the best way to establish native plants. Seed collected from local wildflowers, from a site much like the one where you hope to grow them, have the best chance of germinating, establishing and enduring. Unless you are willing to lavish much attention on the native wildflowers, it is best to try those which are hardy competitors, species such as black-eyed Susan, New England aster or one of the goldenrods. Cultivars of some native wildflowers are available from garden centers and seed houses.

Finally, if you care about preserving natural areas and the native plants and animals found there, contribute to organizations which acquire and protect such sites. Contribute to the Nebraska Game and Parks Commission's Non-game Program through the income tax check-off or direct donations. The program protects natural areas and endangered plants as well as wildlife. Buy a federal waterfowl stamp or Nebraska habitat stamp even if you do not hunt. National wildlife refuges and state wildlife management areas are acquired and maintained by the sale of these stamps and are among the last strongholds of native flora and fauna. Join organizations such as The Nature Conservancy, National Audubon Society or Prairie/Plains Resource Institute, which preserve threatened natural areas.

Farmers and ranchers can directly protect native plants by using herbicides selectively and in the minimum amounts required. Grazing the proper number of animals in a rotation regime not only benefits native plants but, in the long term, is the most productive pasture management. Many of our native wildflowers are highly desirable livestock forage, more nutritious and yielding a greater tonnage than weedy elements which replace them on chronically overgrazed pastures.

But there are even more significant actions with more far-reaching effects which will slow the loss of our dwindling natural flora and the sites where they flourish. Even those who are not landowners rightfully have a say in government policy which contributes to the loss of native plants and natural habitat. When tax dollars are involved, the environment belongs to all of us, not just to those holding a deed. During this century, government farm policy has often encouraged the reckless use of the land, exploiting it for short-term gain rather than long-term sustainability. Tax advantages and subsidies have made the draining of wetlands and plowing of land marginal for crop production economically advantageous. County weed control boards should be aware that not all constituents believe that periodic spraying of road ditches to create pure stands of brome grass is desirable. Mowing, and in some areas of the state, farming of road ditches and railroad rights-of-way, produce a minimal economic return and often destroy the last remnants of native vegetation found within miles. Because government agencies at all levels exercise such widespread controls on both public and private lands, expressing your opinions to appropriate public officials can have a significant impact on preserving what little remains of our natural landscape.

It is human nature to value the rare more than the common. We call some wildflowers weeds, and allocate tax money to eradicate them. Others we call rare, and solicit donations to preserve. Most rare wildflowers are rare because we have destroyed the places where they once grew so abundantly. We value them now only because in the past we destroyed so many.

Green Flowers

Spider Milkweed
Asclepias viridis

OTHER COMMON NAMES: Green antelope-horn, oblong-leaved milkweed.
FAMILY: Milkweed (Asclepiadaceae)
FLOWERING PERIOD: Late May into July.
DISTRIBUTION: Southeastern Nebraska. Southeastern Great Plains.
HABITAT: Dry soils in prairies.
DESCRIPTION: Native perennial growing from a vertical rootstock and woody crown producing lateral roots. Usually several stems, often forming a clump in older plants; erect or lower portions reclining on the ground, slender to stout, usually not branched, 1-2 feet tall. Leaves leathery, mostly alternate; ovate-lanceolate to oblong; 2-5 inches long, less than half as wide. Flower clusters mostly at ends of stems (in umbel-like cymes). Largest flowers of the region's milkweeds; petals do not reflex downward as do those of most milkweeds. Five spreading green petals form a cup in which 5 white and rose-purple hoods encircle the fused anthers and stigma. Seed pod broadly spindle-shaped, erect, 3-5 inches long, usually without tubercles.

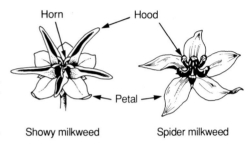

Showy milkweed   Spider milkweed

SPIDER MILKWEED

GREEN MILKWEED

NARROW-LEAVED MILKWEED

Green Milkweed

Asclepias viridiflora

OTHER COMMON NAMES: Green acerates.
FAMILY: Milkweed (Asclepiadaceae)
FLOWERING PERIOD: June and July, but into early August.
DISTRIBUTION: Statewide in Nebraska. Found throughout the Great Plains.
HABITAT: Dry soils in prairies.
DESCRIPTION: Native perennial growing from a vertical rootstock. Stems (1-2) slender to stout, occasionally branched, 1-2 feet or more tall. Leaves mostly opposite on stem; deep green, leathery, often with wavy edges; variable in shape—linear, lanceolate, ovate or oblong; 2-4 inches long. Flowers greenish-white, 20-80 in spherical (umbel-like) clusters on stalks from the upper leaf axils. Like spider milkweed, and unlike most other milkweeds, the flowers lack horns. Seed pod broadly spindle-shaped, erect, 3-5 inches long, without tubercles.

Narrow-leaved Milkweed

Asclepias stenophylla

FAMILY: Milkweed (Asclepiadaceae)
FLOWERING PERIOD: June and July.
DISTRIBUTION: Statewide in Nebraska. Central and southern Great Plains.
HABITAT: Dry soils in prairies and plains.
DESCRIPTION: Native perennial growing from a tuberous root which extends downward as a slender taproot. Stems (1-2) are slender, occasionally branched but usually not, 1-2 feet or more tall. Upper leaves mostly alternate on the stem, lower leaves opposite; narrowly linear, 3-7 inches long, less than .25 inch wide. Flowers greenish-white to yellow, 10-25 flowers in small clusters (an umbel-like cyme) on short stalks from the upper leaf axils. Like spider milkweed, and unlike most other milkweeds, the flowers lack horns. The seed pods are erect, slender, spindle-shaped, 3-5 inches long and without tubercles.

17

JACK-IN-THE-PULPIT

Sand Milkweed
Asclepias arenaria

FAMILY: Milkweed (Asclepiadaceae)
FLOWERING PERIOD: Late June into August.
DISTRIBUTION: Central and western Nebraska. Central and southern Great Plains.
HABITAT: Sandy soils on well-drained upland prairies, roadsides.
DESCRIPTION: Native perennial growing from a rhizome. Stem is stout, usually arching, unbranched; up to 2 feet tall, pubescent. Leaves opposite on stem, ovate to ovate-lanceolate below, oblong to rounded-rectangular above; 2-4 inches long with undulating margins and minute, whitish hairs. Spherical (umbel-like) flower clusters on short stalks from the upper leaf axils, composed of 25-50 small, greenish to cream-colored flowers. Seed pods are broadly spindle-shaped, erect, 3-5 inches long, without tubercles.
GENERAL INFORMATION: About 20 milkweeds are known from the Great Plains, 15 from Nebraska. The Latin name *Asclepias* is from Asklepios, the Greek god of medicine, a reference to reputed medicinal uses of these plants.

SAND MILKWEED

Jack-in-the-pulpit
Arisaema triphyllum

OTHER COMMON NAMES: Preacher-in-the-pulpit, Indian turnip.
FAMILY: Arum (Aracea)
FLOWERING PERIOD: Late April, May, occasionally into June.
DISTRIBUTION: Eastern Nebraska, particularly the Missouri River Valley and lower reaches of its tributaries. Eastern Great Plains.
HABITAT: Moist, rich soils in woodlands; less common on drier woodland slopes.
DESCRIPTION: Native perennial growing from a corm. A thick flowering stalk to 2 feet high. Usually 2 leaves, but occasionally 3, sheathing the flower stalk below and spreading to bear 3 pointed, oval to elliptic leaflets 3-7 inches long. Purplish or green, club-like Jack (spadix) sits in a deep tubular sheath (spathe) which rises behind, becoming the leaf-like hood. Minute flowers clustered at the base of the Jack. Individual plants produce either male or female flowers but not both the same year. Sex of flowers is determined by the plant's age and condition. Plants which stored abundant food in the corm the preceding year usually produce female flowers. Young plants or those with scant root reserves usually produce male flowers or none at all. By early autumn, fertilized flowers develop into a cluster of bright scarlet berries.
GENERAL INFORMATION: The starchy corm contains calcium oxalate crystals, making it inedible until neutralized by drying, boiling or baking. The Pawnee ground the dried corm to make a gruel.

Jack-in-the-pulpit fruit cluster

White Flowers

Bloodroot

Sanguinaria canadensis

OTHER COMMON NAMES: Red Indian-paint, red puccoon, turmeric, redroot, corn-root, sweet-slumber, snake-bite, tetterwort.

FAMILY: Poppy (Papaveraceae)

FLOWERING PERIOD: April and May.

DISTRIBUTION: Extreme eastern Nebraska; principally Missouri Valley, particularly in northeast. Extreme eastern Great Plains.

HABITAT: Moist, rich, well-drained soils in deciduous woodlands.

DESCRIPTION: Native perennial, 6-12 inches tall, growing from a stout, horizontal rhizome up to 1 inch thick with fibrous rootlets. Leaves on long, erect stalks from the rhizome; leaf blade rolled around flower stalk, spreading to a lobed and roughly circular or kidney-shape, 3-8 inches across; leaf stalk lengthens and blade enlarges even after flowering. A single flower, 1 inch or more across, at the end of stalk; 8 (occasionally more) white petals (narrower petals alternating with broader petals) surround the yellow tuft of stamens and a stout, greenish pistil. Flowers close overnight. Pea-like seed capsule 1-2 inches long.

GENERAL INFORMATION: The roots contain a red, latex-like juice once used as a pigment by American Indians; hence the name *Sanguinaria,* from Latin meaning "bleeding," and puccoon, an Indian word applied to a number of dye-producing plants. Roots contain a toxin, sanguinarine. Decoctions made from the roots were used medicinally, principally for the external treatment of skin disorders but also used in small amounts internally for treatment of snakebite and sore throat.

BLOODROOT

20

WHITE FAWN LILY

PRAIRIE FAWN LILY

White Fawn Lily

Erythronium albidum

OTHER COMMON NAMES: Dog's-tooth-violet, adder's tongue, deer tongue, trout lily.
FAMILY: Lily (Liliaceae)
FLOWERING PERIOD: Late March into early May.
DISTRIBUTION: Extreme southeast Nebraska, north in Missouri Valley to Ponca, along Platte River to Fremont. Southeastern Great Plains.
HABITAT: Moist deciduous *woodlands*.
DESCRIPTION: Native perennial growing from a bulb up to 1.5 inches in diameter; *spreading by stolons* and forming patches. Fleshy leaves emerge from the bulb; 6 inches or more long and less than 2 inches wide; sometimes keel-shaped; narrowly elliptic with a pointed tip; usually *mottled with brown*. Plants more than 4 years old produce a pair of leaves; younger plants a single leaf. A leafless flower stalk rises between the leaves, bearing a nodding flower composed of 3 white (or tinged with pink or blue) petals and 3 virtually identical sepals, up to 2 inches long, *conspicuously reflexed* when fully open.
GENERAL INFORMATION: The small bulbs are a favorite food of burrowing mammals and once of native Indians who relished them raw, boiled or roasted.

Prairie Fawn Lily

Erythronium mesochoreum

OTHER COMMON NAMES: Dog's-tooth-violet, midland fawn lily, star-strikers, midland adder's tongue.
FAMILY: Lily (Liliaceae)
FLOWERING PERIOD: Late March and April.
DISTRIBUTION: Southeastern Nebraska and southeastern Great Plains.
HABITAT: Moist *prairies*, open woods.
DESCRIPTION: Native perennial growing from a bulb but *not spreading by stolons*, though may be found in loose colonies. Fleshy leaves emerge directly from bulb; 3-6 inches or more long, less than 2 inches wide; sometimes keel-shaped; narrowly elliptic with pointed tip; *not mottled with brown*. The leafless flower stalk rises between the leaves, bearing a nodding flower composed of 3 white (often tinged with pink or with blue) petals and 3 virtually identical sepals, up to 2 inches long, *spreading only at the tips*. The lengthening flower stalks fall to the ground under the weight of the capsules, depositing seeds away from parent plant.
GENERAL INFORMATION: Bulbs are edible but should not be dug as this plant, as well as white fawn lily, is becoming increasingly uncommon due to the continued destruction of the habitat it requires.

Mountain Lily
Leucocrinum montanum

OTHER COMMON NAMES: Star-of-Bethlehem, sand lily, star lily.
FAMILY: Lily (Liliaceae)
FLOWERING PERIOD: Late April, May.
DISTRIBUTION: Principally the Nebraska Panhandle. West-central Great Plains.
HABITAT: Dry short-grass plains and open ponderosa pine woodlands in a variety of soils.
DESCRIPTION: Native perennial growing from root crown only 1-2 inches underground; with spreading, thick, fleshy roots several inches long. Grass-like leaves, 4-8 inches long; wrapped in a whitish papery sheath underground, spreading at surface. The blossom emerges from between the leaves as a white candle; the 3 sepals and 3 petals unfold to form a star-shaped flower 1-2 inches across with 6 prominent yellow anthers. One plant may bear many flowers and older plants with several crowns may produce dozens of flowers.
GENERAL INFORMATION: While most members of the lily family grow from bulbs, mountain lily has several fleshy, finger-like roots which store food and moisture, permitting a burst of growth in early spring. By midsummer the plants are dormant, having completed their annual cycle before the hot, dry, High Plains summer.

Rocky Mountain Pussy-toes
Antennaria parvifolia

OTHER COMMON NAMES: Rocky Mountain cud-weed.
FAMILY: Sunflower (Asteraceae)
FLOWERING PERIOD: May into July.
DISTRIBUTION: Western and central Nebraska. Central and northern Great Plains.
HABITAT: Dry soils in prairies, pastures and roadsides.
DESCRIPTION: Native perennial growing from creeping stolons and frequently forming dense mats. Shorter, more compact pussy-toe species than those to the east. Basal leaves oblong-lanceolate or spatulate, .5-1 inch long, densely hairy on both upper and lower surfaces, silvery-green. Flowering stalks are seldom more than 6 inches tall, bearing more linear leaves. Minute flowers are gathered into several tight bundles per flower stalk resembling the pads of a cat's foot. Compared to other pussy-toes, this species is small leaved and of short stature.
GENERAL INFORMATION: Male and female flowers borne on separate plants. Plants bearing male flowers are smaller, inconspicuous and infrequently encountered. Female flowers are apparently self-fertile. Because cross-pollination is apparently rare, distinct forms (clones) are common within this species.

MOUNTAIN LILY

Plainleaf Pussy-toes
Antennaria parlinii

OTHER COMMON NAMES: Cat's foot, ladies' tobacco, Indian tobacco, pearly mouse-ear everlasting, poverty weed, white plantain.
FAMILY: Sunflower (Asteraceae)
FLOWERING PERIOD: Late April into June.
DISTRIBUTION: Primarily southeast; sporadic elsewhere in the state. Northern and eastern Great Plains.
HABITAT: Dry soils; woodland edge and openings, thickets, roadsides, occasionally in prairies or pastures.
DESCRIPTION: Native perennial growing from creeping stolons and frequently forming dense mats. Basal leaves in rosettes; ovate to elliptic, on long stalks, up to 3 inches long and half as wide; upper surface dull green and woolly, undersurface silvery and even more densely hairy. Leaves remain green throughout the winter. Male and female flowers usually on different plants. Colonies may be entirely of one sex. Flower stalks up to 15 inches tall (typically shorter); covered with whitish, woolly hairs; bearing several narrow leaves. Tiny, white tubular flowers gathered in dense clusters, several clusters per flower stalk.

Dutchman's Breeches

Dicentra cucullaria

OTHER COMMON NAMES: Butterfly banners, white hearts, blue staggers.
FAMILY: Fumitory (Fumariaceae)
FLOWERING PERIOD: April into May.
DISTRIBUTION: Extreme eastern Nebraska; principally Missouri Valley and lower reaches of its tributaries. Eastern Great Plains.
HABITAT: Rich, well-drained soils in moist deciduous woodlands.
DESCRIPTION: Native perennial growing from a cluster of whitish, flattened, small tubers. Leaf stalks, 3-6 inches long, rise from soil, bearing bluish-green, deeply dissected, coarsely fern-like leaves. Flowers (3-15), borne along a 4-12 inch arching stalk rising above foliage. Each white "breeches" (.5-.75 inch long) hangs from a slender stalk attached at the flower's "crotch." "Legs" are spurs holding nectar. "Waist" open, exposing the stigma and 3 stamens. Long-tongued moths and bees strong enough to force the petals apart visit the flowers for nectar and accomplish cross-pollination. Fruit is an elongated capsule about .5 inch long containing 10-20 shiny black seeds.
GENERAL INFORMATION: Roots contain toxic alkaloids and are poisonous, hence the name "staggers," as the symptoms of cattle having fed on the plant include staggering. Bleeding hearts grown in gardens are a Japanese relative. In spite of its toxic properties, preparations of the plant were used by early settlers to treat urinary disorders and as a poultice for skin diseases.

Wild Strawberry

Fragaria virginiana

FAMILY: Rose (Rosaceae)
FLOWERING PERIOD: Late April into early June.
DISTRIBUTION: Eastern fourth of Nebraska. Eastern and northeastern Great Plains.
HABITAT: Moist to fairly dry, rich soils; prairies, meadows, woodland edge and openings.
DESCRIPTION: Native perennial, 4-8 inches tall, growing from fibrous rhizomes and spreading by stolons to form open colonies. Leaves on long stalks emerge from the soil; 3 leaflets, elliptic or ovate, up to 2 inches long; pubescent, particularly on undersurface; margins serrate. Flowers in clusters on *stalks shorter than leaves;* 5 white petals encircling numerous, conspicuous, yellow stamens. More or less *globular fruit,* .5-.75 inch in diameter with dry seeds (achenes) in pits on the surface; matures from May through early July. Though smaller than garden varieties, fruit has an intense flavor.
GENERAL INFORMATION: Woodland strawberry (*Fragaria vesca*), found across much of Nebraska and the northern and central Great Plains, is similar but usually taller, with flowers often at same level as leaflets and has a more conical-shaped and less intense red fruit with achenes nearer the surface. Rhizomes of woodland strawberry are not so thick and it spreads more aggressively by stolons. It is more frequent in woodlands and thickets. The cultivated garden strawberry is a hybrid between *Fragaria virginiana* and a South American species.

DUTCHMAN'S BREECHES

WILD STRAWBERRY

May-apple

Podophyllum peltatum

OTHER COMMON NAMES: Umbrella plant, mandrake, Puck's foot; hog or Indian apple.

FAMILY: Barberry (Berberidaceae)

FLOWERING PERIOD: May.

DISTRIBUTION: Principally the Missouri River Valley in southeast Nebraska. The southeastern Great Plains.

HABITAT: Moist soils in deciduous woodlands.

DESCRIPTION: Native perennial to 18 inches tall growing from creeping rhizomes to form colonies. Stem thick, smooth; giving rise to one or two ascending leaf stalks. Leaves large, umbrella-like and divided into coarsely toothed lobes. Only mature plants, bearing two leaves, flower. Solitary, nodding flower up to 2 inches across borne on a stalk emerging from the crotch formed by the two leaf stalks; 6-9 white, waxy petals surround conspicuous, bright yellow stamens and a single broad pistil. Flower's odor considered unpleasantly sweet by many. Fruit ripens in July or August; a rounded, yellow-green, many-seeded berry.

GENERAL INFORMATION: The fruit is edible and was used as a flavoring or to make marmalade or preserves. The root, stems, leaves and green fruits are poisonous, but a decoction made from the root was used by some Indian tribes as a laxative as well as other purported medicinal values. Drugs derived from May-apple have been used in cancer research. An old superstition holds that any girl who pulls up the root will soon become pregnant. The true mandrake plant of southern Europe and northern Africa, to which the May-apple bears scant resemblance, has a forked, somewhat "man-like" root (which the May-apple does not) to which aphrodisiac properties were attributed.

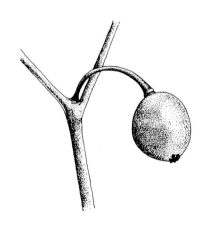

May-apple fruit

White Wild Indigo

Baptisia lactea

OTHER COMMON NAMES: White false indigo, large white wild indigo, rattlepod.

FAMILY: Bean (Fabaceae)

FLOWERING PERIOD: May and June, occasionally later.

DISTRIBUTION: Southeastern Nebraska. Southeastern Great Plains.

HABITAT: Rich, moist soils in prairies, roadsides, stream valleys, ravines.

DESCRIPTION: Native perennial growing from a knobby caudex with rhizomes. Typically a single, erect stem with ascending branches, 2-5 feet tall or more. Unlike plains wild indigo, *not hairy.* Leaves alternate on stem, palmate, three leaflets per leaf. Leaflets are obovate to oblong-lanceolate, 1-3 inches long. Large, white, pea-like flowers openly spaced on erect stalks (racemes) 8-22 inches long. Bladder-like pods are black when mature, .75-1.5 inches long, woody, with a short beak. Seed pods of both wild indigos are ravaged by insects.

GENERAL INFORMATION: Poisonous but usually avoided by livestock. Used extensively as a medicinal plant by American Indians and settlers—as a treatment for cuts, dysentery, scarlet fever, typhus and chronic colds.

WHITE WILD INDIGO

White-eyed Grass

Sisyrinchium campestre

OTHER COMMON NAMES: Prairie blue-eyed grass.

FAMILY: Iris (Iridaceae)

FLOWERING PERIOD: May and June.

DISTRIBUTION: Eastern third of Nebraska. Southeastern Great Plains.

HABITAT: Prairies, grassy woodland edge and openings.

DESCRIPTION: Native perennial growing from fibrous roots. Often grows in tufts, up to 12 inches tall (occasionally taller). Leaves emerge from soil; pale green, linear, grass-like, erect, shorter than flower stalks. Flower stalks leafless, flattened, with two ridges or "wings." Star-shaped flowers less than .5 inch across emerge in clusters from 2 clasping, grass-like bracts (a spathe) 1-2 inches long; 3 petals, 3 virtually identical petal-like sepals, all with sharp tips; white, pale blue or pale rose. Base of petals and sepals, the flower's "eye," is yellow.

WHITE-EYED GRASS

Plains Wild Indigo
Baptisia bracteata

OTHER COMMON NAMES: Long-bracted or cream-colored false indigo, black rattle-pod.
FAMILY: Bean (Fabaceae)
FLOWERING PERIOD: Late April, principally May, into June.
DISTRIBUTION: Southeastern Nebraska. Southeastern Great Plains.
HABITAT: Tallgrass prairie. Well-drained sites, especially gravelly and rocky soils. Often conspicuous on heavily grazed pastures.
DESCRIPTION: Native perennial growing from a knobby caudex with rhizomes. Stems rising obliquely, branched, forming a bushy clump 1-2 feet tall or more. *All parts hairy*. Leaves alternate along stem, palmate, three leaflets per leaf (2 leaflet-like appendages at base of the leaf give the impression of 5 leaflets per leaf). Leaflets oblong-lanceolate to elliptic, 1-3 inches long. Flowers on drooping stalks (racemes) 4-8 inches long. Large, cream to light yellow, pea-like flowers replaced by bladder-like pods with a beak, 1-2 inches long, turning black as they mature. Plants break off at ground level and are tumbled by the wind, aiding seed dispersal.

GENERAL INFORMATION: When exposed to air the sap takes on a dark purple color, hence the name "false indigo." Used medicinally by American Indians, particularly for typhoid and scarlet fevers and colic. The dried pods were used as rattles by young Pawnee, Omaha and Ponca boys.

Plains wild indigo pods

Canada Violet

Viola canadensis

FAMILY: Violet (Violaceae)

FLOWERING PERIOD: May and June.

DISTRIBUTION: Northern Nebraska, particularly northeast. Northeastern Great Plains.

HABITAT: Partial shade in moist soil; woodland edge and openings.

DESCRIPTION: Native perennial often forming patches by rhizomes or stolons. Stems 8-16 inches tall. Stem leaves on stalks about as long as leaf blade, leaves from base on longer stalks; margins toothed: usually cordate shaped (heart-shaped); as wide as long or longer than wide; 2-4 inches long. Flowers on stalks from the upper leaf axils; 5 petals, white with yellow base on inside, purplish tinged on the outside; lower 3 petals with purplish lines at base directing insects to the flower's reproductive parts; lower petal larger than others.

GENERAL INFORMATION: As in Europe, violets were often used by American Indians and early settlers as greens and potherbs. Preparations from violets were considered to be blood purifiers and also were used for various skin disorders. Romans believed that wearing a garland of violets would cure headaches caused by consuming too much wine.

Cow Parsnip

Heracleum sphondylium

FAMILY: Parsley (Apiaceae)

FLOWERING PERIOD: June and July.

DISTRIBUTION: North and northeast Nebraska. Northeastern Great Plains.

HABITAT: Moist, rich soils in woodlands; streamsides, woodland edge and openings.

DESCRIPTION: Native perennial growing from a heavy, branched, fleshy taproot. Stems hollow, erect, stout (approaching 2 inches in diameter at base), grooved, woolly pubescent, 4-6 feet or more tall. Leaves alternate on stem; large, 8-16 inches across, on heavy stalks 4-15 inches long; divided into 3 dark green, lobed, pubescent and coarsely toothed leaflets. Small white flowers in groups of 8-30, gathered into larger, flat-topped clusters (compound umbels) at top of plant. The plant has a rank, unpleasant odor.

GENERAL INFORMATION: American Indians ate the young greens and boiled the fleshy root. The Pawnee prepared a poultice from the root for boils. The Winnebago burned the plant in a smoke treatment for fainting and convulsions. The Omaha apparently attributed great significance to the plant as dried, pulverized roots were mixed with beaver dung and put into the hole where their sacred pole was placed.

Sweet Cicely

Osmorhiza claytoni

OTHER COMMON NAMES: Woolly or hairy sweet cicely.

FAMILY: Parsley (Apiaceae)

FLOWERING PERIOD: May and June.

DISTRIBUTION: Extreme eastern Nebraska. Eastern Great Plains.

HABITAT: Rich soils in moist woods; shade or partial shade.

DESCRIPTION: Native perennial growing from fleshy, swollen, spindle-shaped and fibrous roots. Stems 1-3 feet tall, usually solitary, covered with long, soft hairs. Leaves divided into threes two or three times, the final division resulting in 3 leaf-like leaflets. Leaflets ovate to lanceolate, 1-3 inches long, coarsely toothed. Open clusters (a compound umbel) of small white flowers rise above the foliage on stalks from upper leaf axils.

GENERAL INFORMATION: A similar species, anise root *(Osmorhiza longistylis)*, has a wider distribution across eastern and northern Nebraska and the northern Great Plains. Its stems are usually not as hairy. Sweet cicely either lacks or has only a faint scent of anise, which is strong in anise root. Great Plains Indians and early settlers used an anise root extract as a flavoring and medicine.

Small White Lady's-slipper

Cypripedium candidum

OTHER COMMON NAMES: Little white orchid.
FAMILY: Orchid (Orchidaceae)
FLOWERING PERIOD: May and June.
DISTRIBUTION: Central and eastern Nebraska. Northeastern Great Plains.
HABITAT: Moist, rich soil in meadows and low prairies.
DESCRIPTION: Native perennial growing from fibrous, fleshy rhizomes; often forming clumps. Stems usually single, erect, 6-12 inches tall. Elliptic-lanceolate leaves (3-4) with pointed tips, bases wrapping around stem; 3-6 inches long and 1-1.5 inches wide; somewhat erect. Usually only one flower (occasionally 2) at top of stem. Lower petal is modified into a white, waxy pouch .5-1 inch long, with faint brownish-maroon lines becoming more evident as the flower ages. Other flower parts greenish with brown markings—2 narrow lateral petals, 1-1.5 inches long; twisted upper sepal forming a triangular-shaped hood over the pouch, lower sepals united, wrapping under the pouch.
GENERAL INFORMATION: Although probably once quite common, the conversion of moist, tallgrass prairie sites to cropland has made this one of Nebraska's rarest wildflowers.

Bastard Toad-flax

Comandra umbellata

OTHER COMMON NAMES: False or star toad-flax.
FAMILY: Sandalwood (Santalaceae)
FLOWERING PERIOD: May and June.
DISTRIBUTION: Statewide in Nebraska. Found throughout the Great Plains.
HABITAT: Dry, often sandy or rocky soils on grasslands or open woodlands.
DESCRIPTION: Native perennial growing from extensive rhizomes. Often in clusters or loose colonies. Although capable of manufacturing its own food, partially parasitic on the roots of other plants. Stems stiffly erect, usually less than 1 foot in height. Leaves alternate, linear to elliptic; numerous; some thin and green with conspicuous veins, others are thick and gray-green with inconspicuous veins; .5-1 inch long. Small white flowers in clusters at top of stem; composed of 5 petal-like sepals fused at base.
GENERAL INFORMATION: The fleshy, urn-shaped fruits, up to .25 inch in diameter, are edible raw; sweet and taste best when changing from green to brown. They probably were no more than snacks for Great Plains Indians. The name "bastard" may refer to this plant resembling, but not being, a true toad-flax; being in effect a false or illegitimate toad-flax.

SMALL WHITE LADY'S-SLIPPER

BASTARD TOAD-FLAX

Bluet

Hedyotis purpurea

OTHER COMMON NAMES: Large or mountain houstonia, Venus' pride.

FAMILY: Madder (Rubiaceae)

FLOWERING PERIOD: May and June.

DISTRIBUTION: Reported from one Platte Valley site in eastern Nebraska. Principal range is to the east and southeast of the Great Plains.

HABITAT: Sandy soil; floodplain meadows. Elsewhere in its range found growing on rocky bluffs and slopes.

DESCRIPTION: Native perennial growing from hair-like roots. A slender, delicate plant. Stems are erect, often clustered or in open gatherings; not branched or sparingly so, 4-16 inches tall. Leaves opposite on the stem, *oblong-lanceolate or broadly lanceolate*, leaf bases rounded to heart-shaped; .5-2 inches long, .2-.5 inch wide (3-6 times as long as they are broad); usually *no bundles of smaller leaves* at bases of principal stem leaves. Flowers in clusters at top of stem; white or with lilac tinge; tubular, spreading to 4 pointed lobes; seldom much more than .25 inch long.

GENERAL INFORMATION: The only other bluet reported from Nebraska is narrowleaf bluet (*Hedyotis nigricans*). It is far more abundant and found along the southern border and in the southeast. It is similar except its leaves are

BLUET

filiform or narrowly linear and *bundles of small leaves* are usually found in the axils of the main stem leaves. It grows on sites with a wide variety of soil types and moisture.

False Solomon's Seal

Smilacina stellata

OTHER COMMON NAMES: Spikenard.

FAMILY: Lily (Liliaceae)

FLOWERING PERIOD: May into July.

DISTRIBUTION: Statewide, more common north and east. Central and northern Great Plains.

HABITAT: Full sun or partial shade in moist, especially sandy soils; meadows, ditches, woodland edge, near streams.

DESCRIPTION: Native perennial growing from rhizomes. Forming colonies at favorable sites. Stems erect or arching, sometimes zig-zagging, 1-2 feet long. Leaves alternate, bases clasping stem, lanceolate to oblong-lanceolate, narrowing to a sharp point; 1-4 inches long, parallel veins; often folded into a keel-shape. Flowers on short stalks or stalkless at stem top (a raceme); small (.25 inch across), star-shaped; with 6 white tepals. Fruit a green berry with 6 brownish-black stripes, turning dark blue.

GENERAL INFORMATION: The leaves of false Solomon's seal are arranged in two rows along the stem, similar to Solomon's seal to which it bears a superficial resemblance. The flowers of Solomon's seal, though, are borne on stalks from leaf axils along much of the stem length.

FALSE SOLOMON'S SEAL

SOLOMON'S SEAL WITH FRUIT

Solomon's Seal

Polygonatum biflorum

FAMILY: Lily (Liliaceae)

FLOWERING PERIOD: May and June.

DISTRIBUTION: Statewide except southwest, most common east. Eastern Great Plains.

HABITAT: Rich, moist woodland soils; along streams.

DESCRIPTION: Native perennial growing from a thick, horizontal rhizome. Solitary, arching stems, 3-4 feet long or more. Leaves alternate on stem, without stalks, ovate to elliptic with parallel veins, 2-6 inches long. Flowers in clusters of 2-5 on drooping stalks from upper leaf axils; hidden under foliage. Flowers tubular, greenish-white, less than 1 inch long; replaced by dark blue or black berries.

GENERAL INFORMATION: One stem develops each year, leaving a crater-like, circular scar where it attached to the top of the rhizome. The origin of the common name is speculative. Some say that the scars resemble the seal of King Solomon, who knowing of the root's medicinal value, placed his seal on it. Another version says the crushed root was used to "seale or close up greene wounds," particularly broken bones. The roots were used as a food and for various purported medicinal values by American Indians and white settlers. The starchy rhizomes were gathered and boiled or dried and ground to make flour. The crushed root was believed to heal bruises and a tea brewed from the leaves claimed to be a contraceptive. Spreading the plant on the floors of a house was once believed to rid it of snakes and spiders.

Solomon's seal rhizome

33

ROCK SANDWORT

Rock Sandwort
Arenaria stricta

FAMILY: Pink (Caryophyllaceae)
FLOWERING PERIOD: May and June.
DISTRIBUTION: Extreme south-central Nebraska. Southern Great Plains.
HABITAT: Dry, gravelly or rocky soils in grasslands, often where limestone outcrops.
DESCRIPTION: Native perennial growing from a stout taproot and branched caudex, forming a loose tuft 4-8 inches tall. Numerous branching stems, erect, or bases lying on the ground before ascending. Small linear leaves, somewhat prickly to the touch, less than .5 inch long, mostly clustered low on stems giving the foliage a moss-like appearance. Flowering stalks rise above foliage bearing clusters of small flowers with 5 white petals, yellow centers and protruding stamens.
GENERAL INFORMATION: Rock sandwort differs from sandwort *(Arenaria hookeri)* in forming more open, spreading tufts, having shorter, narrower leaves, and flowers gathered in less compact clusters. Both are drought resistant and most often found growing on rock outcrops or rocky soils. Their ranges in Nebraska apparently do not overlap.

Plains Phlox
Phlox andicola

OTHER COMMON NAMES: Moss or creeping phlox.
FAMILY: Polemonium (Polemoniaceae)
FLOWERING PERIOD: May and June.
DISTRIBUTION: Nebraska Panhandle and western Sandhills. West-central Great Plains.
HABITAT: Dry rocky, gravelly, sandy or alkaline clay soils in grasslands.
DESCRIPTION: Native perennial growing from rhizomes in tufts or spreading in mats, seldom over 4 inches tall. Stems branching, sprawling on ground. Linear, needle-like leaves, ending in a sharp, stiff point; .5-1 inch long. Flowers white, less than .75 inch across; in clusters of 1-3 but most often solitary; tubular, spreading to 5 petal-like lobes.
GENERAL INFORMATION: A similar species, Hood's phlox *(Phlox hoodii)*, is found in the Nebraska Panhandle and the northern Great Plains. Typically it grows in more compact tufts or cushions; its leaves are shorter, more narrow and prickly; its flower lobes smaller, finer and most often do not overlap one another. It is usually associated with rocky outcrops.

Sandwort
Arenaria hookeri

FAMILY: Pink (Caryophyllaceae)
FLOWERING PERIOD: June and July, into August.
DISTRIBUTION: Nebraska Panhandle. West-central Great Plains.

HABITAT: Dry, rocky or gravelly soils, rock out-crops; in full sun.

DESCRIPTION: Native perennial growing from a taproot and branching caudex, forming dense tufts or cushions, usually less than 6 inches across (but up to 1 foot in diameter) and 1-4 inches tall. Leaves linear, rigid, sharp-tipped and usually less than 1 inch long. Small, white, star-shaped flowers, less than .5 inch across. Few to many flowers bloom at one time.

GENERAL INFORMATION: Sandwort is a good example of the "tuft" growth-habit characteristic of many plants found on dry rock outcrops in western Nebraska. The root systems of these wonderfully adapted plants, either deep taproots or extensive, spreading fibrous roots, efficiently extract scant soil moisture. Narrow, rigid leaves, either gray-green to reflect sunlight, or hairy to shade the leaves, reduce water loss from transpiration. Seeds are encased in hard coatings to prolong their viability and discourage germination until adequate soil moisture is available.

PLAINS PHLOX

Miner's Candle

Cryptantha thyrsiflora

FAMILY: Borage (Boraginaceae)
FLOWERING PERIOD: June and July.
DISTRIBUTION: Nebraska Panhandle. Western Great Plains.
HABITAT: Dry, soils; buttes, bluffs, rock out-crops, eroded banks, hilltops in grasslands.
DESCRIPTION: Native biennial or short-lived perennial growing from a woody caudex. Stems (1 or several) are stout, erect, densely covered with long, stiff, whitish bristles; short branches on upper part of plant; 8-16 inches tall. Basal leaves oblong to oblong-lanceolate, 2-4 inches long, silvery-green with a dense covering of relatively long hairs; upper leaves smaller and more narrow. Flowers at ends of branches on upper half of plant; small, like for-get-me-nots in appearance; composed of 5 white petals, united at bases, surrounding a pale yellow, button-like center.
GENERAL INFORMATION: Distinguished from 6 similar species of the same genus found in western Nebraska by height of the inflores-cence, its fullness, small flowers and overall dense covering of stiff hairs.

Platte Thistle

Cirsium canescens

FAMILY: Sunflower (Asteraceae)
FLOWERING PERIOD: Late May and June.
DISTRIBUTION: Central and western Nebras-ka. Central and western Great Plains.
HABITAT: Mildly disturbed sites in grasslands, particularly on sandy or gravelly soils.
DESCRIPTION: Native perennial growing from a deep, fleshy taproot. Stem is erect, often branching; covered with short, woolly hairs; gray-green, 1-2.5 feet tall. Leaves gray-green, cobwebby hairs on upper surface, densely covered with short white hairs below; lower leaves narrowly elliptic, becoming larger and more deeply lobed higher on the plant, 5-10 in-ches long; each lobe tipped with a yellow spine and smaller spines elsewhere on the leaf margins; upper leaves winged, wings extending down stem to next set of leaves. Flower heads, composed of many small tubular flowers, at top of plant, up to 2 inches across, creamy white. Base of flower head bears short yellow spines.
GENERAL INFORMATION: Usually found on grasslands and only on abused pastures does it become abundant.

MINER'S CANDLE

PLATTE THISTLE

White Wild Onion

Allium textile

FAMILY: Lily (Liliaceae)

FLOWERING PERIOD: May and June.

DISTRIBUTION: West half of Nebraska. The common wild onion of the western and northern Great Plains.

HABITAT: Dry grasslands.

DESCRIPTION: Native perennial growing from a bulb less then 1 inch long covered with a fibrous, netted, textile-like "husk." Two narrow, channeled, grass-like leaves arise low on a 4-12 inch tall flower. Flowers in a flat-topped to rounded cluster (an umbel); composed of a dozen or more small white (occasionally pinkish) flowers. Unlike some wild onions, no bulblets produced on flower cluster.

GENERAL INFORMATION: The Cheyenne name for wild onions was "kha-a-mot-ot-ke-wat," literally translating as "skunk testes;" a reference to size, shape and strong scent of the bulb. As with other species of wild onions, bulbs were used for cooking and flavoring (often dried and stored for winter use) as well as medicinal uses.

37

Meadow Anemone
Anemone canadensis

OTHER COMMON NAMES: Crowfoot, round-leaf anemone.
FAMILY: Buttercup (Ranunculaceae)
FLOWERING PERIOD: Late May into July.
DISTRIBUTION: East half of Nebraska, especially eastern third. Northeastern Great Plains.
HABITAT: Wet soils in prairies, grassed-over sloughs, roadside ditches and railways.
DESCRIPTION: Native perennial spreading extensively from rhizomes to form colonies. Hairy stems up to 24 inches but typically 8-14 inches tall. Leaves to 3 inches in length on long stalks; deeply divided into lobes with prominent marginal teeth. Flowers solitary or in clusters, typically standing above foliage; up to 1.5 inches across; composed of 5 white, petal-like sepals spreading nearly flat. Achenes gathered into a bristly, mace-like head.
GENERAL INFORMATION: The root of the meadow anemone was highly prized by the Omaha-Ponca. Ethnobotanist Melvin R. Gilmore wrote that it was called "little buffalo medicine." To touch a buffalo calf was taboo, as was use of the meadow anemone by anyone other than medicine men, hence the name. It was prescribed for many ills but particularly for wounds.

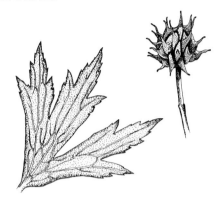

Meadow anemone leaf and fruit head

MEADOW ANEMONE

CANDLE ANEMONE

INDIAN HEMP DOGBANE

Candle Anemone

Anemone cylindrica

OTHER COMMON NAMES: Thimbleweed, tall or long-fruited anemone.

FAMILY: Buttercup (Ranunculaceae)

FLOWERING PERIOD: Late June, early July.

DISTRIBUTION: Statewide except southwest and southern Panhandle. Northern and northeastern Great Plains.

HABITAT: Open grasslands but also at margins of wooded areas in partial shade. On a variety of soils and moisture conditions.

DESCRIPTION: Native perennial growing from a stout caudex with fibrous roots. Single, pubescent, mostly leafless stem 1-2.5 feet or more tall. Basal leaves on long stalks, 2-4 inches wide; deeply divided into a palmate arrangement of 3-7 lobes, which are again divided into smaller lobes. Leaves clustered near top of stem similar but smaller. Flowers usually solitary at ends of long stalks rising from leafy gathering near top of stem. Flowers not showy, less than 1 inch across; composed of 4-6 white or greenish-white sepals surrounding a thimble-shaped fruiting head.

GENERAL INFORMATION: Poncas considered this plant "playing-card medicine" which would bring good luck if the hands were held in smoke over the burning fruits, or the fruits were chewed and rubbed in the palms before playing cards.

Indian Hemp Dogbane

Apocynum cannabinum

OTHER COMMON NAMES: Prairie dogbane, hemp plant.

FAMILY: Dogbane (Apocynaceae)

FLOWERING PERIOD: Late May into July.

DISTRIBUTION: Statewide, less common west. Throughout the Great Plains, less common west.

HABITAT: Moist soils in prairies, stream valleys, roadsides.

DESCRIPTION: Native perennial growing from a deep, branching taproot. Strong, erect, often purplish stems 3-4 feet tall, taller on rich, moist soils. Ascending branches, most on upper half. When cut or broken the plant exudes a milky juice. Leaves opposite on stem; ovate, oblong or oblong-lanceolate; 2-6 inches long; often with a white, waxy coating or bloom as found on plums; undersides may have long, soft hairs; turns golden yellow in the late summer. Small, creamy-white flowers clustered (a cyme) at branch ends or on stalks emerging from leaf axils. Tufted seeds form in spindle-shaped pods, 3-5 inches long.

GENERAL INFORMATION: The milky, latex juices are toxic but because of the plant's bitter taste it is avoided by livestock. Dogbane's toxic glycoside was reportedly used to poison fish for food. Indians used its hemp-like fibers for cordage, fish nets and woven ware.

Poison Hemlock
Conium maculatum

OTHER COMMON NAMES: Spotted parsley, poison parsley.

FAMILY: Parsley (Apiaceae)

FLOWERING PERIOD: June and July.

DISTRIBUTION: Statewide, principally southeastern Nebraska. Principally southeastern Great Plains.

HABITAT: Low-lying, moderately moist, disturbed sites; roadsides, thickets, stream and ditch banks.

DESCRIPTION: Naturalized biennial growing from a stout, carrot-like taproot. Much-branched, erect, pale green stem with purple splotches; 3-6 feet or more in height. Leaves broadly ovate, 6-12 inches long, repeatedly divided until foliage is somewhat fern-like; lower leaves with long stalks, upper leaves with short or no stalks. Abundant small, white flowers in clusters (compound umbels) about 2 inches across, at ends of branches.

GENERAL INFORMATION: Native to Europe, Asia and Africa. Reportedly, the poison used to put Socrates to death was derived from this plant. All parts of the plant, but particularly the seeds, are toxic. Death is not violent as with common water hemlock, commencing with coma and ending with respiratory paralysis. In spite of its potent toxins, in ancient times it was used medicinally in minute doses, particularly as a sedative.

Common Water Hemlock
Cicuta maculata

OTHER COMMON NAMES: Spotted hemlock, cowbane, musquash root, beaver poison.

FAMILY: Parsley (Apiaceae)

FLOWERING PERIOD: June through August.

DISTRIBUTION: Statewide. Throughout most of the Great Plains, more common east.

HABITAT: Wet soils in prairies and meadows; ditches; margins of streams, ponds, marshes.

DESCRIPTION: Native biennial or short-lived perennial growing from a cluster of fleshy, finger-like, tuberous roots. Stout, erect stems, often mottled with purple below, 2-5 feet tall or taller. *Leaflets narrowly lanceolate*, sharply toothed margins, often folded into a keel-shape, 1-5 inches long; arranged on leaf midrib opposite one another (compound pinnate), the leaf terminating with 3 leaflets; lower leaves 1 foot or more in length. Tiny white flowers in small clusters gathered into flat-topped or slightly rounded, larger clusters (compound umbels) 2-5 inches across, at ends of branches.

GENERAL INFORMATION: All parts of the plant are poisonous, particularly the roots. A small portion of the root may be lethal to man or livestock, particularly in spring when toxins are concentrated, although it is not considered as toxic as poison hemlock. Death is reported to be violent, preceded by nausea, diarrhea, restricted breathing and convulsions.

POISON HEMLOCK

COMMON WATER HEMLOCK

Queen Anne's Lace
Daucus carota

OTHER COMMON NAMES: Wild carrot.
FAMILY: Parsley (Apiaceae)
FLOWERING PERIOD: July, with late flowering plants into September.
DISTRIBUTION: East half of Nebraska, particularly southeast. Southeastern Great Plains.
HABITAT: Dry disturbed sites; roadsides, pastures, woodland margins and openings.
DESCRIPTION: Naturalized biennial. Strong, deep, fleshy taproot bears a rosette of leaves the first year; the second year sending up a solitary, erect, branching stem 1-3 feet tall. Lower leaves 2-8 inches long, deeply divided into linear or narrowly lanceolate divisions until somewhat fern-like. Upper leaves smaller and segments reduced until they are like leaf skeletons. Numerous, small white (or pinkish) flowers in small clusters gathered into a flat-topped inflorescence (compound umbels) up to 4 inches across borne on long stalks at top of plant. Flower heads are bristly green globes before unfolding. A *prominent, nest-like cluster of needle-like bracts* envelops the base of the inflorescence.
GENERAL INFORMATION: Introduced from Europe. The cultivated carrot is a race of this species which has been selectively propagated for edible root characteristics.

QUEEN ANNE'S LACE

41

WHITE PRAIRIE-CLOVER

White Prairie-clover

Dalea candida

FAMILY: Bean (Fabaceae)

FLOWERING PERIOD: June and July.

DISTRIBUTION: Statewide, more common east. Central and eastern Great Plains.

HABITAT: Dry soils in prairies and hay meadows, roadsides.

DESCRIPTION: Native perennial growing from a caudex-topped taproot which may extend to a depth of 6 feet. One or more stems from a common base, 1-3 feet tall, occasionally branched above. Leaves alternate on stem, odd-pinnately compound, up to 2.5 inches long. Leaflets (3-5 pairs) obovate to linear-oblong, up to 1.5 inches long with minute glandular dots. Small, white flowers crowded in rings around a green, cylindrical flower head 1-2 inches long. Blooming proceeds from base to tip. Flowers strongly scented.

GENERAL INFORMATION: Highly palatable to livestock and wild grazers. Decreases in abundance under excessive grazing. The Ponca chewed the root for its pleasant taste, Pawnee reportedly bound the tough stems together for use as a broom and a number of Great Plains tribes brewed a tea from its leaves.

Yarrow

Achillea millefolium

OTHER COMMON NAMES: Nosebleed weed, soldier's woundwort, milfoil, old man's pepper.
FAMILY: Sunflower (Asteraceae)
FLOWERING PERIOD: Principally late May and June, into September.
DISTRIBUTION: Statewide, most abundant in the east. Throughout the Great Plains.
HABITAT: Dry soils on moderately disturbed grasslands, pastures, roadsides.
DESCRIPTION: Native perennial growing from fibrous, spreading rhizomes. One or more erect, hairy stems, 1-2 feet tall. Leaves covered with fine hairs; divided into many segments resulting in a fern-like foliage. Strongly aromatic. Small, white to pale-pink flowers gathered into flat-topped clusters (a cyme), 2-4 inches across.
GENERAL INFORMATION: Found in Eurasia as well as North America. Native varieties considered a distinct subspecies. As it was a valued herb in the Old World, Eurasian varieties were introduced to North America. Has been used to treat a variety of ailments including those of the liver and kidneys, gout, influenza and rheumatism. The Winnebagos placed a wad of the leaves in the ear for earaches. The genus name, *Achillea*, is from the mythological Greek warrior Achilles, said to have used the plant to heal wounds. As recently as the Civil War, it was used to stop bleeding, particularly of wounds.

New Jersey Tea

Ceanothus americanus

OTHER COMMON NAMES: Red root, Indian tea, snowbrush, soap-bloom, wild snowball.
FAMILY: Buckthorn (Rhamnaceae)
FLOWERING PERIOD: May into July.
DISTRIBUTION: Southeastern Nebraska. Southeastern Great Plains.
HABITAT: Well-drained, often rocky soils in high-quality tallgrass prairies; hillsides, ravines, roadsides, railways.
DESCRIPTION: An erect, woody, branched shrub 1-2 feet tall or more, growing from deep reddish roots. Often growing in small gatherings of clustered stems. Leaves alternate on stem, broadly oblong, 2-4 inches long, with toothed margins; upper surface dark green, soft pubescence on undersides. The many small, 5-petaled, white flowers in rounded or short-cylindric clusters (a panicle) 1-2 inches long, on 2-4 inch long, leafless stalks (or with only 2 leaf-like bracts) rising from leaf axils on young branches.
GENERAL INFORMATION: Range overlaps with another New Jersey tea, *Ceanothus herbaceous,* which is frequently encountered in the Sandhills region and forms a bushy shrub. Leaves of *Ceanothus herbaceous* do not end in a sharp tip, its flower clusters are flat-topped and the inflorescence stalk usually bears leaves. American Indians dried the leaves to make a tea.

YARROW

NEW JERSEY TEA

Alkali Milk-vetch

Astragalus racemosus

OTHER COMMON NAMES: Creamy poison-vetch, racemed milk-vetch, racemed locoweed.
FAMILY: Bean (Fabaceae)
FLOWERING PERIOD: May and June.
DISTRIBUTION: Northern and south-central Nebraska. Not reported from central or eastern regions. Central and western Great Plains.
HABITAT: Dry to well-drained soils; grasslands, often rocky or disturbed sites, roadsides.
DESCRIPTION: Native perennial growing from a caudex-topped taproot. Few to many stout, erect, hairy stems, 1-2 feet tall; usually branching on upper portion. Leaves alternate, odd-pinnately compound, 2-6 inches long. Leaflets (11-31) linear-lanceolate to ovate, .5-1.5 inches long, minutely hairy on undersides. Flowers, 15-70, yellowish-white (often with tinge of lavender), slender, pea-like, densely crowded on erect stalks (a raceme). Seeds produced in papery, drooping, pea-like pods .5-1 inch long.
GENERAL INFORMATION: Accumulates selenium from the soil. Poisonous to livestock, causing "blind staggers" when consumed in large quantities. Animals may exhibit a variety of symptoms including blindness, aimless wandering, agitation or lethargy. May result in death. Usually avoided by livestock and so is conspicuous in pastures.

Large-flowered Townsendia

Townsendia grandiflora

FAMILY: Sunflower (Asteraceae)
FLOWERING PERIOD: Late May and June.
DISTRIBUTION: Nebraska Panhandle. West-central Great Plains.
HABITAT: Dry, rocky or clay soils in shortgrass plains; eroded banks, ridgelines, rock outcrops.
DESCRIPTION: Native biennial or short-lived perennial growing in a tuft from a substantial, branched taproot. *Stems short,* usually less than 4 inches with few spatulate to oblong-lanceolate leaves 1-2 inches long, most less than .25 inch wide. Leaves originating mostly from root, linear to lanceolate, up to 2 inches long. All leaves gray-green with a whitish pubescence. Single flower head at end of stem; 1-2 inches across; composed of 20-40 white or pinkish petal-like ray florets surrounding a yellow center of disk florets.
GENERAL INFORMATION: A similar species, Easter daisy (*Townsendia exscapa*), is found in western and central Nebraska as well as the western and central Great Plains. It is one of the early flowers of Sandhills uplands. Its flower heads are at ground level, essentially *lacking stems*. Easter daisy blooms from late April through much of May, before large-flowered townsendia, and reportedly was used to decorate pioneer churches at Easter.

ALKALI MILK-VETCH

LARGE-FLOWERED TOWNSENDIA

Death Camass

Zigadenus venenosus

FAMILY: Lily (Liliaceae)
FLOWERING PERIOD: May and June.
DISTRIBUTION: Panhandle of Nebraska. North-western Great Plains.
HABITAT: Dry soils on shortgrass plains; pastures, roadsides, woodland edge and openings.
DESCRIPTION: Native perennial growing from a fibrous bulb . Erect, stiff stem 10-16 inches tall. Leaves grass-like, narrowly linear, bases sheathing stem, often folded, up to 12 inches long. Flowers small (about .3 inch across), composed of 6 creamy-white petals; on short stalks, densely clustered (a raceme) on top 2-4 inches of stem. Each petal has a yellow gland at its base.
GENERAL INFORMATION: All parts of death camass are poisonous but livestock avoid it when adequate forage is available. The bulb could be mistaken for that of a wild onion but it lacks the typical onion odor. A similar plant, white camass *(Zigadenus elegans)* is also found in the Panhandle. It bears a larger inflorescence, its flowers are more showy and nearly twice as large.

DEATH CAMASS

PRICKLY POPPY

WHORLED MILKWEED

Prickly Poppy

Argemone polyanthemos

OTHER COMMON NAMES: Bluestem prickly poppy, thistle poppy.

FAMILY: Poppy (Papaveraceae)

FLOWERING PERIOD: Late May through July, occasionally later.

DISTRIBUTION: Central and western Nebraska. Central and southern Great Plains.

HABITAT: Mildly disturbed sites on grasslands and roadsides. Prefers sandy soil.

DESCRIPTION: Native annual or biennial growing from a taproot. Small plants may establish from seeds the first summer, attaining their full stature and flowering the following growing season. One or several sparsely spiny stems, 2-4 feet tall. Bluish-green leaves, succulent in appearance, covered with a whitish, waxy coating. Leaves alternate, bases clasping the stem; 3-7 inches long; deeply lobed, each lobe ending in a yellowish spine. Principal leaf veins white and on the underside may give rise to occasional prickles. Flowers borne at the ends of branches, 2-4 inches across, composed of 4-6 papery, crinkled, white petals. Yellow cluster of more than 100 stamens in center of flower. Seed capsules, one or more inches long and densely covered with stout yellow spines, appear in midsummer.

Whorled Milkweed

Asclepias verticillata

FAMILY: Milkweed (Asclepiadaceae)

FLOWERING PERIOD: Late June and July, occasionally into September.

DISTRIBUTION: Statewide, more common east. Throughout the Great Plains, becoming infrequent or absent in extreme west.

HABITAT: Dry prairies and plains, particularly on rocky or sandy soils.

DESCRIPTION: Native perennial growing from a shallow root-crown with spreading lateral roots, often forming patches. One to several slender stems, usually not branched, 1-2 feet tall but occasionally taller. Leaves narrowly linear to filiform, 1-3 inches long; arranged in whorls of 3-6 about the stem. Small, greenish-white flowers in clusters of 6-20 at top of stem and from upper leaf axils. Seed pod slender, spindle-shaped, 3-4 inches long with smooth outer surface.

GENERAL INFORMATION: Contains a milky juice reportedly toxic to livestock. Large quantities must be consumed, which is rare, to cause death. The species name is from the Latin *verticillus*, the name given a flywheel of stone or clay used on old, hand-operated spinning spindles to add momentum and stability, a reference to the leaves radiating out from the stem like spokes of a wheel.

Small Soapweed

Yucca glauca

OTHER COMMON NAMES: Yucca, Adam's-needle, soapwell, Spanish bayonet, beargrass.
FAMILY: Agave (Agavaceae)
FLOWERING PERIOD: Late May into July.
DISTRIBUTION: Statewide, most common in central and western Nebraska. Throughout the Great Plains except northeast.
HABITAT: Dry, well-drained, sandy, loess or rocky soils.
DESCRIPTION: Native, semi-woody perennial growing from a thick, woody caudex over a vertical root giving off thick horizontal branches (which give rise to new plants) and numerous slender roots. Older plants with a thick woody stem at ground level. Rosette of stiff, bayonet-like leaves; 16-30 inches long but seldom exceeding .5 inch wide; tapering to a stiff, sharp point; margins with white shedding fibers. Nodding, bell-shaped flowers of 3 petals and 3 sepals, about 2 inches long, crowd the upper half of a stout flower stalk (a raceme), up to 5 feet tall, rising from center of rosette. Flowers creamy-white, greenish-white, occasionally rose tinted. Seed capsules 2-3 inches long; divided into three chambers, each with two rows of flattened black seeds.

GENERAL INFORMATION: Pollination accomplished by a small, night-flying moth which deliberately gathers pollen, flies to another flower, deposits eggs in the flower ovary and spreads the pollen on the stigma to ensure a seed crop. When the moth's eggs hatch, the larvae consume some of developing seeds before boring out and falling to the ground where they winter. Neither moth nor yucca can exist without the other. Crushed soapweed roots agitated in water produce a lather used as a shampoo by American Indians and marketed commercially in the late 1800s. Cord and twine were made from the leaf fibers. Emerging flower stalks resemble and can be eaten like asparagus. Flower buds and immature seed pods were eaten by Great Plains Indian tribes.

SMALL SOAPWEED

47

WHITE BEARDTONGUE

White Beardtongue
Penstemon albidus

OTHER COMMON NAMES: White penstemon, pale beardtongue.
FAMILY: Figwort (Scrophulariaceae)
FLOWERING PERIOD: Late May into July.
DISTRIBUTION: Statewide except southeast, particularly in central and western Nebraska. Throughout the Great Plains except southeast.
HABITAT: Well-drained sandy, sandy loam or gravelly soils in grasslands.
DESCRIPTION: Native perennial growing from a caudex-topped taproot. Stems (1 to 5) *fairly stout*, stiffly erect, not branched, 8-20 inches tall. Leaves opposite, stalkless (somewhat clasping stem), oblong-lanceolate with or without teeth on margins; 1-3 inches long, about .5 inch wide. Herbage may or may not be covered with short stiff hairs. Flowers in clusters of 2-7 on short stalks from upper leaf axils (a thyrse); tubular; flaring to 5 terminal, spreading lobes; white; .5-1 inch long; 4 functional stamens, the 5th only a bearded filament, hence the name "beardtongue."
GENERAL INFORMATION: About 15 species of penstemons found in the Great Plains, 250 or more in North America. Some tribes of Great Plains Indians chewed the root, holding the pulp on an aching tooth to ease the pain.

Slender Beardtongue
Penstemon gracilis

OTHER COMMON NAMES: Slender penstemon, lilac-flowered beardtongue.
FAMILY: Figwort (Scrophulariaceae)
FLOWERING PERIOD: May into July.
DISTRIBUTION: Statewide except southern quarter. Northern half of Great Plains.
HABITAT: Moist to moderately dry, sandy or gravelly soils in grasslands.
DESCRIPTION: Native perennial growing from a slender caudex atop a taproot. Stems (1-4) erect, *slender*, usually not branched; hairy, commonly reddish above; 8-20 inches tall. Leaves dark green; opposite, stalkless (somewhat clasping stem), linear-lanceolate to lanceolate with small or no teeth on margins; 1-3 inches long, less than .5 inch wide; if pubescent, sparingly so. Flowers in clusters of 2-6, on a short stalk from upper leaf axils (a thyrse); tubular, *somewhat flattened;* 5 terminal, spreading to *reflexed lobes;* more papery than fleshy as in white beardtongue; white to *pale lavender;* .5-1 inch long. A rather delicate plant compared to white beardtongue. Inconspicuous and frequently overlooked among tall grasses.

SLENDER BEARDTONGUE

FIELD SNAKE-COTTON

Field Snake-cotton

Froelichia floridana

OTHER COMMON NAMES: Prairie froelichia.
FAMILY: Pigweed (Amaranthaceae)
FLOWERING PERIOD: July into September.
DISTRIBUTION: Statewide in Nebraska. Particularly common in the Sandhills region. Central and southern Great Plains.
HABITAT: Dry, particularly sandy, soil; grasslands, roadsides, railways.
DESCRIPTION: Native annual growing from a taproot. *Stems fairly stout*, erect, often arching; *not branched* or with only a *few erect branches;* mostly leafless; 1.5-3 feet tall. Leaves opposite, without stalks, narrowly oblong, elliptic, oblong-lanceolate or spatulate; 2-4 inches long, about .5 inch wide. Herbage covered with fine soft hairs or matted with woolly hairs. Flowers inconspicuous in woolly spikes at ends of stem or branches, spikes up to 3 inches long. The cottony spike, if not showy, is a curiosity worthy of notice.

GENERAL INFORMATION: A similar species, slender snake-cotton (*Froelichia gracilis*), is also found growing statewide and throughout the central and southern portions of the Great Plains. It has a more delicate stem; is usually more branched at the stem base, with spreading branches; and flower spikes seldom much more than 1 inch long. The two species are known to hybridize producing intermediate forms. Field snake-cotton is frequently found on Sandhills uplands and healing blowouts. Usually growing as single plants or in loose colonies but occasionally forming patches. Their taproots extract subsoil moisture and their sparsity of leaves results in little moisture lost to transpiration. They are plants reduced to the basics, seemingly designed only to endure and produce seed.

False Gromwell

Onosmodium molle

OTHER COMMON NAMES: Marbleseed.
FAMILY: Borage (Boraginaceae)
FLOWERING PERIOD: Late May to July.
DISTRIBUTION: Statewide, less common west. Central and eastern Great Plains.
HABITAT: Dry grasslands, often on sandy, gravelly or rocky (particularly limestone) sites; also in moister river valley soils.
DESCRIPTION: Native perennial growing from a taproot. Stems (1 or more) stout, upright, occasionally branched above, 1-2 feet tall or more. Leaves are coarse, without stalks, alternate on the stem, lanceolate, elliptic or ovate, 2-3 inches long and about 1 inch wide, with prominent rib veins. Herbage gray-green, densely covered with stiff hairs. Drooping flowers clustered at top of plant or branch ends (terminal cymes); composed of 5 pointed, white petals forming a tube about .5 inch long from which a slender style protrudes. Fertilization apparently accomplished within the closed flower. Each flower produces 1-4 glossy nutlets which are extremely hard, hence the name "marbleseed."
GENERAL INFORMATION: Related to, and its herbage resembling that of, hairy puccoon.

FALSE GROMWELL

PRAIRIE FRINGED ORCHIS

White Milkwort
Polygala alba

FAMILY: Milkwort (Polygalaceae)
FLOWERING PERIOD: Late May through July.
DISTRIBUTION: Statewide except east fifth. Throughout the Great Plains, uncommon extreme west and absent east.
HABITAT: Dry, particularly rocky prairie soils; hillsides, bluffs.
DESCRIPTION: Native perennial growing from a woody crown and deep, slender taproot. Usually several slender, unbranched, wand-like stems, 4-16 inches tall, usually less than 1 foot. Leaves few, mostly low on stem; alternate, linear to linear-lanceolate, .5-1 inch long. Small, white flowers densely clustered in narrow spikes (a raceme) 1-2 inches long. Although not showy, an appealing, delicate wildflower.
GENERAL INFORMATION: The dried roots of this plant and a closely related species occurring to the east have the pharmaceutical name "senega;" used by American Indians and white settlers as an antidote for snakebite and for treatment of respiratory ailments. The Sioux used a preparation from the root for earache.

Prairie Fringed Orchis
Platanthera praeclara

FAMILY: Orchid (Orchidaceae)
FLOWERING PERIOD: Late June to mid-July.
DISTRIBUTION: Central and eastern Nebraska. Eastern Great Plains.
HABITAT: Wet to moist soils in tallgrass prairie; meadows, river valleys, swales.
DESCRIPTION: Native perennial growing from coarse, fleshy, somewhat tuberous and fibrous roots. Stout, single stem, 18-30 inches tall. Leaves alternate, lanceolate with bases clasping stem; 4-8 inches long, 1 inch or more wide at base, with parallel veins; reduced in size above. Flowers solitary, in an open arrangement at top of stem (a raceme), up to 40 flowers per stalk, each flower open for a week or more and specialized for insect pollination. Individual flowers 1.25 inches wide, 1.75 inches long; creamy white or greenish; lower lip divided into 3 feathery lobes, smaller upper petals and sepals form a hood, nectar spur (up to 2 inches long) extends back from lower petal. Scent is evident and sweet. Pollination by night-flying hawkmoths.
GENERAL INFORMATION: One of Nebraska's rarest flowers, listed as threatened under the federal Endangered Species Act. Known from only a few sites in eastern Nebraska, the central Platte Valley and northern Sandhills. If found it should be enjoyed where it grows and reported to the Nebraska Game and Parks Commission.

WHITE MILKWORT

51

WHITE WATER-CROWFOOT

White Water-crowfoot
Ranunculus longirostris

FAMILY: Buttercup (Ranunculaceae)
FLOWERING PERIOD: Late May into July.
DISTRIBUTION: Statewide in Nebraska. Throughout the Great Plains.
HABITAT: Shallow water; ponds, lake margins, marshes, ditches, stream margins.
DESCRIPTION: Native aquatic perennial rooting from lower leaf nodes. Stems submerged, floating, 1-3 feet long. Leaves finely divided into hair-like tufts .5-1 inch long. Flowers borne on stalks 1-2 inches above the water surface; about .5 inch across; 5 white petals encircling a yellow center of stamens and numerous pistils. Fruit is a globose head of many achenes.
GENERAL INFORMATION: Frequently covers small ponds or shallow ends of lakes in the Sandhills with white flowers.

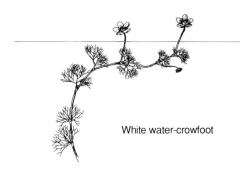
White water-crowfoot

White Waterlily
Nymphaea tuberosa

OTHER COMMON NAMES: Water cabbage, water nymph, American waterlily.
FAMILY: Waterlily (Nymphaeaceae)
FLOWERING PERIOD: June into September.
DISTRIBUTION: Isolated sites, principally eastern half of Nebraska, occasionally found farther west. Eastern Great Plains.
HABITAT: Calm, shallow waters with rich, organic bottoms; river oxbows, ponds, small sandhill lakes or lake margins calmed by emergent and submergent aquatic vegetation.
DESCRIPTION: Native perennial growing from rhizomes with *knotty tubers* which detach to form new plants. May colonize entire surface of small water bodies. Leaves circular, deeply notched to leaf stalk, *greenish on underside*; may stand above water surface when young, floating when mature; up to 1 foot in diameter. Flowers showy, up to 4 inches or more across, rising above or resting on water surface; composed of many white, oval petals surrounding a yellow center of numerous stamens and a single pistil; opening in morning, closing in afternoon, open all day when cloudy. Flowers generally *lack an odor.*
GENERAL INFORMATION: A similar species, fragrant white waterlily *(Nymphaea odorata),* has a similar distribution. Its roots do not bear tubers, leaf undersides are purple or reddish and its flowers are noticeably fragrant.

Halberd-leaved Rose Mallow

Hibiscus laevis

OTHER COMMON NAMES: Marsh mallow, swamp mallow.
FAMILY: Mallow (Malvaceae)
FLOWERING PERIOD: July and August.
DISTRIBUTION: Eastern quarter of Nebraska, principally in the southeast. Southeastern Great Plains.
HABITAT: In shallow water or at the edges of streams, lakes, ponds, ditches.
DESCRIPTION: Native perennial growing from a deep taproot with sturdy lateral roots for support and many fibrous rootlets. Smooth, stout, upright stems, 4-6 feet tall. Leaves alternate on long stalks; triangular or lanceolate, typically, but not always, with a lobe on each side of base; 2-6 inches long with coarsely toothed margins. Flowers on short stalks from upper leaf axils; 5 white to pink petals becoming deep red on interior base; formed into broad funnel about 3 inches across. Flower tube occupied by a stout column lined with pollen-bearing anthers and terminating with 5 joined styles. After a flower's anthers wither, the styles spread to receive pollen brought by bees from other flowers, ensuring cross-pollination. The flowers open in mid or late morning for only a few hours.

GENERAL INFORMATION: A European species of this family was formerly cultivated in the eastern United States for the root's gelatinous substance, used to make marshmallows before synthetics came into use, hence the name of the confection.

HALBERD-LEAVED ROSE MALLOW

WHITE WATERLILY

53

BIG BUR-REED

Big Bur-reed
Sparganium eurycarpum

OTHER COMMON NAMES: Broad-fruited bur-reed.

FAMILY: Bur-reed (Sparganiaceae)

FLOWERING PERIOD: Late May and June.

DISTRIBUTION: Statewide, more common north and east. Central and northern Great Plains, absent in west.

HABITAT: Saturated soils, shallow water; wet meadows, ditches, sloughs, marshes, stream and pond margins.

DESCRIPTION: Native perennial spreading by creeping rhizomes. Stout, erect stem, up to 3 feet tall; sheathed by long, narrow, cattail-like leaves less than .5 inch wide which are V-shaped in cross-section. Flowers in globose heads on zig-zagging stalks; smaller, white male flowers clustered above larger (up to .75 inch in diameter) greenish balls of female flowers. Fruit is a hard, prickly, greenish-brown globe, 1 inch in diameter composed of many achenes.

GENERAL INFORMATION: The fruits are eaten by waterfowl and the entire plant by muskrats.

Watercress
Nasturtium officinale

FAMILY: Mustard (Brassicaceae)

FLOWERING PERIOD: April to October.

DISTRIBUTION: Statewide. Central and southern Great Plains.

HABITAT: Fresh, cool, usually moving waters; shallow springs and streams; saturated soils near springs.

DESCRIPTION: Introduced aquatic perennial rooting at leaf nodes. Stems succulent; branching; submersed, floating or lying on water surface or mud. Occasionally rising 1-2 feet above water surface, filling small springs, but usually not so robust. Leaves somewhat fleshy; deeply divided into 3-9 leaflets; ovate to round, the terminal leaflet largest and rotund. Flowers in clusters (a raceme) at ends of branches; 4 white petals surrounding a stout protruding reddish-brown style.

GENERAL INFORMATION: There has been, and perhaps still is, some disagreement over whether watercress is native to North America or was introduced from Europe. Today, most believe it was introduced. It was widely established by European settlers for use as a salad, garnish, potherb and its purported medicinal values, and since colonial times has spread to most appropriate habitats in North America. During the Middle Ages, watercress was claimed to "kill worms, rectify the intestines, kidneys and bladder; open the liver and spleen; heal and purify internal wounds..." and cure numerous other maladies. It is high in both vitamins A and C.

Watercress leaves

Common Arrowhead

Sagittaria latifolia

OTHER COMMON NAMES: Wapato, broad-leaved arrowhead, duck potato.
FAMILY: Water-plantain (Alismataceae)
FLOWERING PERIOD: July and August.

COMMON ARROWHEAD

DISTRIBUTION: Statewide, more common in eastern Nebraska. Throughout the Great Plains becoming infrequent or absent in west.

HABITAT: Shallow water over organic muds; lake and pond margins, ditches, along slow-moving streams or in backwaters.

DESCRIPTION: Native perennial growing from a rhizome with occasional elongate tubers, 1-2 inches in diameter. Leaf stalks rise from root, typically 1-2 feet long but up to 3 feet; each bearing a single broad, arrowhead-shaped blade 6-12 inches or more long. Flower stalks from roots, more slender and rigid than those of leaves; 3 rounded, white petals around a yellow center of 25-40 stamens; up to 1.75 inches across; lower flowers are female, producing seeds, the upper flowers are male, producing pollen only.

GENERAL INFORMATION: Arrowhead's starchy tubers are slightly bitter if eaten raw but delicious when boiled or roasted. Should be gathered in fall or early spring. They were an important food item for American Indians, early white travelers and for aquatic wildlife. Indians were known to raid muskrat food caches to gather the tubers. This is the most common of several species of arrowheads found in the state and the Great Plains.

Gumbo Evening Primrose
Oenothera caespitosa

OTHER COMMON NAMES: Tufted evening-primrose, gumbo lily, rock rose.
FAMILY: Evening Primrose (Onagraceae)
FLOWERING PERIOD: Early May to August.
DISTRIBUTION: Nebraska Panhandle. Northwestern Great Plains.
HABITAT: Dry clay or rocky soils; buttes, banks, badlands.
DESCRIPTION: Native perennial, 4-6 inches tall, growing from a branching crown over a taproot. Lateral roots may give rise to new plants. *Leaves emerge from ground* forming a rosette; oblong-lanceolate with pointed tip, *coarsely and irregularly toothed*, 2-6 inches long, .5-1 inch wide. Flower stalks emerge from rosette holding flowers above leaves. Flowers 2.5-4 inches across; 4 large, white, *heart-shaped petals*, 8 prominent, pale yellow stamens and a single, even longer style with cross-shaped stigma. Flowers open in late afternoon, usually closing in late morning the following day, withering to pink or red-violet.
GENERAL INFORMATION: There are several white-flowered evening primroses this species could be confused with, but all have distinct stems, none grow in tufts or rosettes.

White-stemmed Evening Primrose
Oenothera nuttallii

OTHER COMMON NAMES: Nuttall's evening primrose.
FAMILY: Evening Primrose (Onagraceae)
FLOWERING PERIOD: June through August.
DISTRIBUTION: Western and central Nebraska. Central and northern Great Plains.
HABITAT: Dry, particularly sandy, soils; grasslands, roadsides.
DESCRIPTION: Native perennial growing from a caudex, spreading by lateral roots. One or more erect stems, usually branching, 1-2 feet tall, whitish "bark" often shedding in thin layers. Leaves alternate, linear to linear-oblong, 1-3 inches long, usually with *smooth margins*. Flowers on stalks from upper leaf axils; buds drooping, opening late in the day; 1-2 inches across; 4 white petals, *not notched;* 8 bright yellow stamens with large anthers, style even longer with cross-shaped stigma. Flower's scent strong and considered unpleasant. Flowers fading to pink or rose.
GENERAL INFORMATION: Identification of western Nebraska's white-flowered evening primroses is difficult, often falling in the realm of the professional botanist. Of those, this species has relatively large flowers and its leaves are usually not toothed.

GUMBO EVENING PRIMROSE

WHITE-STEMMED EVENING PRIMROSE

Combleaf Evening Primrose

Oenothera coronopifolia

FAMILY: Evening Primrose (Onagraceae)
FLOWERING PERIOD: Late May, June, through July.
DISTRIBUTION: Nebraska Panhandle. West-central Great Plains.
HABITAT: Sandy or rocky soils in grasslands; roadsides, floodplains, pastures.
DESCRIPTION: Native perennial growing from a slender caudex and spreading by rhizomes. Stems greenish, erect, branching at base, with sharp, stiff hairs, 4-12 inches tall. Principal stem leaves alternate, *deeply divided* into narrow, lateral lobes (reminiscent of a rooster's comb, hence the common name); .5-1.5 inches long, less than .5 inch wide. Flowers on stalks from upper leaf axils; buds drooping, opening late in the day; .5-1 inch across; 4 white petals only *slightly notched;* 8 bright yellow stamens with large anthers, style longer than stamens with cross-shaped stigma. Flowers fading to pink or rose.
GENERAL INFORMATION: Often locally abundant in years with above average rainfall, filling pastures with white flowers. This species most easily confused with pale evening primrose *(Oenothera latifolia)* which is taller, up to 20 inches; has whitish stems; leaves with coarse teeth and wavy margins; and larger flowers, 1-3 inches across.

COMBLEAF EVENING PRIMROSE

57

Bouncing Bet

Saponaria officinalis

OTHER COMMON NAMES: Soapwort, sweet Betty, old-maid's pink, lady-by-the-gate.
FAMILY: Pink (Caryophyllaceae)
FLOWERING PERIOD: Late June, principally July, into August.
DISTRIBUTION: Statewide, principally east. Scattered throughout the Great Plains, most common southeast.
HABITAT: Variety of soils; roadsides, railways, old farmsteads.
DESCRIPTION: Naturalized perennial spreading by rhizomes and forming colonies. Stems smooth, erect; if branched, only below; leafy, 1-2 feet tall. Leaves opposite, without stalks, ovate-lanceolate, 2-3 inches long; lower ones usually shedding before the time of flowering. Flowers abundant, on short-stalked clusters near top of stem (a cyme); tubular, emerging from a conspicuous (.5 inch or longer) green base (calyx), spreading to 5 notched lobes; pink or white; about 1 inch across. Fragrant.
GENERAL INFORMATION: Bruised leaves agitated in water produce a bubbly lather once used in Europe to clean and whiten fabrics. It was said the white, spreading petals resembled the pinned-up petticoats of a wash woman (given the generic name Bet) bustling about her work. It once was a favorite farmyard flower.

Hoary False Alyssum

Berteroa incana

FAMILY: Mustard (Brassicaceae)
FLOWERING PERIOD: June through August.
DISTRIBUTION: Northern and eastern Nebraska. Principally northeastern Great Plains.
HABITAT: Disturbed sites in a variety of soils; roadsides, railways, pastures.
DESCRIPTION: A naturalized, weedy annual from Europe. Stiff, erect stems, usually branched above, 2 feet or slightly more in height. Leaves alternate on the stem, oblong-lanceolate, occasionally elliptic, up to 2 inches long. All parts pubescent with short, grayish or whitish hairs resulting in gray-green colored herbage. Flowers small, white, on upper branches (a raceme) which continue to elongate throughout the growing season; petals deeply divided into two lobes. Flowers replaced by green, beaked elliptical fruit capsules which line the stalk under the terminal ring of flowers. Capsules are typical of plants belonging to the mustard family, being divided into halves by a thin membrane.
GENERAL INFORMATION: Although probably not considered a wildflower by many, and an outright weed by others, the flowers and fruits are interesting and attractive when viewed closely. It is encountered frequently enough in some regions to warrant knowing its name.

BOUNCING BET

HOARY FALSE ALYSSUM

White Campion
Silene pratensis

OTHER COMMON NAMES: Thunder flower, cow-rattle, snake flower, white cockle.
FAMILY: Pink (Caryophyllaceae)
FLOWERING PERIOD: June into September.
DISTRIBUTION: Potentially statewide except southwest. Northern and eastern Great Plains.
HABITAT: In a variety of disturbed soils; fields, roadsides, occasionally in grasslands.
DESCRIPTION: Naturalized biennial or short-lived perennial growing from a stout taproot. Stems simple or branched below, erect or with base reclining on ground; densely covered with fine white hairs, particularly on upper half; 1-2 feet tall. Leaves opposite, lower leaves on short stalks (but often shed by time of flowering), upper leaves stalkless; lanceolate to broadly elliptic, 1-4 inches long; both surfaces with minute hairs. Male and female flowers on different plants; a flower bears *only stamens or only pistils*. Conspicuous green, tubular structure (calyx) immediately below the white petals; slender in male flowers, inflated and bladder-like in female flowers. Flowers spread over top of plant (a freely branched cyme); .75-1 inch across, petals with a deep cleft, slightly fragrant; open dusk into next morning.
GENERAL INFORMATION: Might easily be confused with night-flowering catchfly *(Silene noctiflora)*, also called "sticky cockle," which has a similar distribution. Both the male and female structures are found on the same flower in night-flowering catchfly. Catchfly, particularly the flowering parts, are sticky to the touch. Both species were inadvertently introduced from Europe.

SEGO LILY

Sego Lily
Calochortus gunnisonii

OTHER COMMON NAMES: Mariposa lily.
FAMILY: Lily (Liliaceae)
FLOWERING PERIOD: Late May, June.
DISTRIBUTION: Northern Panhandle of Nebraska. Great Plains range is northwest Nebraska, southwest South Dakota, eastern Wyoming.
HABITAT: Dry hillsides in grasslands and open areas in pine woodlands.
DESCRIPTION: Native perennial growing from onion-like bulb to height of 10-20 inches. Erect, slender stem with 2-4 linear, flattened leaves 7-10 inches long. Flowers, 1-3, are borne at top of stem; white but occasionally with purplish tinge; composed of 3 large petals up to 1-1.5 inches long and 3 narrower, white sepals. Base of each petal's inner surface yellow with numerous gland-tipped hairs surrounding an *oblong, somewhat arched gland* above which

is a narrow purple band. A second species of sego lily, *Calochortus nuttallii*, is also found in the same region. Differences between them are subtle. Two features observed with a hand lens will aid identification. The gland of *C. nuttallii* is circular. The anther of *C. gunnisonii* is longer than the filament supporting it while the anther of *C. nuttalli* is nearly equal to filament length.
GENERAL INFORMATION: The bulb was a staple of Indian tribes of the region. The bulbs are about 1 inch across and sweet tasting, said by some to resemble a potato in taste when boiled or baked. The Cheyenne dried the bulbs for winter use. Nineteenth century naturalist George Bird Grinnell wrote that the dried bulb "makes a sweet porridge or mush." *Calochortus nuttallii* is the state flower of Utah. When the crops of Mormon settlers were destroyed by plagues of grasshoppers (Mormon crickets), sego lily bulbs, "like manna from heaven," helped sustain them.

Prairie Larkspur
Delphinium virescens

OTHER COMMON NAMES: Plains larkspur.
FAMILY: Buttercup (Ranunculaceae)
FLOWERING PERIOD: Late May into July.
DISTRIBUTION: Statewide. Throughout all but the far northern and northwestern Great Plains.
HABITAT: Grasslands and pastures.
DESCRIPTION: Native perennial growing from fibrous roots, occasionally bearing tuberous enlargements. Usually a single pubescent stem 1-3 feet tall, occasionally in clumps or colonies. Leaves alternate, mostly on lower half of stem; 2-5 inches across, deeply dissected into a palmate arrangement of linear segments. Leaves smaller, on shorter stalks higher on stem. Flowers, 5-30, on short stalks (spike-like racemes) on upper portion of stem. Flower composed of 5 spreading white sepals marked with a purplish-brown spot, the upper sepal arched back in a spur. Within the sepals are 4 smaller white petals; the upper two with nectar-bearing spurs extending into the larger sepal spur. Conspicuous dark brown anthers.
GENERAL INFORMATION: Contains a toxic alkaloid poisonous to livestock if consumed in large quantities. The dried plant is apparently harmless. *Delphinium* is Greek for "dolphin," a reference to the shape of the flower.

PRAIRIE LARKSPUR

Plains Beebalm
Monarda pectinata

OTHER COMMON NAMES: Spotted beebalm, plains or lemon monarda.
FAMILY: Mint (Lamiaceae)
FLOWERING PERIOD: Late May, June, through July.
DISTRIBUTION: Western and central Nebraska. Southwestern Great Plains.
HABITAT: Dry sandy or gravelly soils in grasslands. Increases on overgrazed or on disturbed sites.
DESCRIPTION: Native annual. Stems stiffly erect, single or branching from base, often branching above, 8-16 inches tall. Leaves lanceolate to elliptic, 1-1.5 inches long; sparsely pubescent, toothed margins, densely dotted with oil glands. Flowers in compact, head-like clusters encircling upper portion of stem, each atop a whorl of leafy bracts. Flowers small, white with pinkish tinge; with prominent upper lip and 3-lobed lower lip.
GENERAL INFORMATION: Plant is fragrant and contains thymol, used as an ingredient in antiseptic preparations and as a fungicide. Indian tribes of the southwest used it to season food.

PLAINS BEEBALM

61

Western Fleabane
Erigeron bellidiastrum

FAMILY: Sunflower (Asteraceae)

FLOWERING PERIOD: June and July, into August.

DISTRIBUTION: Western half of Nebraska. Southwestern Great Plains.

HABITAT: Moist, often sandy soil in grasslands; particularly mildly disturbed sites.

DESCRIPTION: Native annual growing from a taproot. Erect, branching stems up to 20 inches tall but usually shorter and somewhat sprawling. Numerous leaves, .5-2 inches long; linear to narrowly oblong-lanceolate; lower leaves often shed by time of flowering. Herbage with minute whitish hairs. Several to many showy flower heads, .5-.8 inch across; 30-70 white to pinkish or pale blue petal-like ray florets surrounding a bright yellow button composed of disk florets.

GENERAL INFORMATION: Flower heads are aster-like, however it has generally finished flowering before asters begin.

Low Fleabane
Erigeron pumilus

FAMILY: Sunflower (Asteraceae)

FLOWERING PERIOD: Late May, June, into July.

DISTRIBUTION: Panhandle and north-central Nebraska. Northwestern Great Plains.

HABITAT: Dry, particularly on rocky soils in grasslands.

DESCRIPTION: Native perennial. Several stiff, erect stems, 4-8 inches tall, rise from a caudex-topped taproot. Leaves linear to narrowly oblong lanceolate, up to 3 inches long but mostly shorter. Herbage has conspicuous white hairs. Showy flower heads (about 1 inch in diameter) terminal on stems and branches; composed of 50 to 100 slender, white, petal-like ray florets surrounding a pale yellow or greenish-yellow button of disk florets. Disk about one-third total width of the flower head.

GENERAL INFORMATION: Flower heads are aster-like, however it has generally finished flowering before asters begin.

WESTERN FLEABANE

LOW FLEABANE

DAISY FLEABANE

Daisy Fleabane

Erigeron strigosus

FAMILY: Sunflower (Asteraceae)

FLOWERING PERIOD: May into August, principally June and July.

DISTRIBUTION: Statewide, more abundant in eastern Nebraska; throughout the Great Plains except in west.

HABITAT: Moist to drier soils, often on sites of moderate disturbance; overgrazed or recovering pastures, roadsides, railways, woodland edge.

DESCRIPTION: Native annual or biennial. Erect, nearly leafless stems, branching above, 1-3 feet tall. Basal leaves *oblong-lanceolate, olliptic to noarly lincar;* up to 5 inches long, less than 1 inch wide; *margins usually without teeth.* Upper leaves alternate on stem, smaller, narrower, margins usually without teeth. Herbage with stiff, whitish hairs. Few to many small flower heads (.5-.75 inch in diameter) borne at ends of branches; composed of 50-100 white, petal-like ray florets surrounding a yellow-green button of disk florets.

GENERAL INFORMATION: Probably our most common fleabane, particularly in the east. Easily confused with a number of similar species, particularly annual fleabane *(Erigeron annuus)* in the eastern third of Nebraska. Lower leaves of annual fleabane, though, are elliptic to broadly ovate and *usually toothed.* The common name comes from the belief that when these plants were dried and stuffed into a mattress they would repel fleas and other insects. Another superstition held that if a pregnant woman planted fleabane, her child would be a boy if the flowers were tinged with blue, a girl if tinged with pink.

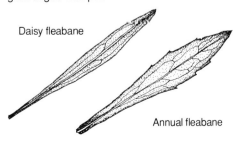

Daisy fleabane

Annual fleabane

WILD LICORICE

WILD LICORICE FRUIT

Wild Licorice

Glycyrrhiza lepidota

FAMILY: Bean (Fabaceae)

FLOWERING PERIOD: Late May into August.

DISTRIBUTION: Statewide in Nebraska. Throughout the Great Plains.

HABITAT: Moist to moderately dry, rich soils; grasslands, stream valleys, roadsides and railways. Often sites of mild disturbance.

DESCRIPTION: Native perennial growing from deep (8-10 feet), spreading, woody rhizomes. Stems stout, erect, branched, 1-3 feet tall. Leaves alternate, odd-pinnately compound; 7-21 oblong or oblong-lanceolate leaflets 1-2 inches long. The stems and leaves dotted with minute glands. Greenish yellow to white, pea-like flowers densely crowded into spike-like clusters (racemes) on stalks emerging from upper leaf axils. Clusters of reddish-brown, elongated, cocklebur-like fruits about .5 inch long, densely covered with hooked prickles. The fruit and flowers are often found at the same time on a plant.

GENERAL INFORMATION: Root or root extracts used by American Indians for a variety of medicinal uses—to reduce fevers in children, as a blood clotting agent, and to induce menstrual flow and aid the expulsion of the afterbirth. It is from a similar European species that commercial licorice is prepared, though the American species has also been used as a flavoring. The roots were eaten raw or roasted by Great Plains Indians, having a taste somewhat like a sweet potato.

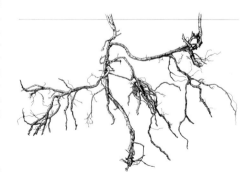

Catnip
Nepeta cataria

OTHER COMMON NAMES: Catmint, catwort, catnep, field balm.
FAMILY: Mint (Lamiaceae)
FLOWERING PERIOD: June through September.
DISTRIBUTION: Statewide, more common in eastern Nebraska. Throughout all but the western and southern Great Plains.
HABITAT: Sunny or shaded disturbed sites; farmsteads, pastures, thickets, open woods, roadsides.
DESCRIPTION: Naturalized perennial growing from a caudex and stout, short taproot; spreading by lateral roots and branching crown. Stems (1 to several) squarish, upright, branched, 2-3 feet tall. Leaves opposite, on stalks about half as long as blade; ovate, triangular to cordate (heart-shaped); 2-3 inches long and half as wide; margins toothed; sparsely pubescent above, densely pubescent below. Flowers small (.25-.5 inch long), in spike-like clusters at ends of branches and upper leaf axils; white with pinkish tinge and red-violet markings; an upper hood and lower lip typical of mints.
GENERAL INFORMATION: When crushed, leaf glands release volatile oil with a musty, minty odor of much interest to cats. Tea made from leaves was considered a general tonic and remedy for many ailments including colic, hives, influenza, and nervous and stomach disorders. Also used as a flavoring.

Virginia Mountain Mint
Pycnanthemum virginianum

OTHER COMMON NAMES: Horsemint.
FAMILY: Mint (Lamiaceae)
FLOWERING PERIOD: Late June through August.
DISTRIBUTION: Central and eastern Nebraska. Eastern Great Plains.
HABITAT: Moist soils; meadows, low prairies, along streams.
DESCRIPTION: Native perennial growing from slender rhizomes. Stems square, branching near the top, hairy, 16-35 inches tall. Leaves numerous, linear-lanceolate, often hairy on underside along mid-vein, .75-2 inches long, fragrantly aromatic when crushed. Flowers small, typical of mints with a hood and lower lip; white, often with lavender tinge; in small, compact, head-like clusters less than .5 inch across; the clusters arranged in a flat-topped inflorescence.
GENERAL INFORMATION: Leaves can be dried and used to make a mint tea.

CATNIP

VIRGINIA MOUNTAIN MINT

SWEET SAND VERBENA

Sweet Sand Verbena
Abronia fragrans

OTHER COMMON NAMES: Heart's-delight, prairie snowball.
FAMILY: Four-o'clock (Nyctaginaceae)
FLOWERING PERIOD: June into August. Flowers open late, persist into the next day.
DISTRIBUTION: Nebraska Sandhills and Panhandle. Southwestern Great Plains.
HABITAT: Sandy soils in grasslands. Often on disturbed sites.
DESCRIPTION: Native perennial growing from a deep, woody taproot. Few to many stems, usually hairy, often reclining; 1-2 feet tall; older plants form open, bushy clumps as wide as tall. Leaves opposite, variable in shape, lanceolate to ovate, dark green on upper surface. Many small, fragrant white flowers in spherical heads 2-3 inches across.

Painted Milk-vetch
Astragalus ceramicus

OTHER COMMON NAMES: Bird's-egg vetch, rattle-weed, painted pod.
FAMILY: Bean (Fabaceae)
FLOWERING PERIOD: Late May into July. Mature pods mostly from late June into July.
DISTRIBUTION: Principally Panhandle and Sandhills in Nebraska. Western Great Plains.
HABITAT: Sandy soils in grasslands. Disturbed sites; often associated with blowouts.
DESCRIPTION: Native perennial growing from a caudex and spreading rhizomes. Stems are weak, stick-like, often reclining on ground and often somewhat zigzag in form, 2-15 inches in length. Leaves mostly reduced to slender, grass-like stalks. Small, inconspicuous, pea-like, white to pinkish flowers; 2-7 per stalk from upper leaf axils (axillary racemes). Fruiting pod showy; 1-2 inches long; bladder-like; cream-colored, mottled with red to reddish-purple; containing several small, brown seeds.

PAINTED MILK-VETCH

Ten-petal Mentzelia
Mentzelia decapetala

OTHER COMMON NAMES: Prairie lily, blazing star, stickleaf, sand lily.
FAMILY: Stickleaf (Loasaceae)
FLOWERING PERIOD: June into September.
DISTRIBUTION: Central and western Nebraska. Much of central and western Great Plains.
HABITAT: Dry soils; particularly rocky, gravelly or clay banks; roadsides and grasslands. Disturbed sites. Usually *not on sandy soils*.
DESCRIPTION: Native biennial or short-lived perennial growing from a strong, deep taproot. Stout, erect stems (1 to several), branching above forming bushy clumps 1.5-3 feet tall. Leaves alternate, gray-green, up to 6 inches long; mostly stalkless, lanceolate or narrowly oblong; deeply toothed with wavy margins; covered with barbed hairs (hence the name stickleaf). Flowers are abundant at ends of branches, 2-4 inches across; 10 creamy-white oblong-lanceolate petals surrounding central mass of yellow stamens. Flowers open and fragrant late afternoon, closing in early morning unless overcast. Pollination by moths or other night-flying insects. Numerous seeds produced in cylindrical capsules, 1-2 inches long.
GENERAL INFORMATION: Bractless mentzelia *(Mentzelia nuda)* is found in the Panhandle, southwest counties and Sandhills *on sandy soils*. It is a more delicate plant in most regards with slightly smaller flowers.

TEN-PETAL MENTZELIA

Gilia
Ipomopsis longiflora

FAMILY: Polemonium (Polemoniaceae)
FLOWERING PERIOD: June through August.
DISTRIBUTION: Nebraska Panhandle and Sandhills. Central and southern Great Plains.
HABITAT: Dry sandy soil in grasslands.
DESCRIPTION: Annual or biennial growing from a strong, deep taproot with fine branching lateral roots. Stems slender, erect, branched above, 1-2 feet tall or more. Leaves not conspicuous; alternate on stem, without stalks, .5-1 inch long; lower leaves deeply divided into 3-5 linear segments. Upper leaves becoming progressively reduced and filiform. Flowers in clusters at ends of branches; trumpet-shaped, narrow tubes about 2 inches long, flaring into 4-5 lobes at end, up to .75 inch wide; white or with bluish tinge.
GENERAL INFORMATION: Well adapted to dry grasslands because of efficient root system and reduced foliage. Pollinated by "long-tongued" night-flying moths.

GILIA

PURPLE MEADOW RUE

CANADA MILK-VETCH

Purple Meadow Rue

Thalictrum dasycarpum

OTHER COMMON NAMES: Maid-of-the-mist.
FAMILY: Buttercup (Ranunculaceae)
FLOWERING PERIOD: June and July.
DISTRIBUTION: Statewide, more common in northern and eastern Nebraska. Northern and eastern Great Plains.
HABITAT: Moist soils, full sun or partial shade; meadows, river valleys, roadsides, shorelines.
DESCRIPTION: Native perennial growing from a caudex with rhizomes and often spreading to form colonies on favorable sites. Stem is erect, branched and leafy toward the top, often with a purplish tinge, 2-6 feet tall. The leaves are compound, divided into leaflets on stalks; most leaflets 1-2 inches long and half as wide with three prominent lobes; dark green above, underside pale and pubescent. Foliage reminiscent of columbine's. Numerous small, white flowers in feathery plumes (panicles) at ends of upper branches. Male and female flowers usually found on separate plants.
GENERAL INFORMATION: Meadow rue is rich in lore. The Pawnee used it as a stimulant for their horses. A root tea was used by other tribes as a stimulant and tonic and to reduce fevers. The seeds were smoked with tobacco to bring good luck when hunting or courting. The Teton Dakota spread the maturing fruits in their lodges and rubbed them on clothing for the pleasant scent.

Canada Milk-vetch

Astragalus canadensis

OTHER COMMON NAMES: Carolina milk-vetch, little rattle-pod (Omaha-Ponca).
FAMILY: Bean (Fabaceae)
FLOWERING PERIOD: July and August.
DISTRIBUTION: Statewide except southwest, more frequent in eastern Nebraska. Eastern and central Great Plains.
HABITAT: Moist prairie soils; along streams and drainages, woodland and thicket edges, roadsides.
DESCRIPTION: Native perennial growing from rhizomes, often forming shrubby patches. Stout, usually erect stems (lower portions occasionally reclining on ground); often branched, 1-4 feet tall, occasionally taller. Leaves alternate, odd-pinnately compound, 2-14 inches long; leaflets, 15-35, lanceolate, oblong or ovate, .5-1.5 inches long. Flowers elongated, pea-like, creamy or greenish white; densely crowded on candle-like stalks (racemes) 2-8 inches long from upper leaf axils. Fruit is a beaked, bean-like pod less than 1 inch long. The largest and most conspicuous of our milk-vetches.
GENERAL INFORMATION: Unlike most milk-vetches, palatable to livestock. Omaha-Ponca boys reportedly used the dried pods as rattles when imitating tribal dances. Fresh meat was laid on cut plants when butchering to keep it clean. Teton Dakota used a decoction of the root to reduce fevers in children.

Illinois Bundleflower

Desmanthus illinoensis

OTHER COMMON NAMES: Prairie mimosa, false sensitive plant.
FAMILY: Mimosa (Mimosaceae)
FLOWERING PERIOD: Late June, peaking in July, into August.
DISTRIBUTION: Statewide except Panhandle and Sandhills. Southern Great Plains.
HABITAT: Dry or moist soils in grasslands; ravines, meadows, edges of wet areas, roadsides.
DESCRIPTION: Native perennial growing from a somewhat woody caudex. Stems 2-4 feet or taller, grooved, *without prickles*, branching at base. Leaves bipinnately compound, 2-4 inches long with numerous tiny leaflets. Flower heads on 1-3 inch stalks from upper leaf axils. Small, creamy-white flowers gathered in pompon-like globes, about .5 inch across, with long, yellow, protruding stamens. Cluster of flattened, brown fruiting pods curve and twist into a globular mass and persist through the winter.
GENERAL INFORMATION: Leaves sensitive to touch, leaflets folding together in strong winds or when handled. Flower heads and foliage are similar to sensitive brier which has *stem prickles* and bears pinkish, ball-shaped flower heads. High in protein, bundleflower is an important native legume for livestock forage, and decreases under heavy grazing.

Illinois bundleflower fruiting pods

INDIAN PLANTAIN

Indian Plantain

Cacalia plantaginea

OTHER COMMON NAMES: Tuberous or prairie plantain.
FAMILY: Sunflower (Asteraceae)
FLOWERING PERIOD: June and July, into August.
DISTRIBUTION: Eastern Nebraska, principally southeast. Southeastern Great Plains.
HABITAT: Moist to wet soils in meadows, prairies and near wetlands.
DESCRIPTION: Native perennial growing from a short, tuberous caudex with fleshy and fibrous roots. Stout, erect, angled-and-grooved stem; 2-4 feet tall or more. Lower leaves alternate, on long stalks; ovate, thick, firm and leathery, usually with smooth margins but occasionally toothed; with prominent, roughly parallel veins; leaf blades up to 6 inches long and half as wide. Flat-topped inflorescence (a cyme) of 50-100 flowers. The most conspicuous part of the flower head is the capsule-shaped gathering of 5 lime-green bracts with whitish ribs which enclose the florets. The outer ends of the 5 tubular disk florets barely emerge from the bracts.
GENERAL INFORMATION: Indian plantain seldom strays far from moist-soiled bottomlands. On upland sites, usually found growing at the base of slopes or in ravines where moisture is plentiful. Most often occurs as isolated plants but occasionally found growing in loose gatherings.

Flowering Spurge

Euphorbia corollata

FAMILY: Spurge (Euphorbiaceae)
FLOWERING PERIOD: Late June, July and into August.
DISTRIBUTION: Eastern Nebraska, principally southeast. Southeastern Great Plains.
HABITAT: Dry soils in prairies, pastures, roadsides, railways.
DESCRIPTION: Native perennial. One or more erect stems, 1-3 feet tall, branching above, growing from a caudex atop a stout, deep root. Leaves alternate; those on the midstem linear, oblong or elliptic on short stalks or stalkless; 1-2 inches long. Lower leaves often shed by time of flowering. Several flower stalks spread from above a whorl of leaves, dividing again at a pair of smaller leaves and bearing shorter stalks with numerous small white flowers. The 5 white, petal-like bracts surround several inconspicuous male flowers and a single female flower. When ripe, the seed capsule snaps open, expelling the seeds some distance from the parent plant.
GENERAL INFORMATION: The plant's milky juice is toxic and causes skin irritation. Early-day herbalists used the powdered root bark to induce vomiting, to clear the respiratory tract of mucus and to purge troubled souls of unwanted emotions, often with violent effects.

SNOW-ON-THE-MOUNTAIN

Snow-on-the-mountain
Euphorbia marginata

OTHER COMMON NAMES: Variegated spurge, wolf's milk.

FAMILY: Spurge (Euphorbiaceae)

FLOWERING PERIOD: July into September.

DISTRIBUTION: Statewide in Nebraska. Throughout all but the northernmost Great Plains.

HABITAT: On dry or moist soils in grasslands, roadsides; abundant in overgrazed pastures.

DESCRIPTION: Native annual. Stout, erect, stems 1-3 feet tall or more, branching near top, sparsely covered with hairs. Leaves alternate, stalkless; oblong, ovate or elliptic; 1-4 inches long. Small, inconspicuous flowers borne in cups with white, petal-like appendages. Whorls of leaves and bracts below the flowers have *prominent white margins.*

GENERAL INFORMATION: Because of its attractive foliage, frequently cultivated in gardens in the East where it is not native, and in Europe. The milky juice is toxic and causes skin irritation. It reportedly has been used to brand cattle. Because of its bitter taste livestock avoid it. In spite of that, Dakota Indians reportedly administered a tea made from the plant to mothers unable to produce milk.

FLOWERING SPURGE

Tall Cinquefoil

Potentilla arguta

OTHER COMMON NAMES: White or glandular cinquefoil.

FAMILY: Rose (Rosaceae)

FLOWERING PERIOD: June and July.

DISTRIBUTION: Eastern and northern Nebraska. North half and southeast Great Plains.

HABITAT: Moist to moderately dry soils; prairies, open woods, roadsides.

DESCRIPTION: Native perennial growing from a stout, branched caudex. Stems erect, not branching until top, 1-3 feet tall. Lower leaves on long stalks, pinnately compound; 7-11 leaflets with sharply toothed margins, most about 2.5 inches long, end leaflets largest. Leaves higher on plant with fewer and smaller leaflets. All parts of herbage covered with soft, white, somewhat sticky hairs. Flowers in compact clusters at top of stem; .5-.75 inch across; 5 white petals; yellow stamens encircling a yellow button of compound pistils.

GENERAL INFORMATION: The common name cinquefoil is derived from Latin and means "five leaves." Some plants of this group have 5 leaflets. *Potentilla* translates from Latin as "potent little plant," a reference to the medicinal values assigned some species of this genus. Indian tribes in the Great Lakes region put the powdered root on duck down and applied it to wounds to stop bleeding.

TALL CINQUEFOIL

FLOWER-OF-AN-HOUR

CAROLINA HORSE-NETTLE

Flower-of-an-hour

Hibiscus trionum

OTHER COMMON NAMES: Modesty, good night at noone, Venice mallow.

FAMILY: Mallow (Malvaceae)

FLOWERING PERIOD: Late June into September.

DISTRIBUTION: Eastern half of Nebraska. Principally the eastern Great Plains but occasional throughout.

HABITAT: Disturbed soils; pastures, field margins, roadsides, railways, farmyards, urban areas.

DESCRIPTION: Naturalized annual weed from Europe. Low-growing, the stem branching and spreading near base, with coarse hairs, usually less than 1 foot tall but occasionally more. Leaves on long stalks, deeply divided into 3-7 palmately arranged segments; each segment roughly lanceolate and lobed. Hairy, ridged, bladder-like bracts open to reveal 5 yellowish-white petals, which are deep red on interior base; 1-2.5 inches across. Cluster of stamens at the flower's center bear bright yellow anthers and surround the pistil with 5 reddish-brown stigmas.

GENERAL INFORMATION: The flowers are open for only a few hours during the early morning, closing before noon unless the sky is overcast, hence the old English name for the plant, "good night at noone."

Carolina Horse-nettle

Solanum carolinense

OTHER COMMON NAMES: Apple-of-Sodom, bull-nettle, tread-softly.

FAMILY: Nightshade (Solanaceae)

FLOWERING PERIOD: May into September.

DISTRIBUTION: Eastern third of Nebraska, principally southeast. Native to southeastern U.S.; apparently introduced and spreading in the southeastern Great Plains.

HABITAT: Disturbed, particularly sandy, soils; cultivated fields, pastures, farmsteads.

DESCRIPTION: Perennial spreading by branching rootstocks and slender, creeping rhizomes. Stems erect, branched, pubescent and sparsely covered with yellow prickles; .5-2 feet or more tall. Leaves alternate, on stalks .5-1 inch long, ovate to roughly triangular with few large lobes, veins on underside with spines; 2-4 inches long. Flowers in one-sided clusters; 5 white, crinkly, petal-like lobes joined at base; 5 conspicuous, bright yellow anthers. Fruit is a yellow, spherical, juicy berry about .5 inch in diameter.

GENERAL INFORMATION: In addition to being a troublesome weed in fields, the plant is poisonous to livestock. The fruit, though attractive, can cause death and *should not be eaten*. The plant contains a chemical which has been used as a sedative.

73

Boneset

Eupatorium perfoliatum

FAMILY: Sunflower (Asteraceae)
FLOWERING PERIOD: Late July, August.
DISTRIBUTION: Statewide, more common in eastern Nebraska. Eastern Great Plains.
HABITAT: Moist to wet prairies, streamsides and river valleys, woodland edge.
DESCRIPTION: Native perennial growing from fibrous roots with branching rhizomes. One to several stout, densely pubescent stems 2-5 feet tall, branching above. Leaves long, tapering lanceolate, in pairs opposite on stem, bases joined to each other and surrounding stem; margin toothed, surface rough and reticulate. Creamy-white florets (9-23) gathered in heads, clustered to form a flat-topped inflorescence at ends of branches.
GENERAL INFORMATION: Boneset tea was a popular folk medicine used to treat a variety of ailments—influenza, malaria, colds, rheuma-

tism and fevers, and a viral disease called "dengue" or "breakbone fever," hence the name "bone-set," implying it would alleviate breakbone fever.

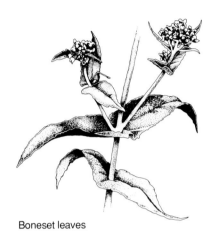

Boneset leaves

BONESET

74

White Snakeroot
Eupatorium rugosum

OTHER COMMON NAMES: Deerwort boneset, snake weed, squaw weed, white sanicle.
FAMILY: Sunflower (Asteraceae)
FLOWERING PERIOD: July into September.
DISTRIBUTION: Eastern third of Nebraska, isolated sites central. Eastern Great Plains, principally southeast.
HABITAT: Moist, rich, disturbed soils in shade or partial shade; urban areas, open woodlands, riverbottoms.
DESCRIPTION: Native perennial growing from a rhizome and fibrous roots; buds from the underground stem forming new plants. Erect, branching stems, 2-3 feet tall or more. Leaves opposite on stem, ovate with rounded to tapering base and pointed tip, 3-6 inches long, 2-4 inches wide, dark green with toothed margins. Stalks emerging from upper leaf axils bear flat-topped or domed clusters of flower heads composed of 12-24 bright white florets.
GENERAL INFORMATION: Pioneers reportedly used the plant to treat urinary disorders, hence the common name "sanicle," a name applied to a number of plants reputed to have healing powers. The herbage contains a toxin called trematol. Snakeroot flourished, and was apparently more frequently eaten by cattle, when woods were cleared by pioneers and other forage was unavailable. When passed on to humans in milk, trematol causes "milk sickness," the disease from which Abraham Lincoln's mother died. During pioneer times, milk sickness was more common than today.

False Boneset
Kuhnia eupatorioides

FAMILY: Sunflower (Asteraceae)
FLOWERING PERIOD: August into October.
DISTRIBUTION: Statewide in Nebraska. Throughout the Great Plains.
HABITAT: Dry prairies and plains, especially sandy soils.
DESCRIPTION: Native perennial growing from a tough, woody caudex atop a taproot to a depth of 15 feet or more. Few to many sturdy, upright stems, branching above, 1-2 feet or more tall; older plants assuming a bushy appearance. Leaves alternate, numerous; lanceolate, may have toothed margins, 1-4 inches long on a short stalk; dotted with resin glands on underside. Flower heads numerous in flat-topped or domed clusters at the top of branches; each composed of 7-33 creamy-white florets. Flowers not showy but the plant is conspicuous long after frost when flower heads become globes of achene plumes.
GENERAL INFORMATION: Common name from the resemblance of this plant's flower heads, composed of tubular florets, to that of the true boneset, *Eupatorium perfoliatum.*

WHITE ASTER

White Aster

Aster ericoides

OTHER COMMON NAMES: Heath or frost aster.
FAMILY: Sunflower (Asteraceae)
FLOWERING PERIOD: September and October. Occasionally still in flower even after the first light frosts.
DISTRIBUTION: Statewide in Nebraska. Found throughout the Great Plains, less common west.
HABITAT: On moist and dry soils; grasslands and roadsides.
DESCRIPTION: Native perennial growing from a spreading network of rhizomes and stolons, often forming colonies. Slender stems branch repeatedly forming bushy plants, 1.5-3 feet tall. Younger plants often recline on neighboring vegetation. Densely leafy; leaves linear, usually less than 2 inches long. Many lower leaves typically shed before flowering. Flower heads are abundant on upper branches; .25-.5 inch

across and composed of 10-20 white, petal-like ray florets surrounding a bright, yellow center disk. Characteristic of the genus *Aster*, both the ray florets and disk florets fertile.
GENERAL INFORMATION: White aster is a prominent plant of prairie uplands. Its extensive system of rhizomes permits it to thrive and spread under drought conditions and it tends to increase under grazing as only the young stems are tender. Older stems are tough and woody. The smallest flowered, hardiest and probably most common of our native asters. Many asters, particularly the white-flowered species, hybridize, producing much variation and making identification difficult. Two other species of white-flowered asters are common in Nebraska. White prairie aster *(Aster falcatus)* grows on moister sites, is not so bushy and tends to have larger flowers. Panicled aster *(Aster simplex)* is more erect, taller (up to 4 feet) and less apt to form clumps.

Fragrant Cudweed
Gnaphalium obtusifolium

OTHER COMMON NAMES: Fragrant ever-lasting, sweet or white balsam, rabbit tobacco, poverty weed.
FAMILY: Sunflower (Asteraceae)
FLOWERING PERIOD: August into October.
DISTRIBUTION: Southeastern Nebraska. Southeastern Great Plains.
HABITAT: A variety of soils, often disturbed sites; prairies, open woods, roadsides.
DESCRIPTION: Native annual, or winter annual (establishing late in the season and over-wintering to flower the following year) growing from a taproot. One or several white, woolly, stiffly erect stems, branching above, 1-2.5 feet tall. Rosette of oblong basal leaves sometimes present. Stem leaves alternate, green above, woolly white beneath; linear-lanceolate, 1-4 inches long and less than .5 inch wide. Inflorescence round-topped or slightly elongate at top of stem; composed of many flower heads with papery bracts; flowers are small, creamy-white quickly taking a brownish tinge.
GENERAL INFORMATION: When crushed, the plant has a balsam-like scent. Indian tribes in the Great Lakes region believed the smoke from burning a closely related plant would revive the fainted and prevent ghosts from causing disturbing dreams.

Nodding Lady's-tresses
Spiranthes cernua

OTHER COMMON NAMES: Drooping lady's-tresses, spike orchid, screw-auger.
FAMILY: Orchid (Orchidaceae)
FLOWERING PERIOD: Late August through September.
DISTRIBUTION: Central and eastern Nebraska. Eastern Great Plains.
HABITAT: Moist to wet soils in prairies; meadows, lake and stream margins.
DESCRIPTION: Native perennial growing from slender, fleshy roots radiating from a crown extending only a few inches into soil. Usually a single, stiffly erect stem, 1-2 feet tall. Leaves grass-like, 3-5, from base of stem, linear-lanceolate, up to 10 inches long, often shed by time of flowering. Flowers in 1- 3 rows, usually spiraling, on upper third of stem; maturing from base of spike upward. Individual flowers less than .5 inch long; white; tubular with a hood, a pair of lateral petals and a reflexed lower lip. Usually sweetly fragrant.
GENERAL INFORMATION: Occasionally found in hay meadows mowed in the summer, where the stems are 6 inches tall or less and almost entirely covered with flowers. Though uncommon, this is the most widespread of the four species of lady's-tresses in Nebraska. The other 3 species are considered rare in Nebraska.

FRAGRANT CUDWEED

NODDING LADY'S-TRESSES

Yellow Flowers

Yellow Wild Buckwheat

Eriogonum flavum

FAMILY: Buckwheat (Polygonaceae)
FLOWERING PERIOD: Late May into July.
DISTRIBUTION: Nebraska Panhandle. Northwestern Great Plains.
HABITAT: Usually found on rocky, gravelly or eroded clay bluffs, outcrops, knolls or ridges.
DESCRIPTION: Native perennial growing from a caudex-topped taproot. Leaves crowded on a short inconspicuous stem; a single rosette in young plants, a tuft of many rosettes, up to 8 inches across in older plants; linear-oblong, thickish; upper surface gray-green, underside silvery, both woolly with hairs; 1-3 inches long, less than .5 inch wide. Small, sulphur-yellow flowers in a tight cluster (an umbel) about .5 inch across above a whorl of small leaves (bracts); at top of 2-10 inch tall, leafless stalk.
GENERAL INFORMATION: Annual eriogonum *(Eriogonum annuum)*, also called umbrella plant, is a common and conspicuous plant in Nebraska's Sandhills. Nearly leafless on the upper portion of the stem, it is stick-like in appearance, silvery white and woolly, 1-3 feet tall. Its flowers are inconspicuous.

Stemless Hymenoxys

Hymenoxys acaulis

OTHER COMMON NAMES: Bitterweed.
FAMILY: Sunflower (Asteraceae)
FLOWERING PERIOD: Late May into July.
DISTRIBUTION: Principally in Nebraska Panhandle. Western Great Plains.
HABITAT: Dry, gravelly or rocky sites.
DESCRIPTION: Native perennial growing from a branched caudex atop a taproot. Young plants solitary, a single rosette of linear, silvery leaves up to 3 inches long, covered with silky hairs; older plants with branching crowns form a tuft of clustered leaf rosettes. Each rosette produces a leafless flower stalk 4-12 inches tall bearing a single flower head .75-1.5 inches across; 8-13 yellow, petal-like ray florets, 3-lobed at tip, usually not overlapping, surround a yellow disk.
GENERAL INFORMATION: "Stemless" seems like an inappropriate name for this plant, however, the slender, leafless "stems" which bear the flower heads are technically flower stalks (scapes). The true stems, bearing leaves, if present at all, are short and inconspicuous, covered by the basal leaves.

YELLOW WILD BUCKWHEAT

Prairie Buck Bean

Thermopsis rhombifolia

OTHER COMMON NAMES: Prairie golden-pea, yellow pea, prairie bean, false lupine.
FAMILY: Bean (Fabaceae)
FLOWERING PERIOD: Late April and May.
DISTRIBUTION: Nebraska Panhandle, occasional farther east. Northwestern Great Plains.
HABITAT: Dry rocky soils to moist sandy soils; grasslands, pine woodland openings and edge, rocky outcrops, buttes, eroded banks, badlands washes.
DESCRIPTION: Native perennial growing from rhizomes. Stem erect, often branched above, 6-12 inches tall. Leaves are alternate, on stout stalks, divided into 3 leaflets; a pair of small leaflet-like stipules where leaf stalk joins stem. Leaflets stiff, gray-green, with fine hairs lying close to surface; broadly lanceolate to ovate, margins without teeth, .75-1.25 inches long. Bright yellow flowers clustered at ends of branches (axillary racemes); pea-like, plump, about .5 inch long, with 5 petals—an erect petal called the banner, 2 lateral petals called wings, 2 fused, lower petals forming the boat-shaped keel housing the stamens and pistil. Smooth, dark brown seeds produced in a sickle-shaped pod 2-3 inches long.
GENERAL INFORMATION: Found in dense patches on badlands washes, sparsely spaced on drier sites. The Lakota burned dried flowers with hair, confining the smoke to portions of arms or legs afflicted with rheumatism to reduce swelling and relieve pain.

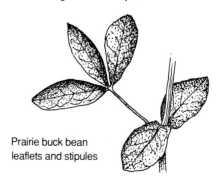

Prairie buck bean
leaflets and stipules

YELLOW STARGRASS

NUTTALL'S VIOLET

Yellow Stargrass

Hypoxis hirsuta

OTHER COMMON NAMES: Hairy stargrass, star-of-Bethlehem.
FAMILY: Lily (Liliaceae)
FLOWERING PERIOD: Late April into June, occasionally later.
DISTRIBUTION: Central and eastern Nebraska. Eastern Great Plains.
HABITAT: Moist, rich soils (occasionally on drier sites); meadows, prairies.
DESCRIPTION: Native perennial growing from a small corm (.25-.5 inch in diameter) with fibrous roots. Narrow, grass-like leaves (3-6) rise directly from the corm; 2-10 inches long. The hairy flower stalk always shorter than leaves; bearing 2 to several flowers on stalks, only 1 or 2 open at same time; up to .75 inch across; 3 petals and 3 similar sepals, green and hairy on outside, bright yellow on inside, surrounding 6 prominent stamens and a single style. Virtually all parts of the plant are covered with stiff hairs, hence the name *hirsuta*, Latin for "bristly." Often hidden among the grasses which it much resembles, particularly when the flowers are closed revealing only their green exterior and grass-like leaves.

Nuttall's Violet

Viola nuttallii

FAMILY: Violet (Violaceae)
FLOWERING PERIOD: Late April into June.
DISTRIBUTION: Western and central Nebraska. Northern and central Great Plains.
HABITAT: Dry soils in grasslands.
DESCRIPTION: Native perennial growing from stout, deep rhizomes. Less than 6 inches tall. Stems often inconspicuous or underground. *Leaf blades lanceolate, ovate or elliptic,* tapering gradually to short stalks, leaf blades 1-3 inches long. Solitary flowers on long stalks rising to height of foliage or above; .5-1 inch across; 5 yellow petals, lower 3 usually with reddish-brown nectar lines.
GENERAL INFORMATION: The only yellow-flowered, grassland violet found in our region.

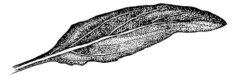

Nuttall's violet leaf

Downy Yellow Violet

Viola pubescens

FAMILY: Violet (Violaceae)
FLOWERING PERIOD: Late April and May.
DISTRIBUTION: East fifth of Nebraska and northern tier of counties. Principally the eastern fifth of the Great Plains; also found in the Black Hills of South Dakota.
HABITAT: Shaded sites in dry to moist soils; woodlands, wooded stream valleys, bluffs.
DESCRIPTION: Native perennial growing from stout, woody rhizomes bearing fibrous roots. Stems, one or more, erect, 6-12 inches tall. Basal leaves (1-2) on long stalks may or may not be present; leaf rounded, kidney-shaped, notched at the union with stalk. Stem leaves on shorter stalks; usually heart-shaped (cordate), notched at union with stalk; leaf blades 1.5-4 inches long and slightly wider. A solitary flower at top of a long stalk from leaf axil; .5-1 inch across; 5 yellow petals, lower 3 usually with reddish-brown nectar lines.

GENERAL INFORMATION: The leaves and stems may or may not be pubescent. Both smooth and pubescent varieties are reported from Nebraska. Pubescent plants are more frequent in the northern part of the species' range. This is the most common yellow-flowered violet found in woodlands of the eastern Great Plains.

DOWNY YELLOW VIOLET

Wild Parsley

Lomatium foeniculaceum

OTHER COMMON NAMES: Carrot-leaf lomatium, biscuit root, whisk-broom parsley.
FAMILY: Parsley (Apiaceae)
FLOWERING PERIOD: Late April and May.
DISTRIBUTION: Principally southeastern and northwestern Nebraska. Found throughout the Great Plains except southwest.
HABITAT: Well-drained, usually rocky soils; grasslands, grassy woodland openings, hilltops and slopes.
DESCRIPTION: Native perennial growing from a strong, deep taproot. Essentially stemless, leaves and flower stalks rising from root crown; 4-20 inches tall. Leaves dissected until fernlike; soft to touch; up to 8 inches long including stalk; *gray-green*. Flowers small, lemon yellow; gathered into flat-topped clusters (compound umbels) at top of the stout stalk which rises above foliage. Aromatic; said to smell somewhat like celery or parsley.
GENERAL INFORMATION: The winged, flattened fruits (about .25 inch long) were used as love charms by some Great Plains Indian tribes. The Pawnee believed that carrying the seeds "rendered the possessor attractive to all persons," he would have many friends and could "win any woman he might desire." The seeds, foliage and roots of this species are edible. Larger-rooted, related species from the northwestern U.S. were dried and ground into a flour used to make biscuit-like cakes.

Narrow-leaved Musineon

Musineon tenuifolium

FAMILY: Parsley (Apiaceae)
FLOWERING PERIOD: May and June.
DISTRIBUTION: Nebraska Panhandle. West-central Great Plains.
HABITAT: Principally on dry, rocky outcrops.
DESCRIPTION: Native perennial growing from a caudex atop a thickened taproot. Stemless leaves rising from root crown to form a compact tuft of foliage. Leaves dissected until *fern-like*. Small, bright yellow (occasionally cream-colored) flowers gathered in flat-topped clusters (compound umbels) about 1 inch across atop a leafless stalk usually less than 6 inches tall.
GENERAL INFORMATION: The fern-like foliage of narrow-leaf musineon easily distinguishes it from leafy musineon. Unlike wild parsley, this species has darker green, shiny leaves and its fruit is not winged.

WILD PARSLEY

NARROW-LEAVED MUSINEON

Leafy Musineon
Musineon divaricatum

FAMILY: Parsley (Apiaceae)
FLOWERING PERIOD: Late April into June.
DISTRIBUTION: Nebraska Panhandle. North-western Great Plains.
HABITAT: Dry, clayey and rocky soils; grass-lands, eroded banks, hillsides, badlands.
DESCRIPTION: Native perennial growing from a thickened taproot. Stems branching in pairs. Leaves basal or appearing basal, 2-6 inches long, deep green; deeply divided, lobes again divided into smaller, rounded lobe segments. Small, bright yellow flowers gathered in flat-topped clusters (compound umbels) about 1-2 inches across, usually less than 6 inches tall.

LEAFY MUSINEON

Leafy musineon leaf

83

WESTERN WALLFLOWER

YELLOW WOOD SORREL

Western Wallflower

Erysimum asperum

OTHER COMMON NAMES: Yellow phlox, prairie rocket.

FAMILY: Mustard (Brassicaceae)

FLOWERING PERIOD: May and June.

DISTRIBUTION: Statewide in Nebraska except east quarter. Throughout the Great Plains, uncommon or absent east.

HABITAT: Dry grasslands, particularly sandy soil; pastures, roadsides.

DESCRIPTION: Native biennial or perennial. Stems are erect, branched above on robust plants; 6-18 inches tall. Leaves numerous; alternate on stem; linear, lanceolate or oblong-lanceolate; often folded in a keel-shape; usually with a few coarse teeth on margins; gray-green with sharp, stiff hairs lying close to leaf surface; 1-3 inches long. Bright yellow flowers with 4 petals; up to 1 inch across, in open, rounded clusters (a raceme) on top third of stem. Pistil continues to elongate even after petals fall; becoming a long (3-5 inches), upward arching, branch-like seed pod present even while flowers still top the stem.

GENERAL INFORMATION: The mustards' former family name was Cruciferae, a reference to petals being roughly arranged in the shape of a cross. Plants of this family contain a pungent juice with a peppery taste. Commercial mustard preparations are from ground seeds of other plants of the mustard family. Better known members of the mustard family include horseradish, radish and turnips.

Yellow Wood Sorrel

Oxalis stricta

OTHER COMMON NAMES: Sheep, poison, toad or lady's sorrel; sour-grass.

FAMILY: Wood Sorrel (Oxalidaceae)

FLOWERING PERIOD: Late April through the summer.

DISTRIBUTION: Central and eastern Nebraska. Central and eastern Great Plains.

HABITAT: Moist soils in sunny or shady, somewhat disturbed sites; farmsteads, yards, gardens, stream banks, prairie ravines, woodland edge.

DESCRIPTION: Native perennial growing from rhizomes; sometimes spreading to form mats. Stem erect or the lower portion reclining on ground, branching near base; 4-20 inches tall. Leaves clover-like; long, stem-like stalks, each bearing 3 heart-shaped leaflets at end, collectively about 1 inch across. Plants with purplish leaves occasionally encountered. Flowers in clusters of 1 to 3 on stalks near the ends of branches; .5-1 inch across; 5 yellow petals with darker nectar lines at bases.

GENERAL INFORMATION: Leaflets and flowers fold at night, a phenomenon called sleep movement. Contains oxalic acid, giving the greens a sour, some say salty, taste. Pawnee children were reportedly fond of eating the foliage of both yellow and violet wood sorrel. Kiowa chewed the leaves to relieve thirst. The leaflets are sometimes added to salads for their tangy taste. Slightly toxic if consumed in a large enough quantity.

Large Yellow Lady's-slipper

Cypripedium calceolus

OTHER COMMON NAMES: Yellow moccasin flower, Noah's ark; Indian, Venus and whip-poor-will shoe.

FAMILY: Orchid (Orchidaceae)

FLOWERING PERIOD: May and June.

DISTRIBUTION: Found in Nebraska's Missouri Valley from Douglas County south. An eastern deciduous forest species which barely enters the Great Plains.

HABITAT: Moist, rich soils in deciduous woodlands. Most often in at least partial shade.

DESCRIPTION: Native perennial growing from stout rhizomes; often forming clumps. Usually single, erect stems, 1-2 feet tall. Bases of 3-6 alternate leaves wrap about the erect stem; ovate-lanceolate with pointed tips and promi-nent parallel veins; 2-8 inches long and half as wide. Typically only 1 showy flower (occasionally 2) at top of stem. Lower petal modified into a yellow, waxy pouch up to 2 inches long, with faint, brownish markings. Other parts of flower greenish to maroon-brown—2 twisted lateral petals (2-3.5 inches long); a triangular sepal as wide as the pouch forming a hood; 2 united sepals curving upward beneath the pouch.

GENERAL INFORMATION: The slipper opening curves inward except near the rear where the flower's reproductive structures are located. Insects entering for nectar found on internal hairs must exit through this gap where they shed pollen on the stigma and are dusted with that flower's own pollen. An increasingly rare wildflower. Exacting in choice of growing sites, they seldom survive when transplanted and should be enjoyed and protected where found.

LARGE YELLOW LADY'S-SLIPPER

HAIRY PUCCOON

Hairy Puccoon

Lithospermum carolinense

FAMILY: Borage (Boraginaceae)

FLOWERING PERIOD: May and June.

DISTRIBUTION: Statewide in Nebraska, most common central. Southern Great Plains, uncommon or absent west.

HABITAT: *Sandy soil* in grasslands.

DESCRIPTION: Native perennial growing from a thick, red taproot. One to numerous stout stems, simple or branched above; 1-2 feet tall. Leaves alternate, without stalks; linear to narrowly lanceolate, *usually with a pointed tip;* 1-2 inches long, less than .5 inch wide. Both stems and leaves gray-green; rough to the touch; densely covered with *coarse, stiff hairs.* Leaf margins often *with a fringe of hairs.* Flowers clustered at end of stems (terminal cymes); tubular, spreading to 5 lobes; deep yellow to yellow-orange; about .75 inch across. Flowers slightly larger and more showy than those of hoary puccoon. Fruit a stone-hard, smooth, white, seed-like nutlet. Older plants may form clumps 2-3 feet across.

GENERAL INFORMATION: Hairy and hoary puccoon are most apt to be confused in eastern Nebraska. Hoary puccoon is uncommon, if present at all, west of Grand Island. East of Grand Island, though, either species may be found. A plant on sandy soil is more than likely hairy puccoon, on a heavier soil hoary puccoon. Both species are "hairy" but to the touch, hairy puccoon is coarse and rough, hoary puccoon fine and velvety. Great Plains Indians extracted a red dye from the root.

Narrow-leaved Puccoon

Lithospermum incisum

FAMILY: Borage (Boraginaceae)

FLOWERING PERIOD: Late April through June.

DISTRIBUTION: Statewide in Nebraska. Found throughout the Great Plains.

HABITAT: In a variety of dry soil types; grasslands, woodland edge and openings, occasionally on disturbed sites.

DESCRIPTION: Native perennial growing from a stout, woody, red taproot. One to several stems, branched above on older plants, 6-16 inches tall. Leaves alternate, without stalks; linear to narrowly lanceolate, with a pointed tip; .5-2 inches long and less than .4 inch wide (noticeably narrower relative to length than the other puccoons). Both the stems and leaves covered with short, fine hairs but not as evident as on the other puccoons as they lie flat. Flowers clustered at end of stems (terminal cymes); *tubular portion longer* than other puccoons (up to .75 inch long), spreading to 5 *crinkly-edged* lobes; lemon yellow; .5-1 inch across. The fruit is a hard, smooth, white, seed-like nutlet.

GENERAL INFORMATION: Indian tribes in the range of this plant extracted a red dye from the root. The genus name *Lithospermum* is from the Greek *lithos*, meaning "stone" and *sperma*, meaning "seed"; a reference to the stone-hard fruit produced by these plants.

Hoary Puccoon

Lithospermum canescens

OTHER COMMON NAMES: Hoary gromwell, Indian paint.

FAMILY: Borage (Boraginaceae)

FLOWERING PERIOD: From late April through June.

DISTRIBUTION: Eastern fifth of Nebraska. Eastern Great Plains.

HABITAT: Found in dry to moderately moist soils; prairies, woodland edge and openings. *Seldom on sandy soils.*

DESCRIPTION: Native perennial growing from a thick, red taproot. One to several stems, usually not branched; 6-16 inches tall. Leaves alternate, without stalks; oblong, linear-oblong or linear, *usually with a blunt tip;* 1-2 inches long, less than .5 inch wide. Both stems and leaves gray-green; densely covered with short, erect, *silky, soft* hairs. Leaf margins *without a fringe of hairs* as in hairy puccoon. Flowers clustered at end of stems (terminal cymes); tubular, spreading to 5 lobes; yellow-orange to deep orange; about .5 inch across. The fruit is a stone-hard, smooth, yellowish-white, seed-like nutlet.

GENERAL INFORMATION: The name puccoon was applied by American Indians to a variety of plants which produce dyes. A red dye was extracted from large roots of this species and used, among more serious applications, by Indian children to color gum from compass plant.

NARROW-LEAVED PUCCOON

HOARY PUCCOON

Prairie Ragwort
Senecio plattensis

OTHER COMMON NAMES: Prairie groundsel, squaw-weed.
FAMILY: Sunflower (Asteraceae)
FLOWERING PERIOD: May and June.
DISTRIBUTION: Statewide in Nebraska. Found throughout the Great Plains, less common west.
HABITAT: Dry soils in grasslands; meadows, pastures, roadsides.
DESCRIPTION: Native biennial or short-lived perennial growing from a caudex; occasionally spreading by stolons to form colonies. Stems usually single, erect, branching above, 1-2 feet tall. Basal leaves on stalks from stem base, blade ovate to broadly lanceolate with a toothed margin; up to 4 inches long including leaf stalk. Leaves few on upper stem, smaller, without stalks, alternate, coarsely toothed or even lobed, sometimes clasping stem. Stem and lower leaves densely pubescent with woolly hairs; or leaves pubescent only when young. Flower heads usually in flat-topped clusters (cymes) at top of stems, .5-.75 inch across; about 8 (occasionally more) slender, yellow, petal-like ray florets surrounding the yellow-orange center of disk florets. Both ray and disk florets are fertile and produce seeds.

GENERAL INFORMATION: The name of this species, *plattensis*, is a reference to the Platte River, where the type specimen was collected. More than a dozen species of *Senecio* are found in the Great Plains. Prairie ragwort is the most common and widespread.

Prairie Parsley
Polytaenia nuttalli

FAMILY: Parsley (Apiaceae)
FLOWERING PERIOD: May and June.
DISTRIBUTION: Southeast Nebraska. Southeastern Great Plains.
HABITAT: Dry to moderately moist soils; meadows, prairie.
DESCRIPTION: Native perennial growing from a long, thickened taproot. Stems stout, erect, branching above, 2-3 feet tall. Lower leaves on stalks up to 6 inches long, base of stalk clasping stem; upper leaves stalkless; deeply dissected to leaf stalk; leaflets deeply divided to their midrib, and lobed, up to 1.5 inches long. Small, yellow flowers are in more or less flat-topped clusters (compound umbels) at ends of the upper branches. By July, the flowers are replaced with conspicuous yellow-green, oblong, flattened fruits about .25 inch long (as seen in photo).

PRAIRIE RAGWORT

PRAIRIE PARSLEY

Golden Alexander
Zizia aurea

OTHER COMMON NAMES: Golden or early meadow parsnip, wild parsley.
FAMILY: Parsley (Apiaceae)
FLOWERING PERIOD: May and June.
DISTRIBUTION: East fifth of Nebraska. Eastern fourth of Great Plains; also in the Black Hills of South Dakota.
HABITAT: Moist, rich soils; meadows, prairie swales, margins of wet areas.
DESCRIPTION: A short-lived, native perennial growing from fibrous, thickened roots. Stems are erect, branching, smooth and often with a reddish tinge; 1-3 feet tall. Leaves alternate on stem. Lower leaves on long stalks, divided into 3 leaflets, or 3 stalks each bearing 3 leaflets (total of 9 leaflets per leaf). Higher leaves on short stalks divided into 3 leaflets. Leaflets ovate to lanceolate, 1-2 inches long and half as wide, with finely toothed margins. Tiny yellow flowers in 10-20 small clusters, gathered into a larger flat-topped or domed inflorescence (compound umbels).
GENERAL INFORMATION: Early settlers believed preparations from this plant could cure syphilis and promote the healing of wounds.

GOLDEN ALEXANDER

STONECROP

Stonecrop
Sedum lanceolatum

OTHER COMMON NAMES: Narrow-petaled stonecrop, live-forever, orpine.
FAMILY: Stonecrop (Crassulaceae)
FLOWERING PERIOD: June and July.
DISTRIBUTION: Nebraska Panhandle. West-central Great Plains.
HABITAT: Thin, dry, gravelly or rocky soils; rock outcrops, road cuts, canyon sides, buttes.
DESCRIPTION: Native perennial succulent growing from slender rootstocks. Ground-level stems and crowded basal rosettes of leaves. Leaves succulent, rounded-linear, less than .5 inch long. Stem leaves alternate, gray-green, reddish to yellow-green; crowded and overlapping. Flowering stalk is erect, 2-6 inches tall, often reddish near the base, flower clusters (cymes) near the top; 5 lemon-yellow, slender, pointed petals spreading into a star-shaped flower .5-1 inch across; flower center a prominent cluster of yellow stamens.
GENERAL INFORMATION: Nebraska's only sedum and one of only several succulents native to the state.

Macoun's Buttercup
Ranunculus macounii

FAMILY: Buttercup (Ranunculaceae)
FLOWERING PERIOD: June and July.
DISTRIBUTION: Principally Nebraska Panhandle, but occasionally farther east. Northern Great Plains.
HABITAT: Saturated soils, sun or partial shade; along stream banks, shorelines, marshes; wet meadows.
DESCRIPTION: Native annual or short-lived perennial growing from thick, somewhat fleshy and fibrous roots. Stem erect, often reclining as plant ages, branching above; with a sparse to dense covering of white hairs; hollow, soft and watery; 1-2 feet tall. Lower leaves larger, on long stalks to 10 inches; divided into 3 leaflets on stalks, which in turn are deeply divided into 3 lobes. Flowers are scattered at the ends of branches; up to .5 inch across; 5 deep yellow, waxy petals surrounding the tuft of yellow stamens and numerous pistils.
GENERAL INFORMATION: Several other yellow-flowered buttercups are found across the state at similar sites. The flower of Macoun's buttercup, though small, is one of the showier buttercups in Nebraska as its petals are usually longer than the green, leaf-like sepals surrounding them. The genus name, *Ranunculus* is from Latin meaning "little frog" or "tapole," no doubt a reference to these plants favoring wet soils and wetland edge.

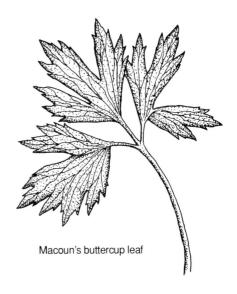

Macoun's buttercup leaf

MACOUN'S BUTTERCUP

Threadleaf Buttercup
Ranunculus flabellaris

OTHER COMMON NAMES: Yellow water-crowfoot, yellow water-buttercup.
FAMILY: Buttercup (Ranunculaceae)
FLOWERING PERIOD: May and June.
DISTRIBUTION: Eastern and north-central Nebraska. Eastern and northeastern Great Plains.
HABITAT: Shallow, fresh, standing water; ponds, lake margins, wet ditches, marshes. Occasionally found stranded on saturated mud flats.
DESCRIPTION: Native aquatic perennial growing from fibrous roots. Stems are hollow, submersed, branching, 1-2 feet long. Lower leaves with stalks up to several times the leaf blade length, the upper leaves with very short stalks having broad bases; submerged leaves are finely dissected into filamentous threads, leaves above water not as finely divided, segments lobed. Flowers on stout stalks which rise above water surface, .75-1 inch across; 5 (occasionally more) glossy, deep yellow petals curve upward forming a small cup surrounding a greenish button of numerous pistils. The flower's color and cup-like shape give rise to the common name buttercup.

THREADLEAF BUTTERCUP

91

Bird's-foot Trefoil

Lotus corniculatus

OTHER COMMON NAMES: Bird's-foot deer-vetch, shoes-and-stockings, crowtoes, sheep-foot, cat's-clover.
FAMILY: Bean (Fabaceae)
FLOWERING PERIOD: June through August.
DISTRIBUTION: Principally eastern Nebraska but also Panhandle. Eastern Great Plains.
HABITAT: Meadows, pastures, roadsides.
DESCRIPTION: Introduced perennial growing from a woody taproot. Several stems, usually reclining on the ground, up to 2 feet long but usually less than 1 foot tall. Leaves alternate on stem. Leaflets elliptic to oblong-lanceolate, .2-.6 inch long and half as wide; 2 at base of leaf stalk, 3 forming a rough triangle at end of stalk. Stems and leaves may or may not be pubescent. Flowers in clusters (umbels) of 3-8 on stalks from upper leaf axils; about .5 inch long, pea-like, yellow or yellow-orange with darker nectar lines; banner nearly as broad as wide. Slender, brown to black seed pods up to 1.5 inches long radiate out from a common point, hence the name "bird's-foot."
GENERAL INFORMATION: Introduced from Europe as a forage crop. Commonly used in roadside seedings to prevent erosion. Much variety in this species as there are many cultivars available commercially.

Sulphur Cinquefoil

Potentilla recta

FAMILY: Rose (Rosaceae)
FLOWERING PERIOD: Late May into July.
DISTRIBUTION: East half of Nebraska. Southeastern Great Plains. Reported to be spreading westward.
HABITAT: Moderately moist to dry soils; meadows, pastures, prairie, roadsides, disturbed sites.
DESCRIPTION: Naturalized perennial growing from a branched and stout caudex. Stems erect, 1-several, branching above; coarse, stiff hairs becoming more abundant above; 1-2 feet tall. Lower leaves on hairy stalks, alternate on stem; leaflets arranged like fingers from the palm (palmately compound) in groups of 5-7, oblong-lanceolate, coarsely toothed, hairy, 1-3 inches long. Flowers in open clusters (cymes) at the ends of branches; .5-1 inch across; 5, usually heart-shaped, pale yellow petals encircling 25-30 stamens and the yellow, cone-shaped cluster of pistils.
GENERAL INFORMATION: Native to Europe and Asia. Plants of this genus have been considered important medicinal plants around the world. The plant's juices are astringent. It was once believed that placing cinquefoil leaves in shoes would prevent blisters. Potentilla tea is reported to relieve fevers and diarrhea, soothe rashes and prevent saddle sores.

BIRD'S-FOOT TREFOIL

Yellow Iris

Iris pseudacorus

OTHER COMMON NAMES: Water, yellow, sword or corn flag; Jacob's-sword, daggers.

FAMILY: Iris (Iridaceae)

FLOWERING PERIOD: Late May into July.

DISTRIBUTION: Scattered sites in Nebraska; potentially could occur statewide. At scattered sites throughout the U.S.; in the Great Plains principally in the southeast.

HABITAT: Marshes, ditches, and shorelines of both flowing and standing water.

DESCRIPTION: Naturalized perennial growing from a thick rhizome. Stems 2-4 feet tall. Leaves are stiff, erect or arching; pale green, sword shaped; usually less than 1 inch wide; equal to or taller than flower stalks. Flowers typically iris; bright yellow with brown markings at base of petals; 2.5-3.5 inches across.

GENERAL INFORMATION: Native of Europe, introduced as a garden plant in North America. Apparently escapes from cultivation or is intentionally introduced into wet areas where it occasionally proliferates. Established and proliferating at sites in Lincoln and Sioux counties in Nebraska and perhaps elsewhere.

Prickly Lettuce

Lactuca serriola

OTHER COMMON NAMES: Wild lettuce, milk or horse thistle, wild opium, compass plant.
FAMILY: Sunflower (Asteraceae)
FLOWERING PERIOD: Late May into September.
DISTRIBUTION: Statewide in Nebraska. Found throughout the Great Plains.
HABITAT: Disturbed sites; field margins, overgrazed pastures, roadsides.
DESCRIPTION: A naturalized winter annual growing from a taproot and fibrous roots. Stem erect, branched, often with bristles on lower third, up to 5 feet tall. Leaves alternate on stem; oblong or oblong-lanceolate, deeply lobed with bristles on margins and midrib on underside; without stalks or bases clasping stem; lower leaves up to 10 inches long and 3 inches wide, reduced in size above. Exudes a milky latex when cut or broken. Flower heads numerous on upper branches (in panicles); less than .5 inch across; composed of 18-25, light yellow, petal-like florets.
GENERAL INFORMATION: Native to Europe. Generally considered the ancestor of our common garden lettuce, having been selected for a reduced content of the bitter, milky latex. This liquid was said to have many medicinal virtues in ancient times—to counteract heartburn, induce sleep, stimulate the appetite and "keepeth away drunkennesse which cometh by the wine." When processed, the plant's juices do have a narcotic effect. In the spring, basal leaves may orient in a north-south direction, hence the name compass plant.

SHOWY PARTRIDGE PEA

Showy Partridge Pea

Cassia chamaecrista

OTHER COMMON NAMES: Large-flowered sensitive pea, locustweed.
FAMILY: Caesalpinia (Caesalpiniaceae)
FLOWERING PERIOD: July and August.
DISTRIBUTION: Eastern half of Nebraska, principally southeast. Southeastern Great Plains.
HABITAT: Disturbed, particularly sandy soils; roadsides, river valleys, woodland edge, field margins.
DESCRIPTION: Native annual. Stems are slender, erect, usually branching low on stem; 1 to 3 feet tall. Leaves even-pinnately compound. Leaflets linear-oblong, less than 1 inch long, 16-30 pairs opposite one another along the midrib. Flowers .75-1.5 inches across; in clusters of 1-6 on short stalks from leaf axils; 5 bright yellow petals, the lower petal largest, upper 4 with reddish spot at base; surrounding a cluster of reddish-brown, drooping anthers. Fruit a narrow, flattened, pea-like pod, 1.5-2.5 inches long; dark brown when dry.
GENERAL INFORMATION: The leaves are somewhat sensitive to touch and fold when handled. The seeds, produced in abundance, are an excellent food for quail and numerous species of seed-eating songbirds.

PRICKLY LETTUCE

CLAMMY GROUND CHERRY

Clammy Ground Cherry
Physalis heterophylla

OTHER COMMON NAMES: Husk or strawberry tomato.
FAMILY: Nightshade (Solanaceae)
FLOWERING PERIOD: Late May into September.
DISTRIBUTION: Statewide except southwest, more common in eastern Nebraska. Central and eastern Great Plains.
HABITAT: Rich, well-drained, disturbed soils; prairies, roadsides, field margins, woodland edge.
DESCRIPTION: Native perennial growing from a branching, deep caudex. Stems erect, thick, often reclining at maturity; branching or not; 1-2 feet tall or more. Leaves on stalks, alternate on stem; mostly ovate with pointed tips, with blunt teeth or not; 2-4 inches long. Herbage pubescence varies from plant to plant; sticky to touch, hence the name "clammy." Flowers solitary on short stalks from upper leaf axils, hidden under upper leaves; nodding, bell-shaped; greenish-yellow with brown center; to 1 inch across. Fruit a yellow berry, less than .5 inch in diameter, enclosed in a papery husk about 1 inch long.
GENERAL INFORMATION: Several other species of ground cherries are found in Nebraska and the Great Plains. This is one of the two most common species. The other, Virginia ground

cherry (*Physalis virginiana*), tends to be less pubescent on the upper portion of the stem; hairs less dense or absent, more stiff and not so sticky. The *green fruit is poisonous* but when ripe in late summer or fall it is edible, either raw or cooked. They were frequently cooked into a sauce by Great Plains Indians. Tomatoes, bell peppers and tobacco are all members of the nightshade family.

Tall Hedge Mustard
Sisymbrium loeselii

FAMILY: Mustard (Brassicaceae)
FLOWERING PERIOD: Late May and June.
DISTRIBUTION: Eastern third of Nebraska. Central and northern Great Plains.
HABITAT: Fields, roadsides, pastures, disturbed soils.
DESCRIPTION: Naturalized annual or winter annual. Stem erect, stiff, branched; coarse, stiff hairs near base; 2-3 feet tall. Lower leaves up to 10 inches long, on stalks; notched nearly to midrib, lobes somewhat triangular in shape; usually with coarse hairs. Leaves progressively smaller higher on stem. Flowers in globular clusters at ends of upper branches (a raceme) which continue to elongate and bear new flowers; about .5 inch across; 4 yellow petals. Slender, .75-1.5 inches long, branch-like seed pods on slender stalks arch out from stem.
GENERAL INFORMATION: Native to Europe and Asia, considered a weed in North America.

TALL HEDGE MUSTARD

95

GOAT'S BEARD

Goat's Beard

Tragopogon dubius

OTHER COMMON NAMES: Western or meadow salsify.

FAMILY: Sunflower (Asteraceae)

FLOWERING PERIOD: May through July.

DISTRIBUTION: Statewide in Nebraska. Found throughout the Great Plains.

HABITAT: Dry to moderately moist soils; disturbed sites, roadsides, margins of cultivated fields, pastures, floodplains.

DESCRIPTION: Naturalized biennial or short-lived perennial growing from a long taproot. A basal rosette of leaves the first year, producing a flowering stem the second. Stem erect, containing a milky sap; 1-3 feet tall. Leaves alternate, clasping stem at base, fleshy, grass-like, tapering gradually to a point, up to 12 inches long, less than .5 inch wide, becoming progres-

sively smaller higher on stem. Young leaves and stems covered with soft, woolly hairs which disappear with age. Solitary flower head at top of stem; 2 or more inches across; pale yellow, dandelion-like; composed only of petal-like ray florets; slender, pointed, green bracts (usually 13) extend out from base of the flower head, longer than the ray florets. Fruits are plumed, parachute-like achenes arranged in a sphere, much like a giant dandelion seed head.

GENERAL INFORMATION: Native of Europe, introduced in North America. Flowers open only in bright sunshine, often only in the morning, closed on overcast days. When closed, some say they resemble a goat's beard. Like some other members of the sunflower family, goat's beard flower heads, to a degree, orient to the sun. Young greens have been used as potherbs and the roots are edible, said to have the flavor of oysters or parsnips.

Field Sow Thistle

Sonchus arvensis

OTHER COMMON NAMES: Corn, tree or perennial sow thistle; milk or swine thistle.
FAMILY: Sunflower (Asteraceae)
FLOWERING PERIOD: June and July.
DISTRIBUTION: Principally northern half of Nebraska. Northern half of Great Plains.
HABITAT: Moist soils; cultivated areas, roadsides, meadows, wetland margins.
DESCRIPTION: Naturalized perennial spreading by deep, creeping roots to form open colonies. Stems erect, hollow, leafy mostly on lower half, branched near top; usually smooth, not hairy; *2-4 feet tall.* Lower leaves on short stalks; deeply divided into lobes opposite one another on leaf midrib; bluish-green with soft prickles on margins; 4-10 inches long. Mid-stem leaves alternate; smaller, not so deeply lobed, bases clasping stem. Stems and leaves often with a whitish, waxy coating which rubs off. Exudes a milky juice when cut. Flower heads in clusters at top of stem; .75-1.5 inches across, bright yellow, *similar to common dandelion.* Flowers close late in day, reopen mid-morning.
GENERAL INFORMATION: Native to Europe and Asia. Although considered a weed, it is not abundant enough to be a problem. Reported to be a good source of nectar and pollen for bees.

FALSE DANDELION

False Dandelion

Microseris cuspidata

OTHER COMMON NAMES: Prairie false dandelion.
FAMILY: Sunflower (Asteraceae)
FLOWERING PERIOD: Late April into June.
DISTRIBUTION: Statewide in Nebraska. Found throughout the Great Plains.
HABITAT: Found in a variety of well-drained soil types; grasslands.
DESCRIPTION: Native perennial growing from a taproot. Stemless above ground. Leaves in a basal rosette; 4-12 inches long, less than 1 inch wide; narrow, grass-like with a whitish midrib; *margins usually wavy* and lined with white hairs. Flower stalk leafless, 2-12 inches tall, bearing a single flower composed of strap-shaped, yellow florets with toothed outer margins. Flower heads are similar to common dandelion but larger, up to 2 inches across. Flowers open mid or late morning, close late afternoon. Unlike common dandelion achenes, which are airborne by parachute-like bristles, false dandelion's one-seeded fruit has many straight, bristly scales.

FIELD SOW THISTLE

BUFFALO BUR

Buffalo Bur

Solanum rostratum

OTHER COMMON NAMES: Beaked or prickly nightshade, prickly potato, Texas nettle, Kansas thistle.
FAMILY: Nightshade (Solanaceae)
FLOWERING PERIOD: June into September, principally July into August.
DISTRIBUTION: Statewide in Nebraska. Found throughout the Great Plains, more common south.
HABITAT: Dry, disturbed soils; fields, overgrazed pastures, roadsides, farmsteads.
DESCRIPTION: Native annual growing from a taproot. Stems erect, branched, often spreading; pubescent and armed with straight, yellow spines; 1-2 feet tall. Leaves alternate on stem; leaf blade 2-5 inches long; *divided nearly to midrib* with rounded lobes or *divided to midrib* with distinct, lobed leaflets; spines mostly on veins, underside of leaf; leaf stalks 1-2.5 inches long with spines. Flowers about 1 inch across, in open clusters at ends of branches; 5 bright yellow petals with wavy edges, joined at the base; 5 prominent stamens, 4 yellow, 1 purplish-brown and usually the longest; flower base (calyx) a spiny, green globe. Fruit is a berry containing many small, black seeds; enclosed by the spiny sepals.
GENERAL INFORMATION: Buffalo bur is native to the plains region and now widely distributed across the continent.

Curly-top Gumweed

Grindelia squarrosa

FAMILY: Sunflower (Asteraceae)
FLOWERING PERIOD: July into September.
DISTRIBUTION: Statewide in Nebraska. Found throughout the Great Plains.
HABITAT: Dry soil, disturbed or overgrazed sites; pastures, roadsides, railways.
DESCRIPTION: Native biennial or short-lived perennial growing from a deep taproot. One to several stout, erect stems; usually much branched above; 1-2 feet tall or more, but flowering plants only a few inches tall where mowed. Leaves alternate on stem; variable but mostly ovate to ovate-oblong; smooth, stiff, with glands exuding a sticky resin; the upper leaves clasping stem, lower leaves on short stalks; margins with equal, rounded teeth; 1-2 inches long, less than half as wide. Flower heads at ends of branches, .5-1.25 inches across; composed of 12-37 yellow, fertile, petal-like, seed-producing ray florets surrounding a center of yellow disk florets which also are fertile. Lower portion of flower head with many green, recurved bracts forming a "curly cup," exuding a "gummy" resin, hence another common name, curly-cup gumweed.
GENERAL INFORMATION: Great Plains Indians used gumweed to treat a variety of ailments. The powdered flower heads were used in asthma cigarettes by early settlers.

PUNCTURE VINE

cipally southern half of the Great Plains.
HABITAT: Dry, particularly sandy or gravelly, soils; disturbed sites, fields, roadsides, railways.
DESCRIPTION: Naturalized annual growing from a taproot. Stems with coarse hairs; sprawling on ground, usually branched, forming mats which may cover several square feet. Leaves opposite on stem. Leaflets, 5-7 pairs, arranged opposite one another along midrib (even-pinnately compound); oblong to ovate, hairy on undersides and margins; less than .5 inch long. Flowers solitary, on short stalks from leaf axils; up to .5 inch across; 5 pale yellow petals. Flowers open only in morning. Fruit a five-part bur, each segment usually bearing a pair of stout spines and smaller spines.
GENERAL INFORMATION: Native to Europe. Sometimes is confused with the true sandbur (*Cenchrus longispinus*) which is a grass 10-20 inches tall, bearing clusters of burs which are *not divided into segments*, with many spines of near equal size.

Puncture Vine
Tribulus terrestris

OTHER COMMON NAMES: Puncture-weed, goat head, ground bur-nut, sandbur.
FAMILY: Caltrop (Zygophyllaceae)
FLOWERING PERIOD: June through August.
DISTRIBUTION: Statewide in Nebraska. Prin-

Sandbur bur   Puncture vine bur

CURLY-TOP GUMWEED

99

Prairie Coneflower
Ratibida columnifera

OTHER COMMON NAMES: Long-headed coneflower, upright prairie coneflower.
FAMILY: Sunflower (Asteraceae)
FLOWERING PERIOD: June and July.
DISTRIBUTION: Statewide in Nebraska. Found throughout the Great Plains.
HABITAT: Dry soils; grasslands, roadsides.
DESCRIPTION: Native perennial growing from a taproot. Stems are erect, single or clustered, branching; covered with stiff, straight hairs; 1-2 feet tall or more. Leaves alternate on the stem, on short stalks or stalkless; mostly 2-4 inches long; dissected into 5-9 linear to lanceolate leaflets arranged opposite one another along the midrib; densely covered with hairs. Upper leaves reduced in size. Single flower heads at the top of long, leafless stalks rising above the foliage. Seed-producing disk florets densely packed in a gray column which turns a rich-brown as it matures, .5-1.5 inches long (*up to 4 times as long as wide*); surrounded at base by 4-11, yellow, infertile, spreading to drooping, .5-1 inch long, petal-like ray florets. Plants with reddish-brown "petals" are occasionally found.
GENERAL INFORMATION: The Oglala brewed a tea-like beverage from prairie coneflower.

Grayhead Prairie Coneflower
Ratibida pinnata

OTHER COMMON NAMES: Drooping coneflower, weary Susan.
FAMILY: Sunflower (Asteraceae)
FLOWERING PERIOD: July into August.
DISTRIBUTION: Eastern fifth of Nebraska, farther west along Elkhorn and perhaps other river valleys. Eastern edge of Great Plains.
HABITAT: Dry to moist soils, full sun or partial shade; meadows, prairie, floodplains, railways, roadsides, woodland edge.
DESCRIPTION: Native perennial growing from woody rhizomes or short caudex. Stems erect, single or clustered, usually branched on upper half; covered with fine hairs; 2-3 feet tall or more. Lower leaves up to 10 inches long (including leaf stalk); alternate on stem, on long stalks; deeply dissected into lanceolate leaflets arranged opposite one another along the midrib; usually with coarse teeth and covered with short, gray hairs. Upper leaves reduced in size. Single flower heads at the top of long, leafless stalks rising above the foliage. Seed-producing disk florets are densely packed on a purplish-brown, *egg-shaped button* which turns a rich brown as it matures; surrounded at the base by 6-13, yellow, infertile, drooping, 1-2.4 inch long, petal-like, ray florets.

PRAIRIE CONEFLOWER

PRAIRIE CONEFLOWER (RED-FLOWERED FORM)

GRAYHEAD PRAIRIE CONEFLOWER

101

GROOVED FLAX

Grooved Flax

Linum sulcatum

OTHER COMMON NAMES: Pale yellow flax.
FAMILY: Flax (Linaceae)
FLOWERING PERIOD: June and July.
DISTRIBUTION: Central and eastern Nebraska. East half of Great Plains.
HABITAT: Dry, especially sandy, soils; grasslands, roadsides.
DESCRIPTION: Native annual. Stem erect, slender, wiry, grooved or angled; branched above, 1-2 feet tall. Leaves inconspicuous, alternate, narrowly linear, less than 1 inch long; lower leaves shed early, stem becoming essentially leafless. Flowers at ends of branches or on short stalks from upper leaf axils; about .5-1 inch across; 5 yellow petals which are shed the same day the flower opens. Each plant bears many flowers but usually only a few each day.
GENERAL INFORMATION: Yellow flax (*Linum rigidum*) is found statewide except in the southeast and throughout the Great Plains. The two species are similar and can be most accurately identified by the number of segments composing the fruit, 10 in grooved flax, 5 in yellow flax. The blue-flowered common flax *(Linum usitatissimum)* of Europe was grown occasionally in northeast Nebraska in past decades as an oil crop.

Common St. John's-wort

Hypericum perforatum

OTHER COMMON NAMES: Tough-and-heal, penny-John, rosin-rose, amber.
FAMILY: St. John's-wort (Clusiaceae)
FLOWERING PERIOD: June into August.
DISTRIBUTION: Principally southeastern Nebraska. Southeastern Great Plains.
HABITAT: Disturbed sites; roadsides, pastures.
DESCRIPTION: Naturalized perennial spreading by rhizomes to form colonies. Stems are erect, much branched above, 16-24 inches tall. Leaves opposite on stem, without stalks, linear to oblong, dotted with oil-filled glands; less than 1 inch long and half as wide. Flowers in clusters (cymes) at ends of upper branches; .5-1 inch across; 5 yellow petals (toothed on one side) with *black dots on margins* surrounding a tufted center of long, numerous yellow stamens.
GENERAL INFORMATION: Introduced from Europe where it was considered a potent herb to ward off illness and evil spirits. Burned on St. John's Day (June 24) and hung in windows to ward off thunderbolts, imps, devils and ghosts. Used medicinally for a number of ailments. Contains the chemical hypericin which if eaten by white-colored livestock reacts with sunlight to produce a skin irritation, hair loss and slow-healing sores.

BLACK-EYED SUSAN

Black-eyed Susan
Rudbeckia hirta

OTHER COMMON NAMES: Brown-eyed Susan, brown Betty, brown daisy, donkey-head.

FAMILY: Sunflower (Asteraceae)

FLOWERING PERIOD: Principally June into July, but through the summer.

DISTRIBUTION: Statewide, more common in eastern Nebraska. Central and eastern Great Plains, sporadic farther west.

HABITAT: Dry to moist soils, particularly sites of mild disturbance; prairie, meadows, roadsides. Frequently used in roadside plantings.

DESCRIPTION: Native biennial or short-lived perennial growing from a taproot or clustered fibrous roots. Stems erect, not branched or branched sparingly above; 1-2 feet or more tall. Leaves alternate on stem, thick, variable in size and shape but mostly oblong-lanceolate to elliptic, 2-7 inches long, less than 2 inches wide, becoming smaller and narrower above; margins may or may not be toothed. Herbage with stiff hairs, rough to touch. Flower heads on long stalks rising above foliage; 2-3 inches across; 8-21, yellow, infertile, petal-like ray florets (up to 1.5 inches long) surrounding a conical, purplish-brown center of seed-producing disk florets, which turn a rich brown as they mature.

COMMON ST. JOHN'S-WORT

Bigroot Prickly Pear

Opuntia macrorhiza

OTHER COMMON NAMES: Beavertail, plains or common prickly pear.

FAMILY: Cactus (Cactaceae)

FLOWERING PERIOD: Late May into July.

DISTRIBUTION: Statewide in Nebraska, most common central, infrequent or absent eastern fifth. Of the two large prickly pears, this species is the most common east of the Panhandle. Central and southern Great Plains.

HABITAT: Dry gravelly and rocky soils, *particularly sandy soils;* grasslands, roadsides, hillsides, banks. Occasionally in partial shade.

DESCRIPTION: Native perennial growing from fibrous roots which are often enlarged and tuberous. Stems in jointed pads or segments, usually less than 10 inches tall, occasionally in clumps several feet across and taller. Segments are obovate or nearly round, flattened, bluish-green; 3-5 inches long, 2-4 inches wide (occasionally larger). Spines in clusters of 1-6, *mostly near segment margins;* spines absent, sparse or only fleshy protuberances in segment center; mostly straight (occasionally twisted), often reddish at base, not barbed, up to 2 inches long; with smaller, hair-like spines which readily detach if touched. Leaves rudimentary and seldom present. Flowers from upper margins of the older segments; 2-3 inches across. Numerous, overlapping, papery, light yellow petals, often reddish at base; surrounding a dense cluster of yellow or reddish stamens and a stout, cylindric style bearing a lobed stigma protruding beyond the stamens. The base of the flower (the ovary) *without spines.* The *fruit is fleshy at maturity,* red or reddish-purple, *without spines;* up to 1.5 inches long.

GENERAL INFORMATION: The mature, seed-filled fruits, the "pears," are edible, sweet and juicy; at their tastiest during September. They were used fresh and dried by Great Plains Indians. When food was scarce, the stems also were eaten after first boiling, permitting the skin with the spines to be easily removed. The pads may, however, be eaten raw, their taste reported to be like cucumber or okra. Early settlers frequently used the fruits to make preserves and wine. The mucilaginous juice of prickly pears was used by Great Plains tribes as a sizing to fix the colors painted on hides.

BIGROOT PRICKLY PEAR

104

PLAINS PRICKLY PEAR

LITTLE PRICKLY PEAR

Plains Prickly Pear

Opuntia polyacantha

FAMILY: Cactus (Cactaceae)

FLOWERING PERIOD: Late May through June.

DISTRIBUTION: Nebraska Panhandle. Probably the most common of the two large prickly pears in the Panhandle. Western Great Plains.

HABITAT: Dry, rocky or sandy soils; grasslands, pastures.

DESCRIPTION: Native perennial growing from fibrous, spreading roots. Stems in jointed pads or segments, usually less than 8 inches tall, occasionally in colonies several feet across. Segments obovate or nearly round, flattened, bluish-green; 2-5 inches long, nearly as wide. Spines in clusters of 1-10, the clusters *evenly spread over all of the segment;* mostly straight, new spines often reddish, not barbed and less than 2 inches long. Leaves rudimentary and seldom present. Flowers from upper margins of older segments; 2-3 inches across. Numerous, overlapping, papery, yellow petals; may or may not be reddish at base; surrounding a dense cluster of yellow or red stamens with yellow anthers and a stout pistil with a green, lobed stigma. The fleshy, green flower base (the ovary) *with spines. Fruit dry at maturity,* red or reddish-purple, smooth-skinned, covered *with spines;* about 1 inch long; not edible.

GENERAL INFORMATION: Bigroot and plains prickly pear hybridize producing intermediate forms and much variation. During the drought years of the 1930s, this species was so abundant that some ranges became worthless for grazing.

Little Prickly Pear

Opuntia fragilis

OTHER COMMON NAMES: Brittle or jumping cactus.

FAMILY: Cactus (Cactaceae)

FLOWERING PERIOD: June and July.

DISTRIBUTION: Central and western Nebraska. Central and northern Great Plains.

HABITAT: Dry, sandy or rocky soils; disturbed sites, grasslands.

DESCRIPTION: Native perennial growing from fibrous roots. Stems in jointed pads or segments which easily break away. Plants usually inconspicuous, composed of 1 to several segments; occasionally forms clumps up to 2 feet across. Low growing, seldom more than 8 inches tall. Segments ovoid (egg-shaped), rounded but somewhat flattened, less than 2 inches long; densely covered with clusters of 1-10 barbed spines, usually less than 1 inch long. The leaves are rudimentary and seldom present. Flowers less than 2 inches across; papery, yellow or yellow-orange petals surrounding the dense cluster of red or yellow stamens and a stout pistil with a green, lobed stigma. Flowers less frequently than other prickly pears; usually on older plants in clumps. Mature fruit a dry berry covered with spines, drying brownish or tan; about 1 inch long.

GENERAL INFORMATION: Because the segments break away readily, seeming to "jump" onto passersby (to root and form new plants if falling at a desirable site), this cactus is often called jumping cactus. The fruit spreads its seeds in a similar fashion. Increases in abundance on heavily grazed pastures.

105

Common Evening Primrose

Oenothera biennis

OTHER COMMON NAMES: Night willow-herb, tree-primrose, king's-cure-all, rampion, scurvish.

FAMILY: Evening Primrose (Onagraceae)

FLOWERING PERIOD: June through September.

DISTRIBUTION: Statewide, more common in eastern Nebraska. Eastern Great Plains.

HABITAT: Dry to moist soils, particularly disturbed sandy or gravelly sites; woodland edge, floodplains, roadsides, field margins.

DESCRIPTION: Native biennial growing from a taproot. Produces a basal rosette of elongate, often lobed and red-spotted leaves the first season, a flowering stalk the second. Stems erect, stout, usually branched, 2-6 feet tall, occasionally shrub-like. Leaves alternate on stem, lanceolate or narrowly ovate with pointed tips and wavy margins; on short stalks or stalkless; 2-6 inches long and less than 1.5 inches wide. Flowers appear singly on stalks from leaf axils near top of the stem; 4 bright yellow, overlapping petals; 1-2 inches across. Flowers appear over a long period of time but never many on same day. Flowers open late in day, closing the following morning never to open again.

GENERAL INFORMATION: The flowers are pollinated by moths and other night-flying insects, and in early morning by bees. To attract night pollinators, the flowers produce a heavy, musky scent and are said to be conspicuous even on dark nights, a phenomenon attributed by some to phosphoric properties. It was one of the earliest North American plants introduced into Europe, reportedly during the early 1600s. There, its thick, parsnip-like root, dug at the end of a plant's first season or beginning of its second, before it became woody, was favored in cooking or used raw in salads. In America, preparations from this primrose were ascribed many medicinal attributes, in fact, in Griffith's **Medical Botany**, published in 1847, one of its names was "cure-all." All parts of the plant were used—leaves, small stems, the bark of larger stems and the taproot. Apparently the principal medical use of the plant was as a dressing or poultice for wounds or skin disorders. Dried plant parts were also steeped in cold water to extract the purported medicinal elements, and used as a sedative and to treat asthma, whooping cough and the hiccoughs.

COMMON EVENING PRIMROSE

Fourpoint Evening Primrose

Oenothera rhombipetala

FAMILY: Evening Primrose (Onagraceae)

FLOWERING PERIOD: June and July.

DISTRIBUTION: Statewide in Nebraska except southeast, principally central and west. South half of Great Plains.

HABITAT: Principally in sandy soils; disturbed sites, roadsides, grasslands.

DESCRIPTION: Native biennial or winter annual growing from a taproot. Stem erect, usually not branched, 2-3 feet tall. Leaves alternate on stem, linear to narrowly lanceolate with pointed tips; essentially stalkless; 1-3 inches long, less than a third as wide. Flowers crowded into a pyramidal spike 4-10 inches long at top of stem; the 4 lemon yellow, roughly diamond-shaped (rhomboidal) petals spreading flatly; prominent stamens and even longer style with stigmas forming a cross-shaped pattern; 1-2 inches across.

GENERAL INFORMATION: During springs with abundant moisture, the yellow flowers of fourpoint evening primrose may blanket low, rolling hills and roadsides in the central and eastern Sandhills region. It is one of the first plants to reclaim sandy soils under abandoned center-pivot irrigation systems in the Sandhills.

FOURPOINT EVENING PRIMROSE

Cutleaf Ironplant

Haplopappus spinulosus

OTHER COMMON NAMES: Ironplant golden-weed, cut-leaved sideranthus.

FAMILY: Sunflower (Asteraceae)

FLOWERING PERIOD: June through September.

DISTRIBUTION: Statewide in Nebraska, uncommon or absent southeast. Throughout the Great Plains, infrequent east fifth.

HABITAT: Dry soil in prairies and plains.

DESCRIPTION: Native perennial growing from a woody caudex atop a woody, often branching, deep taproot. Stems are erect, numerous (rarely solitary), branching above, 1-2 feet tall. Leaves alternate on stem, stalkless, deeply divided (fern-like) into bristle-tipped lobes; narrow, less than 2 inches long, becoming smaller higher on stem. A solitary flower head, .5-1 inch across, at end branches; 15-30 yellow, petal-like ray florets surround a yellow button of disk florets. Both types of florets produce seeds.

GENERAL INFORMATION: A hardy wildflower which can survive drought by virtue of its root system and reduced leaf surface. The stems are tough and wiry, particularly when they dry, hence the name ironweed.

107

LAVENDER LEAF PRIMROSE

Lavender Leaf Primrose
Calylophus lavandulifolius

OTHER COMMON NAMES: Hartweg evening primrose.

FAMILY: Evening Primrose (Onagraceae)

FLOWERING PERIOD: June and July.

DISTRIBUTION: Panhandle and southwest Nebraska. Southwestern Great Plains.

HABITAT: Dry, crusty or rocky soils; grasslands, eroded sites, rock outcrops, bluffs.

DESCRIPTION: Native perennial growing from a caudex-topped, deep taproot. Few to many stems, 6-14 inches long, sprawling on the ground, frequently forming a tuft or small shrub-like plant, seldom more than 1 foot tall. Leaves mostly linear, less than 1.5 inches long, gray-green with hairy pubescence. Flowers from axils of upper leaves; tubular (1-1.5 inches long), spreading to 4, bright yellow, squarish, crinkled petals 1 inch or more in width. Withering flowers turn deep reddish-orange.

GENERAL INFORMATION: In the past, primroses of the genus *Calylophus* have been included with the evening primroses of the genus *Oenothera*. They differ in several observable features. The petals of flowers in the genus *Calylophus* usually are squarish and crinkled. Also, the stigmas are not divided into the cross-shaped lobes as are flowers in the genus *Oenothera*.

Plains Yellow Primrose
Calylophus serrulatus

OTHER COMMON NAMES: Tooth-leaved or cutleaf evening primrose.

FAMILY: Evening Primrose (Onagraceae)

FLOWERING PERIOD: Late May through July. A single plant blooms over a long period as stems elongate and new buds form.

DISTRIBUTION: Statewide in Nebraska. Found throughout the Great Plains.

HABITAT: Well-drained to dry, rocky, gravelly, sandy soils; grasslands, roadsides.

DESCRIPTION: Native perennial growing from a branched, woody caudex atop a taproot. Few to many stems, branched or unbranched, erect to reclining on ground or neighboring vegetation; 6-30 inches tall. Leaves alternate on stem; .5-4 inches long, but most less than 2.5 inches; narrowly lanceolate or narrowly oblong-lanceolate; frequently folded, trough-shape; sharply toothed. Flowers about 1 inch across, on stalks from upper leaf axils; 4 bright yellow petals fading to light yellow or pink; 8 prominent yellow stamens.

GENERAL INFORMATION: Well adapted to dry, hot environments because of its deep root and leaves which expose little surface area, minimizing loss of moisture. Its flowers, unlike most primroses, are open throughout the day.

PLAINS YELLOW PRIMROSE

Common Mullein
Verbascum thapsus

OTHER COMMON NAMES: Flannel or great mullein; velvet or mullen dock; candlewick.
FAMILY: Figwort (Scrophulariaceae)
FLOWERING PERIOD: June through August.
DISTRIBUTION: Statewide, more common in eastern Nebraska. Throughout the Great Plains, more common east and southeast.
HABITAT: Dry to moderately moist, particularly sandy, soils; disturbed sites, floodplains, over-grazed pastures, roadsides.
DESCRIPTION: A robust, naturalized biennial growing from a taproot. Produces a basal rosette of gray-green, densely woolly, obovate to oblong-lanceolate leaves up to 16 inches long and 5 inches wide the first season; a flowering stalk the second. Stem stout (nearly an inch across at base), somewhat woody, woolly, occasionally branched near top where flower spikes emerge, up to 7 feet tall. Stem leaves decreasing in size upwards; thickly covered with woolly hairs; oblong-lanceolate, blades of upper leaves extending along the stem as a wing; Flowers densely crowded on long spikes (up to 2 feet long) at top of stem, but only a few in flower at one time; up to 1 inch across; 5 yellow petals fused at base. An

COMMON MULLEIN

individual flower lasts only one day.
GENERAL INFORMATION: Native of Europe. The Romans reportedly dipped dried flower spikes in tallow to burn as torches. In ancient times, the flowers of common mullein were boiled in lye to make a yellow hair dye.

109

Spotted Touch-me-not
Impatiens capensis

OTHER COMMON NAMES: Spotted jewel-weed, impatience, snapweed, lady's-slipper, silverleaf, wild balsam.

FAMILY: Touch-me-not (Balsaminaceae)

FLOWERING PERIOD: June and July, less frequent later.

DISTRIBUTION: Central and eastern Nebraska. Eastern Great Plains.

HABITAT: Moist to wet soils, usually shady sites; near springs, seeps, streams, marshy areas.

DESCRIPTION: Native annual. Stems weak, watery, branching above, 2-3 feet or more tall. Leaves alternate, on stalks often as long as leaf blades, ovate, coarsely toothed, pale bluish-green, up to 4 inches long. Flowers solitary or in clusters, suspended on slender stalks from leaf axils; funnel-shaped, about 1 inch long with a curved, *forward-pointed nectar spur*, spreading into lobes on open end; *yellow-orange* with reddish-brown dots on interior. Fruit a capsule less than 1 inch long which bursts open when mature, propelling seeds several feet.

GENERAL INFORMATION: The name jewelweed is given because dew gathers on the leaves; impatience and *Impatiens* because when touched, the seed pods "impatiently" expel their seeds. American Indians used the juice from crushed leaves and stems to counteract the effect of contact with poison ivy, nettles and other skin rashes. A similar species, pale touch-me-not (*Impatiens pallida*) is found principally on Nebraska's eastern border. Its flowers are pale yellow and the spur is not as curved and points downward.

Tufted Loosestrife
Lysimachia thyrsiflora

FAMILY: Primrose (Primulaceae)

FLOWERING PERIOD: May into July.

DISTRIBUTION: Central, north-central and north-eastern Nebraska. Northeastern Great Plains.

HABITAT: Wet soils, occasionally in shallow water; marshes, wet meadows, margins of streams and ponds.

DESCRIPTION: Native perennial growing from creeping rhizomes. Stems stout, erect, with a sparse covering of long, soft, white hairs above; 1-2 feet tall or more. Leaves opposite on stem; narrowly lanceolate, without stalks; 2-5 inches long, less than half as wide. Leaves lower on stem much reduced. Small flowers with 5-7 narrow yellow petals and protruding stamens longer than the petals; gathered into club-shaped "tufts" (.5-1 inch long) at end of a long stalk from leaf axils on upper-middle portion of stem.

SPOTTED TOUCH-ME-NOT

TUFTED LOOSESTRIFE

Fringed Loosestrife
Lysimachia ciliata

FAMILY: Primrose (Primulaceae)

FLOWERING PERIOD: Late June through July.

DISTRIBUTION: Statewide in Nebraska except southwest, principally east. Eastern and northeastern Great Plains.

HABITAT: Full sun or partial shade in moist to wet soils; ditches, shorelines, meadows, thickets, woodland edge.

DESCRIPTION: Native perennial spreading by rhizomes to form colonies. Stem slender, erect, branched sparingly above; taller plants often supported by other vegetation; 1-3 feet tall. Leaves opposite, blades ovate-lanceolate to ovate with pointed tips, 2-5 inches long and half as wide; the upper portion of the leaf stalk *fringed with white, kinky hairs* (hence the common name). Flowers *nodding*, up to 1 inch across, on long stalks from upper leaf axils; 5 pointed, yellow petals with reddish bases surround 5 conspicuous stamens. Petals spread flat, giving the flower a flat face.

GENERAL INFORMATION: J.E. Weaver, prairie botanist at the University of Nebraska during the first half of the 20th century, ranked this species as the third most important forb of lowland prairies. It is far less common today.

FRINGED LOOSESTRIFE

Plains Coreopsis
Coreopsis tinctoria

OTHER COMMON NAMES: Common tick-seed, golden or garden coreopsis.
FAMILY: Sunflower (Asteraceae)
FLOWERING PERIOD: Late May, throughout the summer.
DISTRIBUTION: Statewide in Nebraska, most common central. Throughout the Great Plains, less frequent north.
HABITAT: Low-lying, seasonally moist soils, particularly sandy or sandy loam; roadsides, low areas gathering irrigation runoff.
DESCRIPTION: Native annual or short-lived perennial. Frequently found in patches. Erect, slender, branched stems 1-3 feet tall. Leaves opposite, dark green and glossy; divided into linear segments. Flower heads up to 1.5 inches across, on long stalks, numerous at ends of upper branches. Bright yellow, 3-lobed, petal-like ray florets (usually 8) with a *reddish-brown spot at the base* surround a reddish-brown center of seed-producing disk florets.

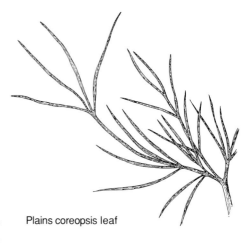
Plains coreopsis leaf

PLAINS COREOPSIS

112

Sneezeweed

Helenium autumnale

OTHER COMMON NAMES: False or swamp sunflower.

FAMILY: Sunflower (Asteraceae)

FLOWERING PERIOD: August through September.

DISTRIBUTION: Statewide, more common in eastern Nebraska. Principally eastern half of Great Plains, sporadic west.

HABITAT: Moist, low ground; shorelines, moist prairies and meadows, roadsides.

DESCRIPTION: Native perennial growing from a crown of fibrous roots. Stems erect, stout, branching above, 2-3 feet or more tall. Leaves alternate, lanceolate to ovate-lanceolate, with or without teeth on the margin; stalkless, leaf blade extending onto stem as narrow wings; 1.5-5 inches long, less than half as wide. Flower heads up to 1.5 inches across; 10-20, three lobed, wedge-shaped, yellow, petal-like ray florets surround a raised, yellow button of disk florets. Both types of florets produce fertile seeds (achenes).

GENERAL INFORMATION: Sneezeweed is bitter and usually avoided by livestock. Can be poisonous if consumed in quantity. These toxic substances are more concentrated in the flowers than in the stems and dried leaves. The dried and powdered flower heads were used as a snuff during pioneer days to induce sneezing which was believed to clear the head of congestion and be a generally good tonic.

Greenthread

Thelesperma filifolium

OTHER COMMON NAMES: Nippleweed.

FAMILY: Sunflower (Asteraceae)

FLOWERING PERIOD: June into August.

DISTRIBUTION: Apparently statewide, uncommon in central Nebraska. South half of Great Plains.

HABITAT: Dry, particularly sandy, gravelly or rocky, soils; disturbed sites, grasslands, roadsides, pastures.

DESCRIPTION: Native annual, winter annual or short-lived perennial growing from a simple or branched taproot. Often found in colonies. Stem slender, erect, branched, smooth; up to 20 inches but more typically 10-15 inches tall. *Leaves divided into narrowly linear segments.* Flower heads solitary at top of a slender, leafless stalk up to 6 inches long; 1.5-2 inches across; 8 broad, *all yellow*, 3-lobed, infertile, petal-like ray florets surround a brownish to yellowish center of seed-producing disk florets.

113

Compass Plant

Silphium laciniatum

OTHER COMMON NAMES: Pilot-weed, gum-weed, turpentine plant, rosinweed.
FAMILY: Sunflower (Asteraceae)
FLOWERING PERIOD: July and August.
DISTRIBUTION: Eastern quarter of Nebraska. Southeastern Great Plains.
HABITAT: Moist soils in low prairies, meadows, and roadsides.
DESCRIPTION: Native perennial growing from a woody taproot extending as much as 10 feet into the soil. Stem stout, erect, not branched; covered with coarse, stiff hairs; 4-7 feet tall or taller. Leaves leathery, clustered at base, up to 15 inches long and about half as wide, deeply notched, nearly to midrib, forming lobes which are likewise notched. Stem leaves alternate, becoming progressively smaller, bases clasping stem. Leaves hairy but not conspicuously so, principally along main leaf veins; rough to touch. Flower heads in clusters on upper third of stem; on short, stout stalks or stalkless, from axils of rudimentary leaves; 3-4 inches across; 15-24 yellow, slender, 1-2 inch long, petal-like, seed-producing ray florets surround the dark brown center of infertile disk florets.
GENERAL INFORMATION: The large, lower leaves often orient in a north-to-south direction, hence the common names of compass plant and pilot-weed. The Pawnee and Ponca believed compass plant attracted lightning and they would not camp near it. Its dried root was burned during electric storms to ward off lightning. When cut or broken, the stem exudes a resinous sap used as chewing gum by Indian and pioneer children. Preparations of compass plant have been assigned various medicinal attributes.

Nodding Beggar-ticks

Bidens cernua

OTHER COMMON NAMES: Stick-tights, tick-seed, small bur marigold.
FAMILY: Sunflower (Asteraceae)
FLOWERING PERIOD: August into October.
DISTRIBUTION: Statewide. Throughout the Great Plains, more common east and north.
HABITAT: Wet soils; ditches, shorelines.
DESCRIPTION: Native annual with branched, erect, often reclining stem, 1-3 feet or longer; rooting where it touches the soil. *Leaves with-*

COMPASS PLANT

out stalks, opposite on stem, occasionally in whorls; linear-lanceolate to oblong-lanceolate, 2-6 inches long, up to 1.5 inches wide; with toothed margins. Flower heads are 1-2 inches across, *nodding when mature*; borne singly or clustered at ends of branches; 6-8 yellow, infertile, petal-like ray florets surrounding the yellow-brown center of disk florets. Dark brown achenes produced by disk flowers cling tenaciously to fur and clothing.
GENERAL INFORMATION: Another beggar-tick common throughout the Great Plains is *Bidens frondosa*. Its leaves are on stalks and deeply divided into lobes; its flower heads not nodding at maturity and not as showy as its petal-like ray florets are rudimentary or even absent.

Nodding beggar-ticks achene

114

CUP PLANT

Cup Plant
Silphium perfoliatum

OTHER COMMON NAMES: Carpenter-weed, square stem, Indian-cup, cup rosinweed.
FAMILY: Sunflower (Asteraceae)
FLOWERING PERIOD: July and August.
DISTRIBUTION: Eastern quarter of Nebraska, principally southeast. East fifth of Great Plains, less common north.
HABITAT: Moist to wet fertile soils; floodplains, meadows, open woodlands, roadsides.
DESCRIPTION: Native perennial. Stems erect, stout, branched near the top or not, *square in cross-section* (which, coupled with the stem's stoutness, explains the name carpenter-weed), if hairy only modestly so, up to 6 feet tall or more. Leaves opposite, the *bases joined around the stem to form a cup*, coarsely toothed; lower leaves up to 10 inches long and 6 inches wide at base, roughly triangular in shape, becoming progressively smaller higher. Flower heads are solitary or in clusters on stout stalks at top of plant; 2.5-3.5 inches across; about 21 or about 34, narrow, .5-1.5 inch long, yellow, petal-like, seed-producing ray florets surround a yellow-green center of infertile disk florets.

NODDING BEGGAR-TICKS

ROSINWEED

FALSE SUNFLOWER

Rosinweed

Silphium integrifolium

OTHER COMMON NAMES: Whole-leaf or entire-leaved rosinweed.
FAMILY: Sunflower (Asteraceae)
FLOWERING PERIOD: Principally July and August, stragglers until frost.
DISTRIBUTION: Eastern quarter of Nebraska. Southeastern Great Plains.
HABITAT: Moderately dry to moist, fertile soils; prairies, meadows, roadsides.
DESCRIPTION: Native perennial growing from a caudex with fibrous roots, forming clumps or open colonies from short rhizomes. Stems erect, stout, usually with bristly hairs, 3-5 feet tall. Leaves dark green, thick and stiff, mostly opposite on stem, without stalks, bases often clasping stem; lanceolate to ovate, without teeth on margins or with small teeth; 3-5 inches long, about a third as wide; coarse hairs on both surfaces, rough to the touch. Flower heads clustered at top of stems; 1.5-3 inches across; waxy, broad, overlapping, leafy bracts encircle about 21 or about 34, yellow, petal-like ray florets which surround the greenish-yellow center of disk florets. Unlike most species of the sunflower family, plants of the genus *Silphium* have ray florets, not disk florets, which are fertile and produce seeds.

False Sunflower

Heliopsis helianthoides

OTHER COMMON NAMES: Ox-eye.
FAMILY: Sunflower (Asteraceae)
FLOWERING PERIOD: July and August.
DISTRIBUTION: Eastern half of Nebraska. Eastern third of Great Plains, scattered farther west.
HABITAT: Dry soils, healing disturbed sites; roadsides, woodland and thicket edge, prairie.
DESCRIPTION: Native perennial growing from a caudex, fibrous roots and short rhizomes. Stems stiff, erect, rough to touch; 3-5 feet tall. *All leaves opposite on stem,* ovate to broadly lanceolate, on short stalks; 2-6 inches long, half as wide; prominently toothed, rough to touch on both surfaces. Flower heads at ends of stems and on stout stalks from upper leaf axils; 1.5-2.5 inches across; 10-16 deep yellow (almost orange), petal-like ray florets surround a *raised, conical center* of yellow disk florets. Individual plants in flower over a long period. Both types of florets produce seeds.
GENERAL INFORMATION: False sunflower is often mistaken for a true sunflower of the genus *Helianthus*. In the sunflowers, only disk florets produce seeds. Also, the petal-like ray florets of false sunflower often persist even when the flower heads have produced fruit.

Tickseed Sunflower

Bidens coronata

OTHER COMMON NAMES: Purple-stemmed swamp beggar-ticks.

FAMILY: Sunflower (Asteraceae)

FLOWERING PERIOD: Late August, September and into October.

DISTRIBUTION: North-central Nebraska, principally Sandhills region. Its distribution in the Great Plains is essentially restricted to north-central Nebraska.

HABITAT: Sandy, wet soils; ditches, floodplains, shorelines.

DESCRIPTION: Native annual 1-5 feet tall. Stem erect, often purplish. Leaves opposite on stem, up to 5.5 inches long; deeply divided to midvein on the lower portion of larger leaves; lobes (leaflets) narrow with serrate margins. Flower heads showy, 1-2 inches across, borne at the ends of branches; usually 8 bright yellow, infertile, petal-like ray florets surrounding the yellow-brown center of disk florets. Black, often sparsely hairy achenes are produced by the disk flowers which usually bear 2 stout awns with barbs not as efficient at sticking to fur or clothing as are those of other beggar-ticks.

Tickseed sunflower leaf

GOLDEN ASTER

Golden Aster

Chrysopsis villosa

OTHER COMMON NAMES: Prairie or hairy golden aster.

FAMILY: Sunflower (Asteraceae)

FLOWERING PERIOD: July into September.

DISTRIBUTION: Statewide in Nebraska; probably most common in the Panhandle and Sandhills. Throughout the Great Plains.

HABITAT: Dry, particularly sandy soils in full sun; upland prairie and plains.

DESCRIPTION: Native perennial growing from a thick, woody caudex and taproot. One or more stems, often sprawling on the ground, forming clumps; usually branched; degree of pubescence varies with subspecies (western plants more hairy); 6-20 inches tall depending on moisture. Leaves are alternate on stem, numerous, oblong-elliptic to narrowly oblong-lanceolate, 1-3 inches long, less than a fourth as wide; gray-green with a dense covering of short hairs making them rough to the touch. Flower heads numerous at ends of branches, 1-2 inches in width; 20-30 bright yellow, petal-like ray florets surrounding a yellow center of disk florets. The fruit is a flattened achene with numerous bristles.

GENERAL INFORMATION: Even though the flower heads are aster-like, hence the common name, they are not true asters. Other closely related species are found in the Great Plains but this is by far the most common. It is a highly variable species, particularly in the degree of pubescence. Several varieties or subspecies have been identified. Prairie botanist J.E. Weaver excavated one golden aster with a main taproot extending to a depth of 13 feet with several large branches reaching 7 to 8 feet into the subsoil. Additionally, he found the upper 18 inches of soil efficiently infiltrated by its roots. Golden aster's extensive and deep system of roots, coupled with its gray-green colored herbage and hairy surface (which minimizes moisture loss through transpiration) make it well adapted to survive and prosper in dry, hot environments. It is considered to have no forage value for most classes of livestock, although sheep are known to graze it. Closely related plants of the same genus are cultivated commercially and sold as ornamentals under the name golden aster.

Grassleaf Goldenrod
Euthamia graminifolia

FAMILY: Sunflower (Asteraceae)
FLOWERING PERIOD: August into October.
DISTRIBUTION: Northern Nebraska. Northern half of the Great Plains.
HABITAT: Moist or drying soils; near streams and lakes, roadsides.
DESCRIPTION: Native perennial spreading by creeping rhizomes to form open patches. Stems slender, branching above. Lower leaves often shed by time of flowering; remaining leaves numerous, linear to linear-elliptic, without stalks; 2-5 inches long, less than .5 inch wide; with *3 prominent, roughly parallel veins*. Small yellow flower heads, each with 20-40 florets, are arranged in *flat-topped clusters* at top of plant.
GENERAL INFORMATION: Differs from *Solidago* species in having minute glandular dots on its leaves and more ray florets than disk florets. Only one species of *Solidago*, rigid goldenrod, in our region has a flat-topped inflorescence. A closely related species, viscid euthamia *(Euthamia gymnospermoides)*, found statewide, has smaller flower heads, usually less than 20 florets, often only one prominent leaf vein and a more gummy and resinous herbage.

Snakeweed
Gutierrezia sarothrae

OTHER COMMON NAMES: Broomweed, rabbit-brush.
FAMILY: Sunflower (Asteraceae)
FLOWERING PERIOD: August and September.
DISTRIBUTION: Central and western Nebraska. Throughout the Great Plains except east fifth.
HABITAT: Dry, particularly rocky, soil on plains. Increases with grazing pressure.
DESCRIPTION: Native perennial growing from a strong taproot, forming a small, 1-2 foot tall, bushy half-shrub. Numerous slender stems, woody at base, branched above. Leaves alternate, linear, .5-2 inches long; lower leaves usually shed before flowering. Herbage somewhat resinous. Small, yellow flower heads in clusters at ends of branches. Stems mostly of the same height producing a yellow-domed, fan-shaped plant when in flower.
GENERAL INFORMATION: Great Plains Indians bound the stems together to fashion brooms. A tea made from the leaves was used to treat rheumatism, stomach ache, snakebite and was given to horses to treat coughs and loose bowels.

GRASSLEAF GOLDENROD

SNAKEWEED

119

Showy-wand Goldenrod
Solidago speciosa

OTHER COMMON NAMES: Showy or noble goldenrod.
FAMILY: Sunflower (Asteraceae)
FLOWERING PERIOD: August and September.
DISTRIBUTION: Eastern fifth of Nebraska, occasionally found in north-central. Principally eastern and southeastern Great Plains.
HABITAT: Dry to moderately moist soils; grasslands, grassy woodland edge and openings, ravines.
DESCRIPTION: Native perennial growing from a stout, woody caudex with numerous fibrous roots. Stems erect, singly or in clusters; usually not branched; hardly visible pubescence on upper stem, rough to touch; often reddish; 1-2 feet tall, occasionally taller. Leaves are numerous, alternate on stem, not hairy or pubescent. Lower leaves on short stalks; ovate to lanceolate to oblong; the margins smooth or slightly toothed; 4-8 inches long; often shed before flowering. Stem leaves smaller, not on stalks; lanceolate, fairly thick. *Veins spreading from midrib*, not parallel. Small, yellow flower heads in a *compact, pyramidal or club-shaped column.* Inflorescence erect, not nodding.
GENERAL INFORMATION: Goldenrods are condemned for aggravating symptoms of hay fever but they are pollinated principally by insects and little of their pollen is wind-borne.

SHOWY-WAND GOLDENROD

Prairie Goldenrod
Solidago missouriensis

OTHER COMMON NAMES: Missouri goldenrod.
FAMILY: Sunflower (Asteraceae)
FLOWERING PERIOD: *Earliest of the goldenrods*; late July into September.
DISTRIBUTION: Statewide. Throughout the Great Plains except extreme southwest.
HABITAT: Dry soils; prairies, roadsides.
DESCRIPTION: Native perennial growing from a spreading caudex or a creeping rhizome. Stems erect, singly or in clusters; *smooth, not hairy;* often reddish; 1-2 feet tall. Lower leaves mostly shed before flowering. Stem leaves numerous, alternate on the stem, essentially without stalks; broadly linear to narrowly elliptic, 2-4 inches long, .5-1 inch wide; margins toothed or not, often only toward tip of blade; 3

PRAIRIE GOLDENROD

prominent, roughly *parallel veins;* thick, somewhat rigid. Small, yellow flower heads arranged along upper side of branches, usually in a *plume-shaped, nodding inflorescence.*
GENERAL INFORMATION: Similar to Canada goldenrod but typically shorter, lacking even minute hairs on stem, and early flowering.

Canada Goldenrod
Solidago canadensis

FAMILY: Sunflower (Asteraceae)
FLOWERING PERIOD: August, September.
DISTRIBUTION: Statewide. Throughout the Great Plains, less common west.
HABITAT: Moist to dry soils; grasslands, thickets, roadsides, railways.
DESCRIPTION: Native perennial growing from a weak caudex or creeping rhizomes. Stems erect, singly or in clusters; *minutely hairy on upper half* and rough to touch, 2-4 feet tall. Leaves numerous, alternate on stem, mostly stalkless; narrowly lanceolate to elliptic, 2-5 inches long, about .5 inch wide; *margins usually sharply toothed;* 3 prominent, roughly *parallel veins.* Small, yellow flower heads arranged along the upper side of branches, usually in a *plume-shaped inflorescence.*
GENERAL INFORMATION: Nebraska's state flower, late goldenrod *(Solidago gigantea),* is more robust and larger, 5-6 feet tall; its stem shiny, often reddish and essentially hairless, particularly below the inflorescence. It too is found throughout the Great Plains.

CANADA GOLDENROD

RIGID GOLDENROD

Rigid Goldenrod
Solidago rigida

FAMILY: Sunflower (Asteraceae)
FLOWERING PERIOD: August, September.
DISTRIBUTION: Statewide. Throughout the Great Plains, infrequent or absent southwest.
HABITAT: Dry soils, often rocky, gravelly or sandy sites; grasslands, roadsides.
DESCRIPTION: Native perennial growing from a stout, branching caudex. Stems erect, stout, not branched; often forming clumps, 1-5 (usually 2-3) feet tall. Rosette of overwintering *basal leaves* with long stalks often exceeding leaf blade in length; blade elliptic-oblong, lanceolate or broadly ovate; 4-12 inches long overall. Leaves on upper stem smaller, without stalks, *bases clasping the stem; thick, leathery, stiff.* Stems and leaves densely covered with short, whitish hairs giving the plant a gray-green color. *Flat-topped inflorescence* of small (but large relative to the other goldenrods), yellow flower heads.
GENERAL INFORMATION: Goldenrods show much variation and some hybridize, complicating identification. Many can only be identified by professional botanists.

PLAINS SUNFLOWER (SHOWING WHITISH CENTRAL SPOT ON DISK)

PLAINS SUNFLOWER

Plains Sunflower

Helianthus petiolaris

FAMILY: Sunflower (Asteraceae)

FLOWERING PERIOD: Early July into September.

DISTRIBUTION: Statewide, but more common central and west. Throughout the Great Plains.

HABITAT: Dry, *particularly sandy*, soil; mildly disturbed sites, grasslands, roadsides.

DESCRIPTION: Native annual growing from a *taproot*. Stems erect, hairy (more so on upper stem), may or may not be branched; *usually less than 3 feet*. All leaves alternate on stem on long stalks; ovate to ovate-lanceolate, usually *not notched* at base of leaf blade; without teeth on margins, or not as pronounced as in annual sunflower; 2-6 inches long and a *third as wide*. Flower heads at ends of branches; usually *less than 3 inches across*; 15-30 yellow, infertile, petal-like ray florets surround a center of seed-producing, dark purplish-brown disk florets. The flat disk usually has a *whitish center spot* of white bearded, chaffy bracts.

GENERAL INFORMATION: Plains sunflower and annual sunflower hybridize producing intermediate forms. Plains sunflower is a diminutive version of annual sunflower—shorter with narrower leaves and smaller flower heads.

Golden Glow
Rudbeckia laciniata

OTHER COMMON NAMES: Tall, cutleaf or green-headed coneflower; thimbleweed.

FAMILY: Sunflower (Asteraceae)

FLOWERING PERIOD: July into September.

DISTRIBUTION: Eastern half of Nebraska. Eastern half of Great Plains, scattered farther west.

HABITAT: Moist soils, usually found in partial shade; woodland edge and openings, floodplains, thickets.

DESCRIPTION: Native perennial growing from a rhizome, often forming colonies. Stem from a coarse, woody base; branched; usually not pubescent; 5 feet or more tall. Lower leaves large, up to 10 inches long including stalks; deeply cut, nearly to midrib, usually into 3-7 lobes, the lobes also deeply cut and coarsely toothed. Flower heads at ends of branches; 2-3 inches across; 6-16 yellow, drooping, infertile, 1-2 inch long, petal-like ray florets surround a *rounded cone of yellow-green,* seed-producing disk florets.

GENERAL INFORMATION: The once common garden flower called golden-glow is a variety of this species selected because of its abundant, petal-like ray florets.

Golden glow leaf

GOLDEN GLOW

123

JERUSALEM ARTICHOKE

Jerusalem Artichoke

Helianthus tuberosus

OTHER COMMON NAMES: Canada potato, earth apple, girasole.
FAMILY: Sunflower (Asteraceae)
FLOWERING PERIOD: August, September.
DISTRIBUTION: Eastern half of Nebraska, infrequent west. Eastern half of Great Plains.
HABITAT: Moist, rich, soils; streamsides, woodland edge, prairie ravines, roadsides.
DESCRIPTION: Native perennial growing from rhizomes bearing tubers. Stems are stout, erect, branched above, usually hairy and rough to the touch; 3-9 feet or more tall. Lower leaves mostly opposite on the stem, upper leaves mostly alternate; leaf blade ovate to broadly lanceolate; thick, dark green and usually coarsely toothed; upper surface rough to touch, undersurface downy; 4-10 inches long, most a third to half as wide as long. Flower heads at ends of branches; 2-3.5 inches across; the 10-20 yellow, infertile, petal-like ray florets surround the center of seed-producing, *yellow disk florets*. Common sunflower, is equally robust, has notched, heart-shaped leaves and a dark, purplish-brown disk.
GENERAL INFORMATION: The name Jerusalem apparently originated from a mispronunciation of the Italian word "girasole," meaning "turning to the sun," a reference to the flower heads following the path of the sun. Tubers form in late summer and early fall. They were an important food of American Indians. Sold commercially today as they contain little sugar and serve as a potato substitute for diabetics.

Sawtooth Sunflower

Helianthus grosseserratus

FAMILY: Sunflower (Asteraceae)
FLOWERING PERIOD: August, September.
DISTRIBUTION: Eastern and north-central Nebraska. Eastern Great Plains.
HABITAT: Moist, rich soils; bottom lands, wet prairies, streamsides, ravines.
DESCRIPTION: Native perennial growing from a woody, spindle-shaped root, spreading by rhizomes and *forming colonies*. Stems erect; pubescent above but mostly smooth below; branching above; 5-8 feet or more tall. Leaves mostly alternate on stem; lanceolate to ovate-lanceolate, *coarsely toothed;* the upper surface rough, undersurface soft with pubescence; 4-8 inches long, one fourth as wide, tapering to a stalk before joining stem. Flower heads at ends of upper branches or on stalks from upper leaf axils; 2-3 inches or more across; 10-20 yellow, infertile, petal-like ray florets surrounding the rounded center disk of seed-producing, *yellow disk florets.*

SAWTOOTH SUNFLOWER

COMMON SUNFLOWER

MAXIMILIAN SUNFLOWER

Common Sunflower

Helianthus annuus

FAMILY: Sunflower (Asteraceae)

FLOWERING PERIOD: Late July into September.

DISTRIBUTION: Statewide in Nebraska. Found throughout the Great Plains.

HABITAT: Disturbed sites; fields, field margins, roadsides, floodplains.

DESCRIPTION: Native annual growing from a taproot. Stems are erect, hairy, with spreading lateral branches; 3-7 feet or more tall. *Leaves mostly alternate* (lowermost leaves are opposite) on long stalks; cordate (heart-shaped) or spade-shaped; toothed; 4-16 inches long and about half as wide. Herbage rough to the touch. Flower heads at ends of branches or on stalks from upper leaf axils; 3-6 inches across; 17 or more yellow, infertile, petal-like ray florets surround the center of seed-producing, *dark purplish-brown disk florets*. The flat disk *does not have a whitish center spot* composed of chaffy bracts, as does the disk of plains sunflower *(Helianthus petiolaris).*

GENERAL INFORMATION: Cultivated by American Indians who selected for plants with large seeds, reportedly increasing seed size 1,000 percent. This species is the wild-growing ancestor of the commercially grown sunflower.

Maximilian Sunflower

Helianthus maximilianii

FAMILY: Sunflower (Asteraceae)

FLOWERING PERIOD: August , September.

DISTRIBUTION: Statewide. Throughout the Great Plains, infrequent or absent west fifth.

HABITAT: Moist, particularly sandy, soils; prairie, river valleys, wet meadows, roadsides.

DESCRIPTION: Native perennial growing from thickened, fleshy roots; spreading by short rhizomes to form compact clumps. Stems are erect, rough to touch because of minute hairs; not branched; sometimes reddish above; 3-6 feet or more tall. Leaves mostly alternate on stem (lower leaves may be opposite); sickle-shaped, usually without teeth on margins; 3-8 inches long, .5-1.5 inches wide; rough to touch on both surfaces; characteristically *folded into a trough shape* and arched. Foliage is bluish-green. Flower heads are on stout stalks from upper leaf axils; 2-3 inches or more across; 10-25 yellow, infertile, petal-like ray florets surround the rounded center of seed-producing, *yellow disk* florets.

GENERAL INFORMATION: First collected on an expedition by German Prince Maximilian of Wied who made extensive scientific explorations of North and South America during the early 1800s.

125

Orange to Red Flowers

WILD COLUMBINE

Wild Columbine

Aquilegia canadensis

OTHER COMMON NAMES: Rock lily, rock bells, honeysuckle.

FAMILY: Buttercup (Ranunculaceae)

FLOWERING PERIOD: Late April and early May, occasionally into June.

DISTRIBUTION: Eastern Nebraska, particularly the Missouri River and lower reaches of its tributaries; occasional along the Niobrara River and in the Pine Ridge. Eastern Great Plains.

HABITAT: Moist, often rocky, woodland soils.

DESCRIPTION: Native perennial growing from a stout caudex. Stems slender; branching to form an open, spreading plant 2 feet or more tall. Principal leaves from base; on long, slender stalks; divided into 3 leaflets on their own stalks, each deeply divided into 3 distinct lobes. Stem leaves alternate, becoming reduced in size, stalkless and not so deeply lobed. Flowers on long stalks at ends of branches or from upper leaf axils; nodding, up to 2 inches long; 5 deep red or crimson, petal-like sepals; 5 tubular petals, mostly reddish but becoming yellow on the outer edges. Protruding bundle of yellow stamens. Petal spurs terminate in a slightly enlarged nectar gland.

GENERAL INFORMATION: Called "black perfume plant" by the Omaha and Ponca, its seeds were crushed, often by chewing, and used as a love charm. The paste was spread on clothes where its fragrance persisted, reportedly reviving in damp weather. Powdered seeds were believed to cause nosebleed, reduce fevers and cure headaches.

Butterfly Milkweed
Asclepias tuberosa

OTHER COMMON NAMES: Orange swallow-wort, pleurisy-root, orange-root.
FAMILY: Milkweed (Asclepiadaceae)
FLOWERING PERIOD: Principally June and July, into September.
DISTRIBUTION: Eastern Nebraska, particularly in the southeast and south-central. Southeastern Great Plains.
HABITAT: Dry to moderately moist, particularly well-drained soils; prairie, prairie remnants, roadsides, railways.
DESCRIPTION: Native perennial growing from a thickened root crown atop a deep taproot. One to several stout, erect stems covered with coarse, stiff hairs; 1-2.5 feet tall. Leaves mostly alternate, lanceolate to narrowly ovate, 2-4 inches long and covered with stiff hairs. *Does not have a milky, latex sap.* Flowers typical of milkweeds; in flat-topped clusters at the top of the stems. Considerable color variation; from a typical, bright red-orange, to a deep reddish-orange, or a rich, dark yellow. Dark red-orange flowers reported to be typical in the heart of its range (eastern Kansas and western Missouri); flowers becoming less red and more yellow at margins of its range. Seed pod spindle-shaped, erect, 3-5 inches long, without tubercles.
GENERAL INFORMATION: The plant has a long history of medicinal uses by both American Indians and early white settlers. Decoctions of its roots were used for respiratory ailments, hence the common name "pleurisy root." Also administered as a laxative, astringent, antirheumatic, antisyphilitic, purgative and emetic.

BUTTERFLY MILKWEED

RED FALSE MALLOW

Red False Mallow
Sphaeralcea coccinea

OTHER COMMON NAMES: Cowboy's delight, scarlet globe mallow, moss rose.
FAMILY: Mallow (Malvaceae)
FLOWERING PERIOD: Late May into August.
DISTRIBUTION: Statewide in Nebraska, but uncommon or absent east fifth. Throughout the Great Plains except east fifth.
HABITAT: Dry, often disturbed soils; roadsides, eroded banks, overgrazed pastures.
DESCRIPTION: Native perennial growing from a woody caudex atop a taproot, spreading by creeping roots to form colonies. Stems, usually several, are erect or somewhat reclining on ground; usually branched and less than 12 inches tall. Leaves alternate on stem; stalks of lower leaves equal to or longer than leaf blade; shorter leaf stalks and smaller leaves above. Leaf blade nearly as wide as long, up to 2 inches; deeply divided, usually to midrib, usually into 3 or 5 discernable leaflets or lobes which in turn are lobed. Stem and leaves gray-green, usually densely pubescent. Flowers in clusters at end of stem; up to 1.5 inches across; 5 salmon to brick-red petals surround a column of yellow stamens. Flower color varies.
GENERAL INFORMATION: Dakota medicine men chewed the plant into a paste which they rubbed over their hands and arms, making them immune to the effect of scalding water, so to the wonderment of beholders they could take pieces of hot meat out of the kettle.

127

TURK'S CAP LILY

Turk's Cap Lily

Lilium canadense

OTHER COMMON NAMES: Canada, Michigan and wild yellow lily.

FAMILY: Lily (Liliaceae)

FLOWERING PERIOD: Late June and July, principally early July.

DISTRIBUTION: Eastern fifth of Nebraska; extreme eastern Great Plains. Extending west from Nebraska's eastern tier of counties along major river valleys.

HABITAT: Moist, rich soil; low prairies, meadows, roadsides, railways, thickets, woodland edge, river valleys.

DESCRIPTION: Native perennial growing from a scaly bulb producing shoots, at the end of which a new bulb may develop; hence often found in colonies. Stems are stout, erect; often branching near top; 2-5 feet or taller. *Leaves in whorls around stem* (upper leaves may be alternate); lanceolate to narrowly elliptic, 2-6 inches long and less than 1 inch wide. *Nodding flowers* on long stalks at top of stem; 3 inches or more across; 6 orange-red tepals (similar or undifferentiated petals and sepals) becoming

yellow at bases, *with numerous brownish spots, reflexed* until nearly touching flower base when mature; 6 stamens with large, pollen-bearing anthers surround a single pistil. Individual flowers often last for several days. A young plant may bear only one flower, older plants 6 or more.

GENERAL INFORMATION: Becoming increasingly rare because of the conversion of low-lying, fertile prairies to farmland, the use of herbicides on hay meadows and roadsides, and road construction.

Leaf whorl of
Turk's cap lily

WESTERN RED LILY

Daylily
Hemerocallis fulva

FAMILY: Lily (Liliaceae)
FLOWERING PERIOD: June and July.
DISTRIBUTION: Principally eastern half of Nebraska, particularly southeast. Eastern half of the Great Plains, principally southeast.
HABITAT: Roadsides, abandoned farmsteads and dump sites.
DESCRIPTION: Introduced perennial spreading to form compact colonies from thickened, fleshy stolons. Leaves basal; linear, often arching; 1-3 feet long, 1 inch or less wide. *Flower stalks leafless*, 3-4 feet tall. Flowers in clusters at top of stalk, each lasting but one day; 2.5-4 inches across; 6 slightly recurved, orange-red tepals (similar or undifferentiated petals and sepals) becoming yellow at bases, *without brownish spots*; 6 prominent stamens, style even longer. Does not produce mature seeds.
GENERAL INFORMATION: A native of Asia, daylily was once a popular garden flower in the United States. Persists where planted or where roots are dumped. Colonies may expand but seldom spread without the help of man.

Western Red Lily
Lilium philadelphicum

OTHER COMMON NAMES: Philadelphia or wood lily, orange-cup.
FAMILY: Lily (Liliaceae)
FLOWERING PERIOD: Late June and July.
DISTRIBUTION: Northern quarter of Nebraska; principally northern Sandhills. Northeastern Great Plains, Black Hills in South Dakota.
HABITAT: Moist to saturated, rich soils; meadows, lake and stream margins, woodland edge.
DESCRIPTION: Native perennial growing from a scaly, fleshy bulb. Stem erect, not branched, up to 2 feet tall. *Leaves alternate to scattered along stem*, uppermost leaves may be in a whorl; linear to narrowly lanceolate, 1-3 inches long, less than .75 inch wide. Flowers, 1-3, at top of stems; erect, *not nodding*, opening skyward, hence the name "orange-cup"; 2-3 inches across. Six orange-red tepals (similar or undifferentiated petals and sepals) becoming yellow at bases, with brownish spots but not as extensive or evident as in Turk's cap lily; tepals constricted into stalks near base, *reflexed only slightly;* 6 stamens surround a single pistil.
GENERAL INFORMATION: Even though the bulbs are small, most about 1 inch in diameter, they were eaten by American Indians. Ethnobotanist Melvin Gilmore wrote that the Dakota Indians pulverized or chewed the flowers and applied the paste as an antidote for the bite of a poisonous brown spider. According to his source, this treatment immediately reduced the inflamation and swelling. Once apparently quite common in northern Sandhills meadows, western red lily is a rare find today. They should not be picked. They seldom survive being transplanted.

DAYLILY

Pink to Red-Violet Flowers

GROUND-PLUM

Ground-plum

Astragalus crassicarpus

OTHER COMMON NAMES: Buffalo bean, plum or pea; prairie apple.

FAMILY: Bean (Fabaceae)

FLOWERING PERIOD: April and May.

DISTRIBUTION: Statewide in Nebraska, more frequent east. Throughout the Great Plains.

HABITAT: On a variety of well-drained soils; hillsides and uplands in grasslands. Declines and disappears when heavily grazed.

DESCRIPTION: Native perennial growing from a branched caudex and woody taproot. Usually several stems, 4-24 inches long; reclining on ground with rising tips, forming a low-growing clump; usually hairy. Leaves alternate, odd-pinnately compound, 2-5 inches long. Leaflets 15-27, oblong-lanceolate to elliptic, usually less than .5 inch long, undersides with tiny stiff hairs lying close to surface and hardly noticeable. Flowers in clusters (racemes) of 5-25 at end of stems or on stalks from upper leaf axils. Relatively long, slender, pea-like flowers; petals white and pinkish, light blue to deeper purple. Plump pods like small plums replace flowers, sprawling on the ground; each fruit .5-1 inch long and nearly as wide; surface exposed to the sun becoming peach to reddish.

GENERAL INFORMATION: The fruits were a food item of American Indians and early settlers who ate them raw, cooked or pickled. It was an unexplained custom of the Ponca and Omaha to soak ground plum fruits with seed corn before planting, discard the ground plums and plant the corn. Various decoctions of the plant were used by American Indians for sore throat, toothache and insect bites. Rodents, particularly prairie dogs, are reported to gather and cache the fruits.

130

Hoary Vetchling

Lathyrus polymorphus

GROUND-PLUM (FRUIT)

OTHER COMMON NAMES: Showy vetchling, showy or hoary peavine, wild or sweet pea.
FAMILY: Bean (Fabaceae)
FLOWERING PERIOD: May and June.
DISTRIBUTION: Statewide in Nebraska except for extreme southeast, most common central. Central and southern Great Plains.
HABITAT: Dry, sandy, often disturbed, soils in grasslands.
DESCRIPTION: Native perennial growing from a caudex and rhizomes. Stems erect, usually branched, 6-12 inches tall. Leaves alternate on stem, even-pinnately compound, *terminating with bristle, not a tendril;* 4-8 pairs of leaflets per leaf, linear, gray-green, .5-1 inch long, less than .25 inch wide. Leaves and stems of plants in western half of Great Plains often pubescent, those in eastern half not. Flower clusters (racemes) on stalks about 2 inches long from leaf axils, 2-5 (up to 8) flowers per cluster; flowers pea-like, deep pink to red-violet, keel lighter in color; about 1 inch long. Stamens and pistil concealed in keel.

HOARY VETCHLING

131

VIRGINIA SPRING BEAUTY

Virginia Spring Beauty
Claytonia virginica

OTHER COMMON NAMES: Fairy spuds, wild potato, ground nut.
FAMILY: Purslane (Portulacaceae)
FLOWERING PERIOD: Late March and April, into early May.
DISTRIBUTION: Principally the Missouri River Valley south of Omaha in Nebraska. Southeastern Great Plains.
HABITAT: Rich soils in shady, deciduous woodlands. Usually midway between bottomlands and bluff tops.
DESCRIPTION: Native perennial growing from a corm, usually less than 1 inch in diameter, with fibrous rootlets. Often found in patches. Each flowering stalk with a pair of dark green, narrow, tapering leaves, 3-7 inches long. The flowering stalks are weak, watery, succulent, often arching, usually less than 6 inches tall, rising from the corm. Flowers usually less than .5 inch across, in clusters (racemes) at top of stalk; 5 white or pinkish petals with darker pink or purple veins. By late June, the above-ground parts have typically disappeared.
GENERAL INFORMATION: The bland-tasting, starchy bulbs were eaten raw or boiled by Indian tribes in the region. They are dug and eaten by small mammals. The plants are uncommon in Nebraska, though, and should not be sacrificed to satisfy curiosity.

Waterleaf
Hydrophyllum virginianum

FAMILY: Waterleaf (Hydrophyllaceae)
FLOWERING PERIOD: May and June.
DISTRIBUTION: Extreme eastern Nebraska, principally in counties which border the Missouri River, most common in northeast. Eastern fifth of the Great Plains.
HABITAT: Rich, moist soils; full or partial shade; deciduous woodlands, river bluffs.
DESCRIPTION: Native perennial forming colonies by spreading rhizomes. Usually a single erect stem, occasionally branched; sparsely covered with short, stiff hairs; watery; 1-2.5 feet tall. Basal leaves on stalks as long as leaf blade; deeply divided nearly to midrib into 5 or more lobes which are in turn often lobed, with toothed margins; minute hairs, mostly on underside; often with white splotches; leaf blade 2-6 inches long. Stem leaves smaller, fewer lobes, on shorter stalks. Flower head roughly spherical, at top of stem or ends of branches (in cymes). Composed of 5-lobed, bell-shaped flowers up to .5 inch long; usually pale lilac, occasionally nearly white or a darker red-violet; each with 5 protruding stamens.
GENERAL INFORMATION: Leaves used as greens by American Indians and early settlers, the plant's juices as an astringent. Genus and common names are a reference to the watery stems and leaves.

Wild Cranesbill

Geranium maculatum

OTHER COMMON NAMES: Shameface, rock weed, spotted geranium.

FAMILY: Geranium (Geraniaceae)

FLOWERING PERIOD: Late April into June.

DISTRIBUTION: Principally southeastern Nebraska. Southeastern Great Plains, but found sporadically farther north and northwest.

HABITAT: Rich, moist soils in open woodlands.

DESCRIPTION: Native perennial growing from a stout, knobby rhizome. Stem is erect, often branched into a fork, 8-15 inches tall. Leaves from plant base on long stalks, divided into 3-5 lobes which radiate out like fingers from the palm, margins coarsely toothed, 2-6 inches wide. Stem leaves are smaller, with fewer lobes, on shorter stalks; typically a pair of leaves immediately under the flower cluster. All herbage is usually hairy. Several flowers at the end of an erect flower stalk less than 2 inches long. Flowers 1 inch or more across; 5 petals, usually a deep pink with delicate and darker nectar lines. The fruit is a beaked capsule, hence the common name cranesbill.

GENERAL INFORMATION: The principal range of this wildflower is in Missouri. Uncommon in Nebraska, reported from several southeastern counties and from Brown County. It is not clear where in Nebraska it is native and where it has been introduced. Carolina cranesbill *(Geranium carolinianum)*, is an annual, and more frequently encountered, its range in Nebraska being principally in the southeast. The flowers of Carolina cranesbill are about half as large as those of wild cranesbill. In most other regards, though, the two species are quite similar.

WILD CRANESBILL

WATERLEAF

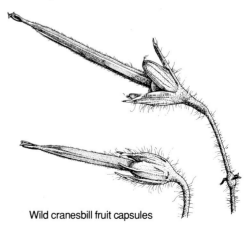

Wild cranesbill fruit capsules

133

Fremont's Clematis
Clematis fremontii

OTHER COMMON NAMES: Leather flower.
FAMILY: Buttercup (Ranunculaceae)
FLOWERING PERIOD: May.
DISTRIBUTION: Found only in extreme south-central Nebraska, north-central Kansas and in east-central Missouri. Considered rare nationally but may be locally abundant.
HABITAT: Well-drained, rocky hillsides in grasslands, usually where fragmented limestone litters soil surface.
DESCRIPTION: Native perennial growing from a stout caudex with many fibrous roots. One to several erect, occasionally branched stems, 10-16 inches tall, often with a purplish tinge, covered with long, soft hairs. Leaves opposite on stem, ovate to elliptic, leathery, with cobwebby hairs on the underside, dark green on upper surface; largest leaves 3-4 inches long. Single, elongated, nodding, urn-shaped flowers, .8-1.5 inches long, at ends of branches or from axils of upper leaves; composed of 4-5 thick, leathery sepals with recurved tips; deep magenta on exterior, white within.

Prairie Phlox
Phlox pilosa

OTHER COMMON NAMES: Downy or hairy phlox.
FAMILY: Polemonium (Polemoniaceae)
FLOWERING PERIOD: May into July.
DISTRIBUTION: Eastern fifth of Nebraska. Eastern fourth of the Great Plains.
HABITAT: Moist, rich soils; low prairies, meadows, roadsides, woodland edge and openings.
DESCRIPTION: Native perennial with stout roots spreading to form colonies. Stems (1 to several) erect; branching mostly below if at all; 1-2 feet tall. Leaves opposite on stem, stalkless, linear and grass-like tapering to a sharp tip; 1-4 inches long, usually less than .25 inch wide. Stems and leaves minutely pubescent. Flowers in clusters (a panicle) at end of stem or branches; tubular, flaring to 5 petal-like lobes; a deep pink, often with darker markings near the center; up to .75 inch across.
GENERAL INFORMATION: Once a common wildflower of low prairies in eastern Nebraska. Varieties of this species are often sold as garden flowers.

FREMONT'S CLEMATIS

PRAIRIE PHLOX

SHOOTING STAR

Shooting Star

Dodecatheon pulchellum

OTHER COMMON NAMES: Cowslip.
FAMILY: Primrose (Primulaceae)
FLOWERING PERIOD: May into June.
DISTRIBUTION: Isolated areas of the Nebraska Panhandle, particularly the North Platte Valley. Northwestern Great Plains.
HABITAT: Moist soils; floodplains, meadows.
DESCRIPTION: Native perennial growing from fleshy, fibrous roots. Leaves form a rosette at ground level; oblong-lanceolate or spoon-shaped, 2-7 inches long. Flowers borne at the top of a leafless flowering stalk up to 20 inches tall (in an umbel). Flowers nodding, about 1 inch long; composed of 5 petals which flare back; each petal a deep pink or a deeper red-violet with a white band or collar just above a yellow base. Stamens tightly clustered in a downward pointing, purplish cone or beak.

135

Wild Onion
Allium canadense

OTHER COMMON NAMES: Meadow or wild garlic, wild shallot.
FAMILY: Lily (Liliaceae)
FLOWERING PERIOD: Late April into July.
DISTRIBUTION: Statewide in Nebraska, less common to the north and west. Of 7 species of wild onions reported from Nebraska, this is the most common in the eastern half. Eastern and southern Great Plains.
HABITAT: Moderately dry to moist soils; prairies, meadows, floodplain grasslands.
DESCRIPTION: Native perennial growing from a bulb covered with a fibrous husk; the bulb seldom more than 1 inch in diameter. Two or more narrow, linear, grass-like leaves, up to a foot or more in length, originate from low on the flowering stalk. Flowering stalks are stout, smooth, up to 2 feet tall depending on the site. The numerous small flowers, white or pinkish-tinged, are gathered in a flat-topped to domed cluster (an umbel) at top of stalk. Distinguished from other native onions in that bulblets, which fall to the ground and may root, establishing new plants, often replace most of the flowers. Flowers also produce small capsules containing tiny black seeds. There is much variation in this species, leading to the recognition of several varieties in the Great Plains.

WILD ONION

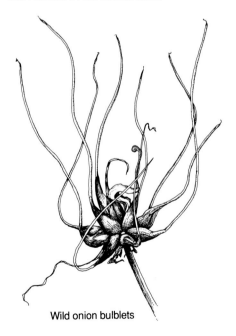
Wild onion bulblets

Pink Poppy Mallow
Callirhoe alcaeoides

OTHER COMMON NAMES: Light or tall poppy mallow.
FAMILY: Mallow (Malvaceae)
FLOWERING PERIOD: Late May, June.
DISTRIBUTION: Principally southeast, west into south-central Nebraska. Southeastern Great Plains.
HABITAT: Dry, often sandy soils in grasslands. Unlike purple poppy mallow, not found on disturbed sites.
DESCRIPTION: Native perennial growing from a thickened taproot. Stems slender, upright, to 2 feet tall, with spreading branches low on the stem. Leaves are alternate on the stem; deeply divided into 5-7 lobes which radiate out like fingers from the palm. The delicate flowers are borne singly or in clusters (a raceme) of 3-5 at the ends of branches; 5 petals overlap forming a deep cup; usually light pink; 1 inch or slightly more in length. A "pompon" of stamens and stigmas in flower center.
GENERAL INFORMATION: Like purple poppy mallow, the root is edible raw or cooked.

136

PURPLE POPPY MALLOW

Purple Poppy Mallow
Callirhoe involucrata

OTHER COMMON NAMES: Wine cup, buffalo poppy, low poppy mallow, cowboy rose.
FAMILY: Mallow (Malvaceae)
FLOWERING PERIOD: Late May, peaking in June, some flowering throughout the summer.

DISTRIBUTION: Central and eastern Nebraska, more common to the south, particularly south-central. Southern half of Great Plains.
HABITAT: Moderately dry to moist, particularly sandy soils; floodplains, grasslands, pastures, roadsides.
DESCRIPTION: Native perennial growing from a substantial, deep, carrot-shaped taproot; occasionally forming mats. Stems lying on the ground or supported by other vegetation; up to 27 inches long. Leaves variable, larger leaves roughly circular; deeply divided into 5-7 lobes which radiate out like fingers from the palm. Solitary, bowl-shaped, intense rose to purple flowers among or rising above foliage; 5 overlapping, inch-long petals, inner surface becoming white near base; surrounding a column of light yellow stamens from which the branched style protrudes.
GENERAL INFORMATION: The Teton Dakota inhaled the smoke of burning, dried roots for head colds. The sweet, starchy roots may be eaten raw or prepared similar to parsnips. Dr. E. James, botanist for the 1819 Long Expedition, noted the plant was found in the Loup Valley and the roots were "by no means ungrateful to the taste."

PINK POPPY MALLOW

137

STANDING MILK-VETCH

Standing Milk-vetch

Astragalus adsurgens

OTHER COMMON NAMES: Prairie or ascending milk-vetch.
FAMILY: Bean (Fabaceae)
FLOWERING PERIOD: June and July.
DISTRIBUTION: Nebraska Panhandle, less common central. Northern half of Great Plains.
HABITAT: Dry, rocky or sandy soils; prairies, pastures, roadsides.
DESCRIPTION: Native perennial growing from a woody caudex and taproot. Stem erect, lower portion often reclining on the ground, often forming low-growing clumps; 4-16 inches tall. Leaves alternate on stem, odd-pinnately compound, 1.5-6 inches long. Leaflets, 9-25, grayish-green, narrowly oblong to oblong-ovate, .4-.8 inch long. Stems and leaves, in varying degrees, covered with stiff, grayish hairs lying close to surface. Flowers pea-like, clustered (racemes) at the ends of short, erect stalks; color variable from light pink, red-violet to blue-violet.
GENERAL INFORMATION: Lower portions of stems often recline on the ground, becoming erect, hence the common names "ascending" and "standing" milk-vetch.

Draba Milk-vetch

Astragalus spatulatus

OTHER COMMON NAMES: Tufted milk-vetch.
FAMILY: Bean (Fabaceae)
FLOWERING PERIOD: May into June.
DISTRIBUTION: Nebraska Panhandle. Northwestern Great Plains.
HABITAT: Dry, rocky soils or in rock crevices; rock outcrops, escarpments, badlands, bluffs, buttes.
DESCRIPTION: Native perennial growing from a caudex atop a taproot. Stems, 1 to several, short, not evident; forming a low, dense mat or tuft, seldom more that 4-5 inches tall. Lower leaves less than .6 inch long, upper leaves up to 2.5 inches long; linear to oblong-lanceolate, sharp-tipped; densely covered with stiff hairs lying close to the surface giving the foliage a silvery color. Flower stalks rise above the foliage; each bearing up to 11 small, red-violet pea-like flowers (in racemes).
GENERAL INFORMATION: Reported to be long-lived. Occasionally propagated as a rock-garden plant. There are about 20 species of milk-vetch found in Nebraska and nearly 30 in the Great Plains.

Purple Locoweed
Oxytropis lambertii

OTHER COMMON NAMES: Lambert or stem-less locoweed, crazyweed, rattleweed.
FAMILY: Bean (Fabaceae)
FLOWERING PERIOD: Late April and May, well into June.
DISTRIBUTION: Statewide in Nebraska except southeast. Throughout the Great Plains except extreme southeast.
HABITAT: Dry or at least well-drained, particularly rocky or sandy soils. Often on somewhat disturbed or eroded sites; grasslands, road-sides, badlands, eroded banks.
DESCRIPTION: Native perennial growing from a caudex atop a taproot. Often forming tufts or mats. *Stems are not evident*, short, crowded in a crown at ground level. Leaves erect or angling upward, 2-8 inches long; odd-pinnately compound, 7-19 leaflets. Leaflets are silvery-green, linear to narrowly oblong, with sharp tips, less than 1.5 inches long, *less than .2 inch wide.* Flowering stalks and leaves hairy. Clusters (racemes) of 10-20 flowers at the top of a *leafless stalk* up to 12 inches tall, rising above leaves. Flowers pea-like, *keel with a pointed tip;* red-violet to blue-violet, about .75 inch long. This species shows much variation in flower color, shape and size of leaflets, and the amount of pubescence.

PURPLE LOCOWEED

GENERAL INFORMATION: Locoweeds of the genus *Astragalus* have stems bearing leaves, and the tips of the flower's keels are rounded. Generally avoided by livestock if other forage is available but if eaten, animals become addicted to it. Eaten in large quantities, animals, particularly horses, become spooky, disoriented and eventually may suffer paralysis and death.

DRABA MILK-VETCH

SCORPIONWEED

CRESTED BEARDTONGUE

Scorpionweed

Phacelia hastata

FAMILY: Waterleaf (Hydrophyllaceae)
FLOWERING PERIOD: Late May into July.
DISTRIBUTION: Nebraska Panhandle. West-central Great Plains. Rather uncommon.
HABITAT: Dry, sandy or rocky, usually disturbed soils; rock outcrops, roadcuts, buttes.
DESCRIPTION: Native perennial growing from a caudex atop a taproot. Stems pinkish, stout, erect or with bases somewhat reclining on the ground; branched or not; up to 18 inches tall. Leaves mostly basal, on stalks; lanceolate to elliptic; silvery-green and 1.5-3.5 inches long. Stem leaves smaller, on short stalks or stalkless, alternate on the stem. All herbage hairy to pubescent. Florets tubular, densely clustered on a short, *coiled flower inflorescence* (a cyme) at top of stem and branches; dusty pink to pale lavender, with conspicuous, protruding stamens.
GENERAL INFORMATION: Claude Barr, author of **Jewels of the Plains**, described the flower color "a hue as indefinable in its neutral lavender as the shadow of a vanished hope." The coiled flower inflorescence is reminiscent of a ram's horn or scorpion's tail. The genus name is from the Greek word *phakelos*, which translates as "bundle," a reference to the cluster of flowers at the top of the flowering stalk.

Crested Beardtongue

Penstemon eriantherus

OTHER COMMON NAMES: Fuzzy-tongue penstemon.
FAMILY: Figwort (Scrophulariaceae)
FLOWERING PERIOD: June.
DISTRIBUTION: Nebraska Panhandle, isolated locations farther east. Northwestern Great Plains.
HABITAT: Dry, sandy, gravelly, rocky or clayey soils; eroded sites, roadsides, pastures, rock outcrops.
DESCRIPTION: Native perennial growing from a woody caudex atop a taproot. Stems (1-5) erect, stout, not branched, up to 16 inches tall. Leaves opposite on the stem, firm, often purplish on undersides; margins may be toothed. Basal leaves are on short stalks, oblong-lanceolate to spatulate; 1.5-3 inches long including stalks, less than 1 inch wide. Leaves above smaller, without stalks, bases somewhat clasping stem. All portions of the plant pubescent in varying degrees. Flowers densely clustered at top of stem (a thyrse); tubular, flaring into a 2-lobed upper lip and 3-lobed lower lip; deep pink to a darker red-violet with darker nectar lines; up to 1.5 inches long. *Flower throat filled with hairs; a sterile stamen covered with yellow hairs (the bearded tongue) protrudes from the throat.*

Sawsepal Penstemon

Penstemon glaber

OTHER COMMON NAMES: Large smooth beardtongue.
FAMILY: Figwort (Scrophulariaceae)
FLOWERING PERIOD: June and July.
DISTRIBUTION: Nebraska Panhandle. West-central Great Plains, extending farther west in the Dakotas.
HABITAT: Dry, rocky or gravelly soils; eroded banks, roadcuts, bluffs, grasslands.
DESCRIPTION: Native perennial growing from a woody, branched caudex atop a taproot. Stems (several to many) are erect, stout, not branched, 15-26 inches tall. Leaves opposite on stem; glossy, dark green; *thick, smooth and waxy;* margins not toothed. Basal leaves are less than 3 inches long and less than .75 inch wide, oblong-lanceolate to obovate narrowing to stalks which are usually winged. The upper leaves slightly larger, 2-4 inches long, .5-1.5 inches wide; broadly to narrowly lanceolate, without stalks and often clasping the stem. Flowers densely clustered along top third to half of stem (a thyrse), usually *arranged along one side of the stem;* tubular, flaring into a 2-lobed upper lip and 3-lobed lower lip; red-violet or blue-violet with darker nectar lines; 1 inch or more long. The sterile stamen is only sparsely bearded with yellow hairs.

GENERAL INFORMATION: Claude Barr, author of **Jewels of the Plains**, noted that in wet periods the flower color is pale, and more intense during times of dry weather. Barr found sawsepal penstemon to be one of the longer-lived penstemons, individual plants surviving up to 10 years. Its thick, glossy, waxy leaves are characteristic of plants which evolved in regions of low rainfall and humidity, an adaptation which minimizes the loss of moisture from the leaves by transpiration.

SAWSEPAL PENSTEMON

HAYDEN'S PENSTEMON

Hayden's Penstemon

Penstemon haydenii

OTHER COMMON NAMES: Hayden's beard-tongue, blowout penstemon, blowout bluebells.
FAMILY: Figwort (Scrophulariaceae)
FLOWERING PERIOD: Late May to mid June.
DISTRIBUTION: Known only from the Sand-hills region of Nebraska.
HABITAT: Loose sand; usually in or on the margins of blowouts.
DESCRIPTION: Native perennial growing from a caudex atop a taproot. Stems (1 to many) often reclining on ground with ascending tips; *stout*, 10-30 inches tall; often in multi-stemmed clumps. Stems root when covered by shifting sand. Leaves with a slight waxy bloom, margins not toothed, thick and firm; linear-lanceolate with broad bases clasping the stem, tapering to a long, narrow tip; 2-5 inches long, up to .5 inch wide. Stems and leaves not pubescent or hairy. Non-flowering, vegetative shoots with long, very narrow linear leaves; distinctly different from flowering stems. Flowers densely grouped in clusters at top of stems (a thyrse); each cluster of 4-6 flowers rising opposite on stem from the axil of a *spoon-shaped, sharp-tipped, leaf-like bract;* bracts up to 2.5 inches wide and 3 inches long. Flowers tubular (appearing inflated), flaring into a 2-lobed upper lip and 3-lobed lower lip; pink to a milky blue with darker nectar lines (rarely white); about 1.25 inches long; *strongly fragrant.* A sterile stamen bearded with golden-yellow hairs near the tip.
GENERAL INFORMATION: Hayden's penstemon is perhaps Nebraska's rarest wildflower and is the only plant in the state listed as endangered under the federal Endangered Species Act. It apparently has declined in abundance as wild fires and disturbance by large herds of buffalo, which promoted the formation of blowouts, became increasingly rare occurrences in the region.

Cobaea Penstemon
Penstemon cobaea

OTHER COMMON NAMES: Cobaea beard-tongue, wild foxglove.
FAMILY: Figwort (Scrophulariaceae)
FLOWERING PERIOD: Late May and June.
DISTRIBUTION: Southeastern Nebraska. Southeastern Great Plains.
HABITAT: Most frequently in dry to moist (but well-drained) sandy loams or soils formed from limestone. Prairie hillsides and banks.
DESCRIPTION: Native perennial growing from a frequently large, woody rhizome. Stems (1-3) are erect, stout, not branched, 1-2 feet tall. Leaves opposite on stem, thick, usually toothed. Basal leaves on short, winged stalks, spatulate to oblong-lanceolate, 2-6 inches long and less than 2 inches wide; often absent or withered by the time of flowering. Leaves above smaller, lanceolate to ovate, bases clasping stem. Pubescence most noticeable near top of plant. Flowers on short stalks; in clusters of 2-6 from axils of leafy bracts at top of stem (a thyrse); tubular, bulging in the middle, flaring into a 2-lobed upper lip and 3-lobed lower lip; nearly white, pink to pale red-violet with darker nectar lines; up to nearly 2 inches long.
GENERAL INFORMATION: Cobaea and shell-leaf penstemon are the largest flowered members of the genus on the Great Plains.

Shell-leaf Penstemon
Penstemon grandiflorus

OTHER COMMON NAMES: Large or large-flowered beardtongue.
FAMILY: Figwort (Scrophulariaceae)
FLOWERING PERIOD: Late May and June.
DISTRIBUTION: Statewide in Nebraska except southern Panhandle and southwest. Perhaps most abundant in the eastern Sandhills. Eastern half of Great Plains, extending farther west in Nebraska and the Dakotas.
HABITAT: Dry to moist but well-drained, particularly sandy soils; grasslands, roadsides.
DESCRIPTION: Native perennial growing from a woody caudex atop a taproot. Stems (1-3) erect, stout, not branched, 2-3 feet tall. Leaves opposite on stem; blue-green, fleshy, smooth, with a waxy bloom, margins not toothed. Basal leaves broadly ovate to spatulate, on stalks, up to 6 inches long. Stem leaves are broadly ovate to nearly round, bases clasping the stem; 1-3 inches long. Flowers on short stalks from axils of leafy bracts near top of stem (a thyrse); tubular and appearing inflated, flaring into a 2-lobed upper lip and 3-lobed lower lip; usually pink to lavender (occasionally more blue-violet, crimson or white) with darker nectar lines; 1-2 inches long. The sparingly bearded, sterile stamen is golden-yellow. Leaves and flowers evenly spaced on stem, not crowded.

COBAEA PENSTEMON

SHELL-LEAF PENSTEMON

143

Violet Wood Sorrel

Oxalis violacea

OTHER COMMON NAMES: Sheep or sour grass; sheep, lady's or toad sorrel.

FAMILY: Wood Sorrel (Oxalidaceae)

FLOWERING PERIOD: May and June, occasionally flowering again in September or early October.

DISTRIBUTION: Eastern half of Nebraska. Eastern half of the Great Plains.

HABITAT: Dry to moderately moist soils; prairie, woodland edge and openings, roadsides, mildly disturbed sites.

DESCRIPTION: Native perennial growing from a scaly bulb. Stems absent, leaves and flowering stalk rising directly from the bulb. Leaves are clover-like, on stalks 2-5 inches long; 3 rounded, heart-shaped, somewhat succulent leaflets, notched on outer margin, collectively about 1 inch across. Flower stalks are up to 8 inches tall, rising above the leaves; typically several flowers per stalk. Flowers composed of 5 pink or deeper red-violet petals; seldom much more than .5 inch across. Seeds are produced in a capsule less than .25 inch long. When mature, the capsule splits, explosively scattering the seeds.

GENERAL INFORMATION: Leaflets and flowers close at night or on cloudy days. Like yellow wood sorrel, this plant contains oxalic acid giving it a sour taste. Great Plains Indians utilized the plant in several ways. Its ground bulbs were fed to horses in the belief it would make them faster. Various preparations of the plant were used as a wormer, to increase the flow of urine and reduce fevers. All parts of the plant are edible.

VIOLET WOOD SORREL

SHOWY ORCHIS

WEDGELEAF FOG-FRUIT

Showy Orchis
Galearis spectabilis

FAMILY: Orchid (Orchidaceae)
FLOWERING PERIOD: May into June.
DISTRIBUTION: In Nebraska, found principally in the Missouri River Valley from Burt County south. Southeastern Great Plains.
HABITAT: Moist, rich, upland soils in deciduous woods. Generally in shaded sites on bluff sides between bottomlands and ridgelines.
DESCRIPTION: Native perennial growing from a cluster of thickened, fleshy roots and a short rhizome. Stem short, inconspicuous. Usually 2 basal leaves; narrowly obovate to broadly elliptic; smooth, somewhat succulent; clasping stem at ground level; 3-7 inches long, half as wide. Flowering stalk rises from between the leaves; 4-8 inches tall; bearing lanceolate to elliptic, leaf-like bracts and 2-8 flowers .5-1.5 inches long (in a raceme). Lower petal mostly white, arching sharply downward; 2 lateral petals and 3 sepals united, forming a pinkish to rose-colored hood. A thickened, tubular spur, .5-.75 inch long, projects back and downward from the base of the lip.
GENERAL INFORMATION: Once one of the more abundant of the native orchids, but becoming increasingly uncommon in its limited Nebraska range as overgrazing and timber cutting destroy its woodland habitat.

Wedgeleaf Fog-fruit
Lippia cuneifolia

FAMILY: Vervain (Verbenaceae)
FLOWERING PERIOD: Late May and June.
DISTRIBUTION: Principally Nebraska's southern third. Southern half of the Great Plains.
HABITAT: Variety of moist, mildly disturbed sites.
DESCRIPTION: Native perennial growing from a woody caudex. Stems lying on soil surface, branching near base, occasionally rooting at nodes, up to 3 feet long; with short and erect branches bearing leaves and flowers, usually less than 6 inches tall. Leaves opposite on the stem, without stalks, thick, with *2-6 sharp teeth on outer half;* wedge-shaped to linear; 1-1.5 inches long, less than .25 inch wide. Flower spike is solitary, at top of stalk rising from stem node; up to .5 inch across. Heads are at first spherical with a ring of small flowers, but later elongating to nearly 1 inch, the ring of flowers moving up the cylindric head. Flowers small; upper lip with 2 lobes, lower lip with 3, the middle lobe largest; pale red-violet (or whitish) with deeper colored throats.
GENERAL INFORMATION: Northern fog-fruit (*Lippia lanceolata*) is similar and found in eastern and southern Nebraska. Its flower spikes are smaller; stems often erect but supported by surrounding vegetation; leaf blades lanceolate with the entire margin toothed.

145

PINCUSHION CACTUS

Pincushion Cactus
Coryphantha vivipara

OTHER COMMON NAMES: Ball, purple, nipple and cushion cactus.
FAMILY: Cactus (Cactaceae)
FLOWERING PERIOD: May and June.
DISTRIBUTION: Central and western Nebraska. Throughout the Great Plains; infrequent or absent in eastern fifth.
HABITAT: Dry, sandy or rocky soils on hillsides and upland grasslands.
DESCRIPTION: Native perennial growing from fibrous roots. One to several stems grow from the same root; highly modified into a somewhat elongated globe composed of many cylindrical tubercles which are tipped with several central, brown spines surrounded by more numerous and smaller, white or gray spines. The plants are rarely more than 3 inches tall. Leaves are lacking; photosynthesis taking place in the enlarged stems. One to several flowers appear among the upper tubercles. Flowers are composed of many narrow and sharp-tipped, red-violet petals surrounding a center of yellow-orange anthers and the slightly taller, white, comb-shaped stigmas; 1-1.5 inches across. Most often found as a single globe but occasionally forming a dense cluster of many plants.
GENERAL INFORMATION: The species name, *vivipara*, means "producing live young"; a reference to basal tubercles rooting to form new plants. The fruit is fleshy, oblong, up to 1 inch long, green and edible.

Wild Begonia
Rumex venosus

OTHER COMMON NAMES: Winged, veined or sand dock.
FAMILY: Buckwheat (Polygonaceae)
FLOWERING PERIOD: Late May into July.
DISTRIBUTION: Statewide in Nebraska except southeast, most common Sandhills and Panhandle. Throughout the Great Plains, infrequent or absent extreme east.
HABITAT: On sandy, moist to moderately dry soils; disturbed sites, grasslands, roadsides, river bluffs and bottoms. One of the first plants to begin recolonization of blowouts.
DESCRIPTION: Native perennial often forming colonies from spreading rhizomes. Stems erect or reclining on the ground, branched or unbranched, often reddish tinged, usually less than 8 inches tall. The leaves are alternate on short stalks; ovate to ovate-lanceolate; somewhat leathery with smooth surfaces; 1-5 inches long. The flowering stalks rise above foliage. Flowers are greenish and not conspicuous. Becoming showy and colorful in fruit. The achene is enclosed by enlarged, deep pink to crimson wings (sepals). The leaves and fruits are frequently ravaged by insects.

SKELETONWEED

WILD BEGONIA

Skeletonweed

Lygodesmia juncea

OTHER COMMON NAMES: Rush or prairie pink, rush skeleton plant.

FAMILY: Sunflower (Asteraceae)

FLOWERING PERIOD: June through August.

DISTRIBUTION: Found statewide in Nebraska. Throughout the Great Plains, infrequent or absent extreme southeast.

HABITAT: Dry, particularly sandy, sandy-loam or loess soils; disturbed sites on grasslands, banks, roadsides.

DESCRIPTION: Native perennial growing from a deep, vertical rhizome. Stems gray-green, erect, much branched at base, 10-20 inches tall. *Leaves sparse, not conspicuous*; those low on stems linear, less than 1.5 inches long; absent or reduced to scales on mid-stem and higher. Flower heads are solitary at the top of branches, .5-.75 inch across; usually 5 strap-shaped, seed-producing, pink, petal-like ray florets with toothed outer margins. Disk florets absent. Few flowers in blossom at one time.

GENERAL INFORMATION: Frequently found with globose enlargements, the result of a gall wasp depositing an egg in the stem where the larva develops. A tea brewed from this plant was used by several Great Plains Indian tribes to increase the flow of milk in nursing mothers, a custom probably fostered by the milky juice exuding from the plant's broken stems. This approach to herbal medicine is very close to the European "doctrine of signatures" which was formalized by a Swiss physician in the mid 1600s. It suggested some plants have signatures or clues to their medicinal uses; that whatever part of the human body a plant or plant part resembled, it could cure. When hardened, the milky sap was used as chewing gum by Indian children, turning a bright blue color when chewed.

147

WESTERN WILD ROSE

Western Wild Rose
Rosa woodsii

FAMILY: Rose (Rosaceae)
FLOWERING PERIOD: Late May into July.
DISTRIBUTION: Statewide except southeast. Northern two-thirds of the Great Plains.
HABITAT: Sandy or light clay soils, sun or partial shade; prairie ravines, river valleys, bluffs, woodland edge and openings.
DESCRIPTION: Native woody shrub often growing in dense thickets. *Stems upright* and much branched; *usually with 1-2 spines immediately under base of leaf stalk;* up to 5 feet tall. Stems red, often with a purplish tinge; prickles mostly on lower portion of older stems; in general not as densely covered with prickles as prairie wild rose. Leaves alternate on stem, odd-pinnately compound; *5 to 9 leaflets*, oval to obovate, margins toothed, .5-1 inch long, less than .4 inch wide. Flowers are solitary or in clusters on lateral branches from previous year's growth; 5 broad, overlapping, pink to deeper red-violet petals surrounding a center of many bright yellow stamens. Flowers 2 inches or more across. When fully open, the flower is saucer-shaped, *not as flat as prairie wild rose.* Flowers fragrant. Fruit fleshy, orange-red, urn-shaped hip about .5 inch in diameter, containing many seeds.
GENERAL INFORMATION: A third species, smooth wild rose (*Rosa blanda*), is uncommon but found in the eastern half of Nebraska.

Prairie Wild Rose
Rosa arkansana

OTHER COMMON NAMES: Arkansas rose.
FAMILY: Rose (Rosaceae)
FLOWERING PERIOD: Late May into July.
DISTRIBUTION: Statewide, but more frequent east. Throughout the Great Plains, infrequent or absent extreme south, less common west.
HABITAT: Found in a variety of dry to moderately moist soils; grasslands, roadsides.
DESCRIPTION: Native woody shrub occasionally spreading by stout horizontal roots to form patches. Stems are reddish-brown; they may, but usually do not, die back partially or even to ground level over winter. Lower stem *densely armed with yellowish spines.* Usually less than 20 inches tall. Leaves alternate on stem, odd-pinnately compound; *7 to 11 leaflets*, oval to obovate, margins toothed, .5-1 inch long, less than .4 inch wide. Flowers generally in clusters of 2-3, at ends of new-growth stems and on short side branches from older stems; 5 broad, overlapping, pink petals surrounding a center of many bright yellow stamens; 2 inches or more across. When fully open, petals spread widely, the *flower face becoming nearly flat.* Flowers fragrant. Fruit fleshy, bright red, urn-shaped hip about .5 inch in diameter, containing many seeds.
GENERAL INFORMATION: This is the most common wild rose of the Great Plains.

PURPLE CONEFLOWER

Purple Coneflower
Echinacea angustifolia

OTHER COMMON NAMES: Black Samson.
FAMILY: Sunflower (Asteraceae)
FLOWERING PERIOD: Late June to mid-July.
DISTRIBUTION: Statewide in Nebraska. Found throughout Great Plains, less common west.

HABITAT: Well-drained or dry soils; hillsides, upland prairie and plains, roadsides.

DESCRIPTION: Native perennial growing from a strong, dark brown to black taproot known to extend as deep as 10 feet into the subsoil. Stems, 1 to several, are stiffly upright, 10-20 inches tall, leafless for several inches below the flower heads. Prominently veined, dark green leaves; mostly near base of the stem. Lower leaves on stalks; broadly lanceolate to narrowly elliptic; 3-8 inches long and usually less than 1 inch wide. Upper leaves stalkless, progressively smaller. Stems and leaves covered with short, bristly hairs. Flower heads solitary at top of stem, 1.5-2.5 inches across; 12-20, infertile, pale pink to a deeper red-violet, petal-like ray florets surround a domed, reddish-brown center of disk florets. Ray florets point skyward when they emerge but are pushed progressively downward as the center disk enlarges. Sharp-tipped bracts on the disk persist long after the seeds have been dispersed.

GENERAL INFORMATION: An important medicinal plant of Great Plains Indians. In 1885 a Pawnee City, Nebraska, doctor marketed an extract of the roots as "Meyer's Blood Purifier"; promoted as a cure for tumors, syphilis, ulcers, piles, fevers, typhus and other ailments. Today, extracts of the plant are being studied for the treatment of bacterial infections.

PRAIRIE WILD ROSE

LONG-BRACTED SPIDERWORT

Long-bracted Spiderwort

Tradescantia bracteata

FAMILY: Spiderwort (Commelinaceae)
FLOWERING PERIOD: Late May into July.
DISTRIBUTION: Statewide in Nebraska, becoming infrequent or absent in the west. Throughout the Great Plains, most common east.
HABITAT: Moist soil; mildly disturbed sites, meadows, railways, roadsides, floodplains.
DESCRIPTION: Native perennial growing from fleshy roots and sometimes spreading by rhizomes. Stems are erect, fairly stout and *usually not branched;* up to 16 inches tall. Grass-like, linear-lanceolate leaves alternate on the stem; *rarely folded;* 4-10 inches long, usually less than .5 inch wide. Stems and leaves smooth to sparsely covered with soft, thin hairs; *without a whitish, waxy bloom.* Several to many flowers in clusters (cymes) at top of stem, subtended by bracts similar to, and as large or larger than stem leaves, which may be folded. *Sepals hairy;* 3 red-violet to blue-violet petals; 6 conspicuous stamens tipped with bright yellow anthers, filaments same color as petals, hairy at base.
GENERAL INFORMATION: The common name spiderwort refers to the mucilaginous juice in the stems which can be drawn out into slender threads which resemble a spider's silken strands. Even less flattering local names include snot-weed and cow-slobbers.

Prairie Spiderwort

Tradescantia occidentalis

FAMILY: Spiderwort (Commelinaceae)
FLOWERING PERIOD: Late May into July.
DISTRIBUTION: Statewide in Nebraska, infrequent or absent east fifth. Throughout most of the Great Plains except extreme east.
HABITAT: Sandy, dry to moderately moist, soil; disturbed sites, roadsides, grasslands.
DESCRIPTION: Native perennial growing from slender or thick, fleshy roots. Stems are erect, *often branching,* up to 20 inches tall. Grass-like, linear-lanceolate leaves alternate on the stem; smooth, not pubescent, *with a whitish, waxy bloom; often folded;* 4-10 inches long and less than .5 inch wide. Several to many flowers in clusters (cymes) at top of the stem or ends of branches, subtended by bracts similar to but not as large as stem leaves. *Sepals hairy;* 3 red-violet to blue-violet petals; 6 conspicuous stamens with bright yellow anthers, filaments same color as petals, hairy at base. Like the dayflowers, which belong to the same family, spiderwort flowers close by midday and last but one day.
GENERAL INFORMATION: The ranges of long-bracted spiderwort and prairie spiderwort overlap over much of the Great Plains where they intergrade. These hybrid plants cannot clearly be called one species or the other.

Ohio Spiderwort

Tradescantia ohiensis

FAMILY: Spiderwort (Commelinaceae)
FLOWERING PERIOD: May into July.
DISTRIBUTION: Southeastern Nebraska, at least as far north as the Platte River. Southeastern Great Plains.
HABITAT: Moist soil on mildly disturbed sites; meadows, railways, roadsides, floodplains.

DESCRIPTION: Native perennial growing from thick, fleshy roots. Stem erect, slender, *sometimes branched*, 2 feet or more tall. Grass-like, linear-lanceolate leaves alternate on stem; 4-12 inches long, less than .75 inch wide. Stems and leaves are smooth, not hairy or pubescent; with a whitish, *waxy bloom*. Several to many flowers in clusters (cymes) at top of stem or ends of branches, subtended by bracts similar to, but shorter than the stem leaves. *Sepals smooth,* not pubescent or hairy except for a tuft of hairs at tip; 3 deep red-violet to blue-violet petals; 6 conspicuous stamens bearing bright yellow anthers, filaments same color as petals, hairy at base.

GENERAL INFORMATION: The spiderwort genus was named in honor of John Tradescants, the royal gardener to Charles I of England. His son, John Tradescants Jr., who was also an accomplished botanist, took a spiderwort *(Tradescantia virginiana)* native to the eastern United States, to England from Virginia. The petals of all spiderworts are delicate, lasting but one day. Rather than shriveling and falling from the plant, however, the petals are acted on by enzymes and liquify, turning into a mucilaginous mass.

Dakota Vervain

Verbena bipinnatifida

FAMILY: Vervain (Verbenaceae)
FLOWERING PERIOD: May until frost.
DISTRIBUTION: Principally central Nebraska, probably most common south-central and north-central; occasionally farther east or west. Southern two-thirds of the Great Plains.
HABITAT: Found on a variety of soils in grasslands, pastures, roadsides, hillsides.
DESCRIPTION: Native perennial growing from a taproot. Stems branching near base, usually lying on ground with rising tips, less frequently erect; sometimes rooting at the nodes, forming new plants; with long, stiff, whitish hairs; up to 2 feet long but rarely exceeding 10 inches tall. Stems continue to elongate throughout the growing season, producing new flowers. Leaves on stalks, opposite on stem; deeply divided nearly to the leaf midrib, the segments again deeply divided and lobed; stiff white hairs mostly on margins and underside; .5-2 inches long and nearly as wide. Flowers at the ends of branches, initially in flat-topped clusters, elongating into spikes as fruit matures. Flowers tubular, flaring into 5 lobes which spread flat up to .5 inch across; tip of lobes usually notched, pink to deep red-violet with a darker center.

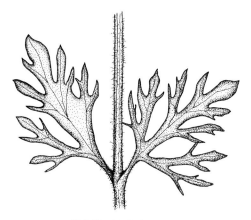

Dakota vervain leaves

DAKOTA VERVAIN

Hoary Vervain

Verbena stricta

OTHER COMMON NAMES: Hoary, woolly or mullein-leaved verbena.

FAMILY: Vervain (Verbenaceae)

FLOWERING PERIOD: June into September.

DISTRIBUTION: Statewide in Nebraska. Found throughout the Great Plains, becoming infrequent north, southwest and extreme west.

HABITAT: Dry to moderately moist soils; disturbed sites, overgrazed pastures, roadsides. Found on drier sites than blue vervain.

DESCRIPTION: Native perennial growing from extensive, branching, fibrous roots. Stems are often in clusters, stiffly erect, may be branched above, somewhat square in cross-section; 1-3 feet tall. Leaves numerous, essentially stalkless, opposite on the stem, prominently veined; ovate to elliptic; margins coarsely toothed; 1-4 inches long. Leaves and stems are usually densely covered with soft, whitish hairs and soft to the touch. Flowers on slender spikes up to 10 inches long at top of stem. Small, tubular flowers .25-.5 inch long and equally wide; pink to a deeper red-violet or blue and rarely white. Flowers mature from the base of the spike to the top.

GENERAL INFORMATION: The vervains contain a bitter-tasting juice, and are avoided by livestock. Hoary vervain is frequently abundant on chronically over-grazed pastures.

Blue Vervain

Verbena hastata

OTHER COMMON NAMES: Blue verbena, false or American vervain.

FAMILY: Vervain (Verbenaceae)

FLOWERING PERIOD: June into September.

DISTRIBUTION: Statewide in Nebraska, more common east. Throughout the Great Plains, infrequent or absent extreme south and west.

HABITAT: A variety of moist soils; low prairies, meadows, shorelines, wet ditches, roadsides.

DESCRIPTION: Native perennial growing from fibrous roots. Stems erect, tough, often sparingly branched above, rough-pubescent with short hairs, somewhat square in cross-section; 2-4 feet or more tall. Leaves on stalks, opposite on the stem; lanceolate to oblong-lanceolate, often with two smaller side lobes near the base; coarsely toothed; 2-6 inches long. Flowers on numerous, slender spikes (2-6 inches long) at top of the stem. Small, tubular flowers less than .25 inch long; a deep red-violet to blue, occasionally paler, rarely white.

GENERAL INFORMATION: The Teton Dakota Indians boiled the leaves to make a tea for stomach ache. A 16th century European herbal claimed preparations of the plant were a "perfect gem for the treatment of all wounds, be they fresh or putrid, and for all ulcers, wens [obstructed sebaceous glands] and hardened arteries."

Purple Loosestrife
Lythrum salicaria

FAMILY: Loosestrife (Lythraceae)
FLOWERING PERIOD: July and August.
DISTRIBUTION: Sporadically across Nebraska; Missouri, Platte, Niobrara and Elkhorn valleys and other sites not associated with rivers. Principally eastern and northern Great Plains.
HABITAT: Moist to wet organic soils; shorelines, marshes, wet ditches, wet meadows.
DESCRIPTION: Naturalized perennial growing from a taproot and extensive fibrous root system giving rise to new plants. Stem stout, erect, *roughly square in cross-section;* usually much branched, forming a bushy plant 3-6 feet or more tall. Leaves are opposite on stem or in whorls of several leaves; lanceolate, stalkless; up to 4 inches long, less than .5 inch wide; becoming smaller and narrower above. Flowers in spikes 4-12 inches long, at top of branches; composed of 4-6 slender, deep red-violet petals.
GENERAL INFORMATION: Introduced accidentally as seeds and intentionally as a garden plant during the early 1800s. An aggressive competitor, replacing more desirable native plants in wetlands. Its range and abundance in the Great Plains are expanding. Difficult to eradicate once established.

Winged Loosestrife
Lythrum alatum

FAMILY: Loosestrife (Lythraceae)
FLOWERING PERIOD: June into August.
DISTRIBUTION: Statewide in Nebraska except Panhandle, more common east. Eastern and southeastern Great Plains.
HABITAT: Moist to wet soils in low prairies and meadows; along ditches and shorelines.
DESCRIPTION: Native perennial growing from a slender, branching, horizontal rhizome with fibrous roots. Stems are erect with numerous slender, willowy branches; roughly square in cross-section; 1-3 feet tall. Leaves alternate above, opposite below; lanceolate, dark green, stalkless; lower leaves up to 2.5 inches long, less than half as wide; becoming smaller and narrower above. Flowers from leaf axils on the upper portion of stems; solitary or in pairs; up to .5 inch across; 6 pale pink or deeper red-violet petals with darker nectar lines.
GENERAL INFORMATION: The common name loosestrife (also applying to fringed and tufted loosestrife of the genus *Lysimachia*) is attributed to a legend of King Lysimachus of ancient Sicily, who calmed a charging bull by pulling up a European plant of this genus and waving it in front of the bull, "loosing him of his strife."

Sensitive Brier

Schrankia nuttallii

OTHER COMMON NAMES: Shame-vine, cat-claw or bashful sensitive brier.

FAMILY: Mimosa (Mimosaceae)

FLOWERING PERIOD: Principally June and July, occasionally later.

DISTRIBUTION: Principally central Nebraska, particularly south-central. South half of Great Plains but as far north as south-central South Dakota and north-central Nebraska.

HABITAT: Dry, or at least well-drained, sandy, gravelly or loess soils; usually on somewhat disturbed sites; grasslands, banks, bluffs, road-sides, hillsides, ravines.

DESCRIPTION: Native perennial growing from a somewhat woody caudex on top of a taproot. The stems typically are weak and sprawling, arched or lying on the ground and surrounding vegetation; *armed with hooked prickles* (hence the name catclaw); up to 3 feet long. Leaves alternate on stem, the central leaf stalk with 4-8 pairs of side stalks, each bearing 8-15 pairs of leaflets (bipinnately compound). Leaflets are oblong to elliptic, about .25 inch long. *Leaves touch-sensitive,* the leaflets folding when touched or jostled by strong winds. Numerous small, tubular flowers at the center of a spherical flower head up to 1 inch across; but not conspicuous because of the even more numerous (8-12 per flower) protruding pink stamens, each tipped with a yellow anther. Flower heads on prickly stalks up to 1.5 inches long from leaf axils.

GENERAL INFORMATION: Because of its attractive foliage and flowers and the novelty of its touch-sensitive leaves, sometimes used as a landscape plant. Why the leaflets close is speculative; perhaps a moisture conserving response in summer's strong, hot winds.

SENSITIVE BRIER

Bush Morning-glory
Ipomoea leptophylla

OTHER COMMON NAMES: Man-root, man-of-the-earth, bush moon-flower.
FAMILY: Morning Glory (Convolvulaceae)
FLOWERING PERIOD: Late June into August.
DISTRIBUTION: Principally western and central Nebraska, occasionally farther east. Southern half of the Great Plains except eastern fifth.
HABITAT: Dry to moderately moist, particularly sandy or gravelly soil; grasslands, roadsides, banks, often somewhat disturbed sites.
DESCRIPTION: Native perennial growing from an enlarged taproot. Stems, several to many, erect; usually arching as they lengthen, the ends lying on the ground; 3 feet or more long; forming a bushy clump up to 3 feet tall, twice as wide. Leaves alternate, linear, on short to inconspicuous stalks; 2-4 inches long and less than .25 inch wide. Flowers, 1-4, on stout stalks from leaf axils; funnel-shaped; deep pink to a rich red-violet, the throat darker; about 2 inches wide, 3 inches long.
GENERAL INFORMATION: Several inches below the soil surface, the root enlarges into an enormous, spindle-shaped, moisture-storage organ up to 2 feet in diameter and 3 feet long. Roots of young plants were eaten raw, roasted, boiled or dried for later use by Great Plains Indians. The Pawnee burned the root in a smoke treatment believed to remedy nervousness and bad dreams.

Canada Thistle
Cirsium arvense

FAMILY: Sunflower (Asteraceae)
FLOWERING PERIOD: June into September.
DISTRIBUTION: Statewide in Nebraska except southernmost counties. Central and northern Great Plains.
HABITAT: Moist, disturbed soils; roadsides, pastures, field margins, river valleys.
DESCRIPTION: Naturalized perennial spreading to form colonies from deep lateral roots which frequently send up new shoots. *Stems more slender* than most thistles; erect, usually much branched above, *without spines;* 2-4 feet tall. Lower leaves usually lobed, sometimes only shallowly so; variable in shape, oblong to lanceolate; 2-7 inches long; surfaces either smooth or slightly hairy (particularly on underside); usually with wavy margins and bearing *a few spines.* Upper leaves smaller, usually with less prominent lobes, bases clasping the stem. *Flower heads small* compared to other thistles, 1 inch or less long; on branches at top of the plant; composed of many small tubular flowers; light lavender to violet-blue; *base of flower head essentially without spines.* Male and female flowers on separate plants. Male flower heads up to 1 inch across; female heads smaller, about .5 inch. Flowers fragrant.
GENERAL INFORMATION: Native to Europe, Asia and North Africa. A noxious weed, particularly troublesome in the western Platte Valley.

BUSH MORNING-GLORY

CANADA THISTLE

COMMON BURDOCK

Common Burdock

Arctium minus

OTHER COMMON NAMES: Wild rhubarb, hard dock, beggar button, cuckoo button.

FAMILY: Sunflower (Asteraceae)

FLOWERING PERIOD: July and August into September.

DISTRIBUTION: Principally eastern Nebraska. Eastern Great Plains.

HABITAT: Moist, rich soils in full sun or partial shade; disturbed sites, floodplains, abandoned farmsteads, pastures, wooded areas.

DESCRIPTION: Naturalized biennial growing from a stout, fleshy, carrot-like taproot. Produces a rosette of basal leaves the first year; a stout, usually reddish, much-branched flowering stalk 2-5 feet tall the second year. Basal leaves ovate or cordate (heart-shaped), superficially resembling those of rhubarb; 11-22 inches long, nearly as wide. Leaf margins smooth or toothed and generally wavy. Woolly, grayish hairs cover leaf underside. Upper leaves smaller and less coarse. Small, tubular, rose-purple flowers gathered in thistle-like heads less than 1 inch in diameter; flower heads clustered at branch ends; when dry, becoming a bur with hooked bristles which readily attach to animal fur, aiding seed dispersal. Unlike the thistles, which employ feathery bristles to disperse their achenes by the wind, the achenes of common burdock have a cluster of bristles shorter than the achene itself.

GENERAL INFORMATION: This is the most common of several burdocks introduced from Europe and Asia. In Japan, the root of a larger species, great burdock *(Arctium lappa)* is valued as a pot vegetable and the young leaves are used as greens. This species, with flower heads twice the size of those of common burdock, has been reported in Custer and Sarpy counties in Nebraska. Common burdock apparently spread rapidly in North America, the burs probably hitching rides on livestock. Various burdock medicines were once widely acclaimed as blood purifiers, and reported to be "very good for those who have been bitten by vipers, mad dogs and other poisonous animals." Folklore has it that eating the stems raw would "stir up lust."

Flodman's Thistle

Cirsium flodmanii

OTHER COMMON NAMES: Prairie thistle.
FAMILY: Sunflower (Asteraceae)
FLOWERING PERIOD: July and August.
DISTRIBUTION: Statewide in Nebraska except southwest, more common north. Northern half of the Great Plains.
HABITAT: Moist or poorly drained, lightly disturbed soils; prairies, meadows, roadsides.
DESCRIPTION: Native perennial spreading by rhizomes. Stem is erect, sparingly branched, *white with short, woolly hairs, without spines*; 1-2 feet or more tall. Leaves in basal rosette and lower on stem 5-9 inches long; gray-green with short hairs on upper surface; a *whitish, dense tangle of hairs on underside;* becoming more deeply lobed higher on the stem; each lobe ending in a spine. Basal leaves and some stem leaves without lobes, oblong-lanceolate. Leaves reduced in scale and clasping higher on stem. Flower heads at the top of branches, 1-2 inches across; composed of many small tubular flowers, pinkish to red-violet. Base of flower head bears short, yellow spines.
GENERAL INFORMATION: Flodman's thistle is a rightful constituent of native prairies and begins the recolonization of disturbed grasslands. On properly managed rangelands it is not a problem plant.

FLODMAN'S THISTLE

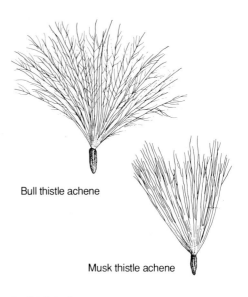

Bull thistle achene

Musk thistle achene

Bull Thistle

Cirsium vulgare

FAMILY: Sunflower (Asteraceae)
FLOWERING PERIOD: Late July, August and into September.
DISTRIBUTION: Statewide in Nebraska. Found throughout the Great Plains, more common east.
HABITAT: Roadsides, pastures, floodplains and other disturbed sites.
DESCRIPTION: Naturalized biennial growing from a fleshy taproot. Stem stout, erect, hairy, with leafy branches; 2-5 feet or more tall. Leaves extend along the stem as *spiny wings*. A rosette of low-growing leaves produced the first year; flowering stalk the second. Leaves deeply lobed with crinkled margins, lobes tipped with spines. *Upper leaf surface smooth with yellow prickles,* undersurface green to gray-green, pubescent but not woolly pubescent as in some thistle species. Upper leaves smaller, not so deeply lobed. Plump, rounded flower heads at ends of branches; often numerous and clustered, 2 inches or more across; composed of many small, tubular red-violet flowers. Flower head constricted immediately below flowers. Base of flower head is covered with many *long, yellow-tipped spines. Cobwebby strands* usually evident between the spines. The achenes of bull thistle, and most thistles, are carried by feather-like plumes.
GENERAL INFORMATION: Native of Europe and Asia.

158

BULL THISTLE

MUSK THISTLE

Musk Thistle

Carduus nutans

OTHER COMMON NAMES: Nodding thistle.
FAMILY: Sunflower (Asteraceae)
FLOWERING PERIOD: Principally June and early July; less frequent through the summer.
DISTRIBUTION: Eastern half of Nebraska, common in southeast; reportedly spreading north and west. Southeastern Great Plains.
HABITAT: Thrives on moist alluvial soils but also on drier, less fertile soils; disturbed areas, roadsides, ravines, overgrazed pastures, occasional in grasslands.
DESCRIPTION: Naturalized winter annual or biennial growing from a stout, fleshy taproot. Usually establishes a rosette of spiny leaves its first season, a flowering stalk the second. Stem is stout, erect, branched and covered with hairs, or cobwebby; 3-6 feet or more tall. Leaves 2-10 inches long; lanceolate, elliptic or oblong; wavy, white margins; lobed, each lobe ending in a spine. Lower portions of *leaves extend onto the stem as a "wing."* Unlike other thistles, the leaves are essentially smooth on both upper and lower surfaces, not pubescent. Hemispherical flower heads on long and mostly naked stalks at top of the plant, *nodding;* deep pink to a red-violet; *sharp-tipped, reflexed bracts cover base of flower head;* 1-2 inches or more across. Stems, leaves and base of the flower heads all bear spines. *Achene with fine, hair-like bristles*, not feather-like plumes. The achenes of other Great Plains thistles, both native and naturalized, are carried by feather-like plumes.
GENERAL INFORMATION: Introduced from Europe and western Asia. Apparently uncommon during the 1930s, it was placed on Nebraska's noxious weed list in 1959.

Musk thistle leaf wing

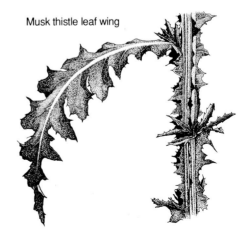

159

largest lobe serving as a landing pad for insects; shorter, arching, 2-lobed upper lip forming a hood over 4 stamens and the pistil.

GENERAL INFORMATION: Unlike the true nettle, which the leaves of this wildflower resemble, the hairs do not sting. Marsh hedge-nettle was once considered an important medicinal plant, used to promote the healing of wounds and clear mucus from the respiratory tract.

MARSH HEDGE-NETTLE

Marsh Hedge-nettle
Stachys palustris

OTHER COMMON NAMES: Marsh or clown's woundwort, marsh betony.
FAMILY: Mint (Lamiaceae)
FLOWERING PERIOD: June into August.
DISTRIBUTION: Statewide in Nebraska except the Panhandle, southwest and extreme south-central; most common north and east. Northern half and east-central Great Plains.
HABITAT: Moist soils in grasslands; meadows, shorelines, wet ditches, sloughs.
DESCRIPTION: Native perennial spreading by rhizomes and sometimes bearing whitish tubers. Stem is erect and usually not branched, roughly square in cross-section; with *long, soft, white hairs*; 1-3 feet tall. The leaves are opposite on the stem, most lacking stalks, margins toothed, hairy to densely pubescent; lanceolate to broadly lanceolate; 2-4 inches long and less than 1 inch wide. Flowers in groups of 2-8 from the axils of leaf-like bracts near top of the stem. Flowers are about .5 inch long; pale lavender with darker markings; lower lip with

Self-heal
Prunella vulgaris

OTHER COMMON NAMES: Heal-all, dragonhead, blue-curls, heart-of-the-earth.
FAMILY: Mint (Lamiaceae)
FLOWERING PERIOD: Late May until frost.
DISTRIBUTION: Statewide in Nebraska except the southwest, most common southeast. Principally southeastern Great Plains, sporadically farther north and west.
HABITAT: Moist soils; full sun or partial shade; meadows, roadsides, woodland edge and openings; wetlands and stream margins.
DESCRIPTION: Native perennial growing from a short caudex or short, slender rhizomes. Stem usually erect, often with the lower portion reclining on the ground and occasionally putting down roots forming patches. Stems are sometimes branched; roughly square in cross-section; usually covered with soft hairs, at least near top; usually less than 1 foot tall. Leaves on short stalks, opposite on stem; margins with shallow, rounded teeth or smooth; leaf blade lanceolate, 1-4 inches long, usually less than 1 inch wide. Flowers at top of stem or branches, in a short, cylindrical cluster (a dense terminal spike) 1 inch or more long, .5 inch across with numerous, leafy bracts. Flowers up to .5 inch long; upper lip a red-violet to blue-violet hood; lower lip mostly white and 3-lobed, the center lobe largest and fringed on outer margin.
GENERAL INFORMATION: This species is widely distributed in northern North America, Asia and Europe. As implied by its common name, it has been attributed with numerous medicinal applications, principally in Europe. Preparations were used as a treatment for sore throat, boils, hemorrhages, diarrhea, gas, colic; stomach, liver and urinary disorders. The species name, *vulgaris*, is from Latin meaning "common," the implication being that it was a medicine for the common man.

American Germander

Teucrium canadense

OTHER COMMON NAMES: Wood sage.

FAMILY: Mint (Lamiaceae)

FLOWERING PERIOD: Late June, principally July, as late as early September.

DISTRIBUTION: Statewide in Nebraska. Found throughout the Great Plains, infrequent or absent extreme west and southwest.

HABITAT: Moist soils; full or partial shade; grasslands, meadows, sloughs, shorelines, woodland edge and openings.

DESCRIPTION: Native perennial forming colonies by spreading rhizomes which may bear whitish tubers. Stems erect, usually not branched, roughly square in cross-section; pubescent; 1-3 feet tall. Leaves opposite on stem, on stalks less than .5 inch long, margins toothed, pubescence most noticeable on underside; lanceolate to ovate-lanceolate; 2-4 inches long, less than 1 inch wide. Flowers in a spike-like inflorescence 6-12 inches tall at top of stem; .5 inch or more long; pale lavender with darker markings; upper lip formed into a *pair of erect horn-like projections;* lower lip with a pair of lateral lobes and a larger, downward directed middle lobe. Stamens and pistil not mature at the same time, ensuring cross-pollination.

GENERAL INFORMATION: While the stems are pubescent, they are not covered with long, soft, white hairs as are those of marsh hedge-nettle. In both species, though, there is much variation in the degree of pubescence or hairiness. The pair of horn-like projections on American germander is a good identification feature for this species. The flowers are well designed to accommodate visiting bees and when abundant this wildflower is a valuable honey plant. The extended lower lip serves as a perch for bees and other insects coming for nectar found deep in the flower tube.

SELF-HEAL

AMERICAN GERMANDER

161

SHOWY MILKWEED

Showy Milkweed
Asclepias speciosa

FAMILY: Milkweed (Asclepiadaceae)

FLOWERING PERIOD: June and July.

DISTRIBUTION: Central and western Nebraska. Throughout the Great Plains, infrequent or absent in extreme southeast.

HABITAT: Moist, particularly sandy soils; grasslands, meadows, roadsides.

DESCRIPTION: Native perennial growing from a deep rhizome. Stems stout, not branching or sparingly branched on upper portion of plant; densely pubescent above, sparingly so below; 1.5-3 feet tall. Leaves usually opposite on stem; broadly lanceolate to ovate or ovate-oblong; bluish-green, pubescent, particularly on underside; 3-7 inches long. Spherical clusters of 10-40 flowers at top of stem and on stalks from the axils of upper leaves. Flowers hourglass-shaped: the lower part composed of 5 reflexed, rose or rose-and-white colored petals; the upper part composed of 5 long, pointed, creamy-white hoods which are nectar receptacles. Emerging from near the base of each hood is an inward arching horn. The *hoods are exceptionally long* in this species making the flower heads showy (see illustration on page 16). Seed pod broadly spindle-shaped, erect, 3-4 inches long, the outer surface usually covered by tubercles.

Smooth Milkweed
Asclepias sullivantii

OTHER COMMON NAMES: Sullivant's milkweed.

FAMILY: Milkweed (Asclepiadaceae)

FLOWERING PERIOD: Late June and July occasionally into August.

DISTRIBUTION: Eastern Nebraska, principally southeast. Southeastern Great Plains.

HABITAT: Moist, rich soils in low prairies, meadows, roadsides.

DESCRIPTION: Native perennial growing from an enlarged crown atop a deep and fleshy rhizome. One to several stout, erect stems, 2-4 feet tall. Leaves distinctive: ovate to oblong, with rounded ends and sharp tips; thick, somewhat succulent, *smooth,* the principal veins often tinged with pink; 2-6 inches long and half as wide. Domed clusters of 15-40 flowers at top of plant and on stalks from upper leaf axils. Flowers are hourglass in shape, relatively large compared to other milkweeds, rose-pink and pinkish-white. Seed pod broadly spindle-shaped, erect, 3-4 inches long; tubercles, if present at all, only on upper half.

GENERAL INFORMATION: Decreases and disappears under excessive grazing. An indicator of high-quality, low prairie sites. Usually found in loose colonies but seldom many at one site.

Common Milkweed

Asclepias syriaca

OTHER COMMON NAMES: Silkweed, silky swallow-wort.

FAMILY: Milkweed (Asclepiadaceae)

FLOWERING PERIOD: June through August.

DISTRIBUTION: Principally eastern half of Nebraska. Eastern Great Plains.

HABITAT: Moderately dry to moist, often somewhat disturbed sites in a variety of soils; grasslands, roadsides, fields and floodplains.

DESCRIPTION: Native perennial growing from a deep rhizome. Stems are stout, usually not branched; sparsely to densely pubescent; 2-5 feet tall. Leaves mostly opposite on the stem; ovate, elliptic or oblong; bluish-green, pubescent, particularly on the underside; 4-7 inches long. Spherical clusters (up to 4 inches in diameter) of 20-130 flowers at top of the stem and on stalks from the axils of uppermost leaves. Flowers are hourglass-shaped, both the upper and lower parts are usually a dull pinkish-rose, hoods may be more whitish. *Hoods are not enlarged* as those of showy milkweed, the flower heads are not so striking. Seed pod broadly spindle-shaped, erect, 2-4 inches long, and usually *densely covered with tubercles.*

GENERAL INFORMATION: The Sioux reportedly extracted the juice from the flowers and boiled it down to make a brown sugar. Common milkweed (as well as showy milkweed) shoots, when less than 8 inches tall, can be eaten much the same as asparagus, as can flower buds and green seed pods. All, though, must be boiled in several changes of water as they contain a mildly toxic substance. During World War II, the latex from milkweeds was tested as a rubber substitute and the plumy seed hairs were used as a substitute for kapok in life jackets. In recent years there has been a renewed interest, particularly in central Nebraska, in using the silky seed plumes of milkweeds in a mix with bird down as a filler for garments and quilts. It is being cultivated on an experimental basis. Showy and common milkweed are known to hybridize, producing plants with intermediate characteristics.

SMOOTH MILKWEED

COMMON MILKWEED

SCARLET GAURA

Scarlet Gaura
Gaura coccinea

OTHER COMMON NAMES: Wild honeysuckle, butterfly weed.
FAMILY: Evening Primrose (Onagraceae)
FLOWERING PERIOD: Late May, principally June, occasionally as late as August.
DISTRIBUTION: Statewide in Nebraska, but *infrequent southeast and Sandhills.* Throughout the Great Plains, infrequent or absent southeast.
HABITAT: On a variety of dry soils; grasslands, woodland edge and openings, roadsides, often on somewhat disturbed sites.
DESCRIPTION: Native perennial growing from a branched caudex atop a deep taproot and spreading by horizontal roots to form colonies. Usually several stems, *branching near base,* leafy, *1-2 feet tall.* Leaves alternate on stem; lanceolate to narrowly oblong or narrowly elliptic; leaf margins smooth or with a few shallow teeth; less than 1.5 inches long, smaller upward. Stems and leaves may or may not be covered with grayish hairs. Flowers in a spike-like inflorescence 2-12 inches long; blooming from the bottom to top; only a ring of flowers in bloom at one time. Flowers resemble those of honeysuckle; *.25-.5 inch across;* 4 petals, at first white fading to pink and finally scarlet, all in the same day; narrow sepals reflexed back; 8 protruding stamens with reddish-brown anthers. Sweetly fragrant.
GENERAL INFORMATION: This species varies in degree of branching, pubescence, size and flower color. Velvety gaura (*Gaura parviflora*), also called small-flowered gaura, is an annual found across most of the southern and central Great Plains. Velvety gaura is seldom less than 2 feet in height and is usually not branched. Its leaves are 2-3 times as large as those of scarlet gaura and more tapering, lanceolate-elliptic. Leaves and stems of velvety gaura are densely pubescent and soft. The flowers of velvety gaura are less than .25 inch wide, those of scarlet gaura larger than .25 inch.

SWAMP MILKWEED

Swamp Milkweed

Asclepias incarnata

OTHER COMMON NAMES: Water nerve-root, rose or swamp silk-weed.
FAMILY: Milkweed (Asclepiadaceae)
FLOWERING PERIOD: July and August.
DISTRIBUTION: Statewide in Nebraska, more common east. Throughout the Great Plains, becoming infrequent west.
HABITAT: Wet soils in low prairies, meadows and ditches; margins of streams, lakes, ponds and marshes.
DESCRIPTION: Native perennial growing from shallow but extensive fibrous roots. Usually single stemmed; branched mostly above; 4-5 feet tall, taller on some sites or when crowded by other plants. Leaves opposite on the stem; *linear-lanceolate with pointed tips, thin*, deep green; 3-6 inches long and 1 inch or less wide. Pubescent but inconspicuously so. Exudes a milky sap when cut or broken but only in small amounts. Pinkish-rose and white, hourglass-shaped flowers gathered into flat-topped or domed clusters at the top of the plant. Seed pod slender, spindle-shaped, erect, 2-4 inches long, without tubercles.

Large-flowered Gaura

Gaura longiflora

OTHER COMMON NAMES: Butterfly weed.
FAMILY: Evening Primrose (Onagraceae)
FLOWERING PERIOD: July into September.
DISTRIBUTION: *Principally southeast* Nebraska. Southeastern Great Plains.
HABITAT: Moist to dry, often disturbed soils; prairies, roadsides, railways, woodland edge and openings.
DESCRIPTION: Native annual or winter annual growing from a fleshy taproot. Stems erect, branching above, 2-6 feet tall. Outer layer of lower stem often peeling. Leaves narrowly elliptic, may or may not be shallowly toothed, 1-5 inches long, less than 1 inch wide. Usually a *cluster of small leaves in axils of principal leaves*. Leaves and stems are covered with minute, stiff hairs. Flowers in clusters at the ends of branches, in *an open, spreading inflorescence;* .5-1 inch across; 4 petals which narrow abruptly at the base, white fading to pink or rose, arranged in an irregular pattern; 8 protruding, white stamens with long, yellow to reddish-brown anthers and an even longer style bearing a 4-lobed stigma. Flowers open late in the day.

Alleghany Monkey-flower

Mimulus ringens

OTHER COMMON NAMES: Square-stemmed monkey-flower
FAMILY: Figwort (Scrophulariaceae)
FLOWERING PERIOD: June through August, principally July.
DISTRIBUTION: Eastern half and northern third of Nebraska. Eastern fourth of Great Plains, extending farther west in Nebraska and Kansas.
HABITAT: Wet to moist soils in full sun or partial shade; stream banks, sandbars, lake and marsh edge.
DESCRIPTION: Native perennial growing from fibrous roots, often spreading by rhizomes or stolons to form colonies. Stems erect, may be branched above, *roughly square in cross-section*, 1-3 feet tall. Leaves opposite, stalkless or even somewhat clasping stem, lanceolate with toothed margins; 1-3 inches long and a third as wide. Flowers are solitary, on stalks about 1 inch long, from axils of upper leaves; a deep red-violet to blue; tubular, spreading into a 2-lobed, erect upper lip and a 3-lobed lower lip; the throat of the flower nearly closed by an arch-ed, yellowish ridge (the palate) on the lower lobe. Bumblebees are strong enough to force open the flower lips and reach the nectar, in the process accomplishing pollination.
GENERAL INFORMATION: It is said, by those with fertile imaginations, the flower resembles the face of a monkey, particularly when the sides of the flower are squeezed; hence the common name and the genus name, *Mimulus*, from Latin, roughly translating as "little buffoon" or "mimic."

Wild Bergamot

Monarda fistulosa

OTHER COMMON NAMES: Horsemint, bee-balm, Oswego-tea.
FAMILY: Mint (Lamiaceae)
FLOWERING PERIOD: June into August.
DISTRIBUTION: Statewide in Nebraska. Found throughout the Great Plains except southwest.
HABITAT: Rich, moist soils, full sun or partial shade; floodplains, pastures, woodland edge, roadsides, ravines, shorelines.
DESCRIPTION: Native perennial spreading into colonies from creeping rhizomes. Stems stout, erect, may be branched above, roughly square in cross-section, pubescent above, up to 5 feet tall. Leaves on stalks, opposite along the stem, ovate to lanceolate; leaf margin unevenly, shallowly toothed or not toothed; undersides hairy; 1-4 inches long and .5-1.5 inches wide. Leaves bearing many glandular dots which secrete a fragrant oil. Flower heads solitary on stalks at the ends of branches, up to 1.5 inches across; fragrant when crushed, even when dry in the winter. Petals are usually pink or lavender, occasionally a blue-violet or rarely white; fused into a slender tube which divides into an erect and tubular upper lobe (from which stamens and the style protrude) and a reflexed, slightly spreading lower lobe. This is a highly variable species, particularly in the degree of branching and flower color.
GENERAL INFORMATION: The leaves were boiled by the Teton Dakota to make a tea to cure abdominal pains, by the Lakota for sore throat. The Winnebagos made a preparation from the leaves for pimples. The leaves were dried and used as a seasoning by early settlers, the crushed flower heads used in sachets. The tender, early leaves are best for brewing a tea. Later leaves can be used as an oregano-tasting seasoning.

ALLEGHANY MONKEY-FLOWER

CANADA TICKCLOVER

WILD BERGAMOT

Canada Tickclover
Desmodium canadense

OTHER COMMON NAMES: Canada or showy tick-trefoil, beggar's lice or ticks, stick-tights.
FAMILY: Bean (Fabaceae)
FLOWERING PERIOD: Principally July, into September.
DISTRIBUTION: Eastern half and north-central Nebraska. Eastern third of the Great Plains, extending west across northern Nebraska and the Dakotas.
HABITAT: Moist, particularly sandy or rocky soils; floodplains, stream banks, thicket edges, roadsides, ravines. Often found on mildly disturbed or healing sites.
DESCRIPTION: Native perennial growing from a branching caudex atop a woody taproot. Stems are erect and often in clusters, usually not branched below the inflorescence; hairy mostly on upper portion; 3-4 feet or more tall. Leaves alternate, on *stalks 1 inch long or less* becoming shorter or absent near top. Each leaf with 3 broadly lanceolate to ovate leaflets; middle leaflet largest, 2-4.5 inches long, half or less as wide. Leaves hairy, particularly the underside, and rough to the touch. Unlike some other tickclovers, though, the leaves do not have many hooked hairs and so they do not cling to clothing. Flowers are arranged along the arching stem tip and *on short stalks or branches emerging from it,* forming an inflorescence composed of several arching flower stalks (racemes). Flowers pea-like, pink to a rich red-violet to blue-violet, up to .5 inch long. Flattened, segmented seed pods, up to 1 inch long; covered with hooked hairs which cling to fur and clothing.
GENERAL INFORMATION: This is the largest-flowered and showiest of 6 tickclovers occurring in Nebraska (8 in the Great Plains). Illinois tickclover (*Desmodium illinoense*), found principally in southeast Nebraska and the southeastern Great Plains, has smaller flowers and is not as showy. Its leaf stalks are nearly as long as the leaflets; leaves are leathery and rough to the touch on both the upper and lower surfaces because of numerous hooked hairs, hence the leaves cling to clothing. The flowers appear along the *unbranched stem top.* Tickclovers are considered good honey plants. When young they are eaten by livestock and native grazers. They decrease in abundance under heavy grazing pressure.

SILKY PRAIRIE CLOVER

Silky Prairie Clover
Dalea villosa

FAMILY: Bean (Fabaceae)

FLOWERING PERIOD: July into August.

DISTRIBUTION: Statewide in Nebraska except extreme western Panhandle and southeast, most common central, particularly in the Sandhills. Throughout the Great Plains, infrequent or absent eastern and western fifths.

HABITAT: Loose, dry to moderately moist, sandy soils; disturbed sites, roadsides and margins of blowouts.

DESCRIPTION: Native perennial growing from a woody, branching caudex atop a taproot. A low-growing, sprawling plant, usually less than 16 inches tall. Stems, 1-several, erect, or more frequently with the lower portions reclining on ground; branching above. Numerous leaves, alternate on stem, up to 1.5 inches long, odd-pinnately compound; 11-25 leaflets, narrowly elliptic and less than .5 inch long. Stems and leaves silvery-green, densely woolly with short, white hairs. Flower spikes solitary at ends of short branches near top of the plant; minute, pinkish flowers with protruding yellow stamens encircle a spike up to 4 inches long; flowers mature from base to tip. As much as half of the flower head in blossom at one time.

GENERAL INFORMATION: A subtly attractive plant because of its compact growth habit; its arrangement of numerous small, silvery leaflets and its delicate flower color.

Purple Prairie Clover
Dalea purpurea

OTHER COMMON NAMES: Thimbleweed, red tassel-flower, violet prairie clover.

FAMILY: Bean (Fabaceae)

FLOWERING PERIOD: June and July.

DISTRIBUTION: Statewide in Nebraska, more common in the east. Throughout Great Plains, less frequent west.

HABITAT: Dry to moderately moist grasslands; roadsides, railways, hillsides, pastures, meadows, floodplains.

DESCRIPTION: Native perennial growing from woody roots forming a caudex in older plants. Stems, several to many, are slender, erect, frequently branched; 1-3 feet tall. Leaves alternate, up to 1.5 inches long, odd-pinnately compound; 3-7 (usually 5) leaflets, linear, up to 1 inch long. Stems and leaves occasionally with minute, soft, whitish hairs; but usually not, or not noticeably so. Flower spikes at the ends of short branches at top of plant; minute red-violet to pink flowers with protruding yellow stamens encircle a compact columnar spike .5-1.5 inches long; flowers mature from base to tip.

GENERAL INFORMATION: A preferred forage for livestock and native grazers. Decreases and disappears under overgrazing. The Oglala brewed a tea-like drink from the leaves. The Ponca chewed the roots for its pleasant taste. The tough stems were bundled and used as brooms by the Pawnee.

Rocky Mountain Bee Plant
Cleome serrulata

OTHER COMMON NAMES: Spider flower, Indian pink, stink flower, pink cleome

FAMILY: Caper (Capparaceae)

FLOWERING PERIOD: Principally July and August but into September.

DISTRIBUTION: Statewide in Nebraska, most common in the central and west. Throughout the Great Plains.

HABITAT: Moderately dry to moist, particularly sandy or rocky soils; disturbed sites, roadsides, near windmills, grasslands.

DESCRIPTION: Native annual. Stem is erect, usually leafless and not branched on the lower portion of plant; branching and leafy above; 2-5 feet tall. Leaflets in threes, narrowly lanceolate, 1-2 inches long, smaller higher on plant. Flower clusters (racemes) roughly spherical to elongated, at the ends of branches, continuing to elongate during the growing season. Individual flowers are composed of 4 pink petals with 6 conspicuous pink stamens which protrude up to 1 inch beyond the petals. Seed capsules are slender with pointed tips, up to 3 inches long, and often fully formed while the upper portion of the inflorescence is still flowering.

GENERAL INFORMATION: As the common name implies, Rocky Mountain bee plant is an excellent honey flower and is sometimes cultivated for that purpose. The common name spider flower is probably a reference to the long, spreading stamens which, with a bit of imagination, could be seen to resemble the legs of a spider. Plants of this genus have a pungent, mustard-like taste and a scent most consider unpleasant, hence another common name, stink flower. Members of this genus have been cultivated as garden ornamentals. The leaves and the young, tender shoots were eaten by western American Indians. Stems were boiled down to a thick black syrup which was dried into hard cakes to be revived later in hot water and used as a black paint or dye for pottery decoration. Because it produces seeds so abundantly, it is an important food plant for doves and other small birds.

PURPLE PRAIRIE CLOVER

ROCKY MOUNTAIN BEE PLANT

Spotted Joe-Pye Weed

Eupatorium maculatum

OTHER COMMON NAMES: Purple boneset.
FAMILY: Sunflower (Asteraceae)
FLOWERING PERIOD: Principally late July and August, into September.
DISTRIBUTION: Statewide in Nebraska, more common north. Principally northeastern Great Plains but reported west across Nebraska and South Dakota.
HABITAT: Moist to wet soils, full sun or partial shade; shorelines, stream banks, wet meadows, ditches.
DESCRIPTION: Native perennial growing from a branched rhizome with fibrous roots. Stem erect, blotched or evenly tinged with purple, 2-5 feet or more tall. *Leaves in whorls* of 4-5, on short stalks; narrowly ovate to broadly lanceolate with pointed tips; rough textured, margins toothed; leaf blade 3-6 inches long and half as wide. Small, dusty pink to red-violet florets (9-22) clustered in flower heads; the flower heads gathered *into a somewhat flat-topped inflorescence* (a cyme) at top of stem.

GENERAL INFORMATION: Origin of the common name is generally attributed to an Indian medicine man, Joe Pye, who lived in colonial New England. It was claimed he cured typhoid fever with decoctions made from plants of this group. Two other species of Joe-Pye weed are found in Nebraska and the Great Plains. Both tall Joe-Pye weed *(Eupatorium altissimum)* and sweet Joe-Pye weed *(Eupatorium purpureum)* are found principally in southeastern Nebraska and in the southeastern Great Plains. The inflorescence of sweet Joe-Pye weed is typically dome shaped and bears only *5-7 florets per flower head;* the leaves of tall Joe-Pye weed are opposite on the stem, not whorled.

SPOTTED JOE-PYE WEED

BALDWIN'S IRONWEED

WESTERN IRONWEED

Baldwin's Ironweed

Vernonia baldwinii

FAMILY: Sunflower (Asteraceae)
FLOWERING PERIOD: Late July and August, into September.
DISTRIBUTION: Southern half of Nebraska, becoming less frequent west. Southern half of the Great Plains, infrequent or absent west fifth.
HABITAT: *Dry soils*; pastures, roadsides, disturbed sites.
DESCRIPTION: Native perennial growing from rhizomes with thickened and fibrous roots. Stem single or in clusters, erect, stout, pubescence most noticeable below, branching only in the inflorescence, 2-5 feet tall. Leaves are numerous, alternate on the stem; on short stalks or lacking stalks, margins with small teeth; narrowly lanceolate to narrowly ovate; 2-6 inches long, 1-2 inches wide. Flower heads at ends of short branches near the top of the plant; usually forming a *loose and irregularly shaped (but occasionally flat-topped) inflorescence.* Each flower head is composed of 17-34 bright, red-violet disk florets.
GENERAL INFORMATION: Because of their bitter taste, ironweeds are not browsed by cattle. They are resistant to drought and can become abundant on overgrazed pastures.

Western Ironweed

Vernonia fasciculata

FAMILY: Sunflower (Asteraceae)
FLOWERING PERIOD: July into September.
DISTRIBUTION: Statewide in Nebraska, becoming uncommon in the Panhandle. Throughout the Great Plains except west fifth.
HABITAT: *Moist soils;* low prairies, meadows, roadsides, wetlands edge.
DESCRIPTION: Native perennial growing from elongate rhizomes with thickened and fibrous roots. Stems single or in clusters, erect, stout, often reddish, not noticeably pubescent, branching only in inflorescence, 2-5 feet or more tall. Leaves numerous, alternate on the stem, on short stalks or stalkless, the margins sharply toothed; lanceolate; 2-6 inches long, less than 1.5 inches wide. Flower heads at the ends of short branches near top of plant; usually forming a *flat toppod inflorescence.* Each flower head is composed of 10-26 usually deep, red-violet disk florets.
GENERAL INFORMATION: A hand lens is necessary to reliably identify the ironweeds. Under magnification the underside of western ironweed leaves are conspicuously pitted. The underside of Baldwin's ironweed leaves are not conspicuously pitted.

PINK SMARTWEED

Pink Smartweed
Polygonum bicorne

FAMILY: Buckwheat (Polygonaceae)
FLOWERING PERIOD: Principally July and August but through September.
DISTRIBUTION: Central and eastern Nebraska. Southern half of the Great Plains.
HABITAT: Wet soils or shallow, standing water; marsh edge, shorelines, wet ditches.
DESCRIPTION: Native annual growing from a taproot. Stem slender, erect, much branched; 3 feet or more tall. Leaves alternate on stem, narrowly lanceolate with a pointed tip; lower leaves on stalks, upper leaves stalkless; up to 4.5 inches long, less than 1 inch wide. Flowers are densely crowded in *numerous*, elongated clusters (racemes) up to 2 inches long at ends of branches and on stalks from axils of upper leaves. Flowers small; fused at the base, pink; sepals form a cup with 4-5 blunt lobes from which *5 stamens protrude slightly.* The fruit is a small, shiny, dark brown achene.
GENERAL INFORMATION: Over 20 species of knotweeds and smartweeds occur in the Great Plains. Of these, several grow in wet soils or in shallow water, and bear elongated clusters of small pinkish flowers. Two of these species are found throughout the Great Plains and are the most likely to be confused with pink smartweed. Water smartweed (*Polygonum amphibium*) usually has only *1 or 2 clusters of flowers*. Pennsylvania smartweed (*Polygonum*

pensylvanicum) is the most similar to pink smartweed. Its flowers may be pink or a darker red-violet and its stamens *do not* extend beyond the flower cup. The small, dry fruits of smartweeds are an important food of waterfowl and other birds.

Slender Gerardia
Agalinis tenuifolia

FAMILY: Figwort (Scrophulariaceae)
FLOWERING PERIOD: August and September.
DISTRIBUTION: Statewide in Nebraska. East half of the Great Plains.
HABITAT: Moist or wet soils; low prairies, roadside ditches, shorelines, stream banks.
DESCRIPTION: Native annual. Stems erect, usually with numerous branches producing an open, bushy plant; up to 2 feet tall. Leaves opposite on stem, narrowly linear with sharp tips; 1-2.5 inches long. Stems and leaves often are wine-red or reddish brown, particularly later in the season. Flowers from leaf axils on slender stalks. The flower is tubular, spreading to five prominent lobes, the upper two forming a hood over the stamens; pink to deep red-violet, becoming white at the base and mottled with darker spots; *about .5 inch long*.
GENERAL INFORMATION: This is the most frequently encountered of the Great Plains gerardias. Slender gerardia is known to be parasitic on other forbs or grasses.

Rough Purple Gerardia

Agalinis aspera

OTHER COMMON NAMES: False foxglove, rough purple agalinis.

FAMILY: Figwort (Scrophulariaceae)

FLOWERING PERIOD: August through September.

DISTRIBUTION: Statewide in Nebraska except southwest; more frequent east half. East half of the Great Plains.

HABITAT: Dry soils in grasslands, roadsides, open woods.

DESCRIPTION: Native annual. Stems erect, many upward-angling branches (with clusters of small axillary leaves) forming a bushy plant; 1-2 feet tall. Leaves opposite on stem; edge of leaves rolled under; narrowly linear with sharp tips; up to 1.5 inches long. Stems and upper surface of leaves with short, stiff hairs; rough to touch. Flowers large and showy; borne singly on stalks from leaf axils on upper stem; *stalk bearing the flower longer than the calyx.* Flower is bell-shaped with spreading lobes, pink or red-violet, up to 1 inch long.

GENERAL INFORMATION: Large purple gerardia (*Agalinis purpurea*), is less common but similar. The stalk bearing its flower is *shorter than the calyx.* Its flower is slightly larger.

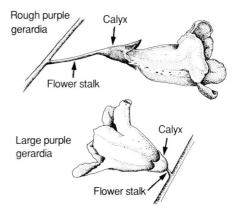

Rough purple gerardia — Calyx — Flower stalk

Large purple gerardia — Calyx — Flower stalk

HAIRY FOUR-O'CLOCK

Hairy Four-o'clock

Mirabilis hirsuta

FAMILY: Four-o'clock (Nyctaginaceae)
FLOWERING PERIOD: July and August.
DISTRIBUTION: Statewide in Nebraska, infrequent or absent in extreme south. Central and northern Great Plains.
HABITAT: Found on a variety of dry to moderately moist, particularly sandy soils; mildly disturbed sites, roadsides, pastures, grasslands.
DESCRIPTION: Native perennial growing from a branching caudex on top of a sturdy taproot. Stems erect or angling upward, 1 or more from same base, *usually not branched;* 2-3 feet tall. Leaves are opposite on stem, stalkless or lower ones on short stalks, *mostly lanceolate with a broad base,* 2-4 inches long. *All parts of herbage with stiff, short hairs.* Flowers at end of stem and on stalks from axils of upper leaves; in clusters of 2-5; emerging from a conspicuous, angular cup composed of 5 united bracts (which spread flat and persist after the flower tube has fallen); *pink, petal-like sepals* fused into a bell-shaped tube lobed on the outer margin; 3-5 pink, protruding filaments with bright yellow anthers, a solitary style exceeding stamens in length. Flowers open late in the day and last only into the next morning.

Wild Four-o'clock

Mirabilis nyctaginea

FAMILY: Four-o'clock (Nyctaginaceae)
FLOWERING PERIOD: May through August.
DISTRIBUTION: Statewide in Nebraska. Found throughout the Great Plains.
HABITAT: On a variety of soil types; disturbed sites, roadsides, field margins, pastures, floodplains, urban areas.
DESCRIPTION: Native perennial growing from a branching caudex atop a thick, fleshy taproot. Stems slender, erect or angling upward; *much-branched, repeatedly forking,* particularly near the top; nodes conspicuously swollen; 2-3 feet tall. Leaves opposite on the stem, on stalks .5-2 inches long, more or less *heart-shaped* (cordate) leaf blades 2-4 inches long. *Herbage not noticeably pubescent.* Flowers at ends of branches; in several clusters of 3-5, emerging from an angular cup composed of 5 united bracts (which spread flat and persist after the flower tube has fallen); *red-violet, petal-like sepals* are fused into a bell-shaped tube, lobed on the outer margin; 3-5 red-violet, protruding filaments with yellow anthers, a solitary style exceeding stamens in length. Flowers open in late afternoon, hence the name four-o'clock, and wilt before noon the following day.

Blazing Star
Liatris squarrosa

OTHER COMMON NAMES: Scaly blazing star, rattlesnake-master, colic-root.

FAMILY: Sunflower (Asteraceae)

FLOWERING PERIOD: June and July. One of the earliest flowering *Liatris.*

DISTRIBUTION: Statewide in Nebraska. Southern half of the Great Plains.

HABITAT: Dry to moderately moist, particularly sandy soils in grasslands.

DESCRIPTION: Native perennial growing from a corm with fibrous roots. One or more stems, erect, not branched, 10-24 inches tall. Leaves alternate, not as numerous as in most other species of *Liatris*, linear, *extending to top of stem; 2-6 inches long, less than .5 inch wide, becoming progressively smaller higher on stem. Stems and leaves are *not hairy* except in the variety found in extreme southeastern Nebraska and Great Plains which may be pubescent, particularly in the flowering spike. *Flower heads few and openly spaced* in a spike along top of stem; .5-1 inch long. Conspicuous, green turning red-violet, *sharp-tipped, reflexed bracts* at the base of each flower head; enclosing 20-40 deep red-violet, tubular disk florets with protruding styles. The fruit is an achene with short, feathery plumes.

GENERAL INFORMATION: The stout, parsnip-shaped taproot of dotted gayfeather and the bulbous corms of the other blazing stars and gayfeathers enhance drought tolerance and allow recovery from the loss of above-ground parts. Those with shallow corms are less drought resistant and may disappear during prolonged drought. Plants with enlarged roots seldom escaped the attention of American Indians. The ample roots of *Liatris* species were ascribed numerous medicinal virtues, including countering the effect of venomous snakebite, hence the common name rattlesnake-master. The roots were apparently used for food, but only as a last resort, as the roots of older plants are woody and essentially inedible.

WILD FOUR-O'CLOCK

BLAZING STAR

DOTTED GAYFEATHER

Dotted Gayfeather
Liatris punctata

OTHER COMMON NAMES: Blazing star, dotted button-snakeroot, starwort.
FAMILY: Sunflower (Asteraceae)
FLOWERING PERIOD: August into October.
DISTRIBUTION: Statewide in Nebraska. Found throughout the Great Plains.
HABITAT: Dry soils; grasslands, roadsides.
DESCRIPTION: Native perennial growing from a *stout taproot* extending 4-16 feet into subsoil. Stems may be solitary, but typically in a cluster; erect, not branched, *1-2 feet tall*. Leaves alternate, numerous, extending into flower spike; linear; lower leaves up to 6 inches long, less than .25 inch wide and becoming progressively smaller higher on the stem. The leaves usually have a conspicuous, whitish midrib. Stems and leaves usually without hairs except for a fringe on leaf margins. Flower heads *tightly clustered* in a spike on top third or half of stem (but not as close together as in thick-spike gayfeather), about .5 inch long; 4-8 pink, tubular disk florets with protruding styles. The fruit is an achene with short, feathery plumes. Because of its deep taproot, this species is the most drought resistant of the gayfeathers and blazing stars.

Thick-spike Gayfeather
Liatris pycnostachya

OTHER COMMON NAMES: Prairie or hairy button-snakeroot, prairie blazing star, Kansas or tall gayfeather.
FAMILY: Sunflower (Asteraceae)
FLOWERING PERIOD: July into August.
DISTRIBUTION: Eastern third of Nebraska, most common in southeast. Eastern fourth of Great Plains.
HABITAT: Moist, rich soils in low prairies, meadows, roadsides.
DESCRIPTION: Native perennial growing from a woody corm. One or several erect and unbranched stems *2-5 feet tall*. Leaves alternate, numerous, linear; lower leaves up to 12 inches long and usually less than .5 inch wide, becoming progressively smaller higher on stem. The leaves usually have a distinct, whitish midrib. Stems and leaves may be pubescent with stiff hairs on upper portion of the plant, usually not below. Flower heads *densely clustered* in a club-shaped spike up to 18 inches long on top fifth to half of stem; heads .5 inch or less long; 5-7 pink, tubular disk florets with protruding styles. Fruit a bristly-barbed achene. Our tallest *Liatris*, and one of the earliest to flower.

176

Rough Gayfeather

Liatris aspera

OTHER COMMON NAMES: Tall gayfeather, button snakeroot, rattlesnake-master.
FAMILY: Sunflower (Asteraceae)
FLOWERING PERIOD: Late August into early October.
DISTRIBUTION: Eastern half, particularly eastern third of Nebraska. Eastern third of the Great Plains.
HABITAT: Well-drained prairie soils; roadsides, upland prairie, ravines, banks.
DESCRIPTION: Native perennial growing from a knobby corm with fibrous roots. One or more erect and unbranched stems, up to 3 feet tall. Leaves alternate on the stem, numerous, linear; lower leaves up to 8 inches long and 1 inch wide, becoming progressively smaller higher on stem. Ends of leaves blunt or rounded, not tapering to a point. The leaves usually have a distinct, whitish midrib. The stems and leaves usually have stiff, short hairs making the plant rough to the touch, hence the common name. Flower heads in a spike along top of stem; *distinctly spaced, not densely clustered;* 1 inch or more long and almost as broad. Conspicuous, green to red-violet, *rounded bracts* at base of flower head form a cup around the 16-35 pink to red-violet tubular disk florets with protruding styles. Prior to opening, flower heads are slightly elongated spheres with rounded bracts. Fruit is a bristly achene.

GENERAL INFORMATION: The Pawnee boiled the corm and leaves to make a medicine for children with diarrhea. The ground flower heads, mixed with shelled corn, were fed to horses in the belief it would make them swifter, and the corm was chewed into a paste which was blown into a horse's nostrils to increase endurance. In the southeastern United States, the corms were crushed into a paste and applied as a poultice, or prepared with milk and taken internally, to counteract snakebite.

THICK-SPIKE GAYFEATHER

ROUGH GAYFEATHER

177

Aromatic Aster

Aster oblongifolius

FAMILY: Sunflower (Asteraceae)

FLOWERING PERIOD: September and early October.

DISTRIBUTION: Statewide in Nebraska except southwest, more common in central and east. Throughout the central and eastern Great Plains.

HABITAT: Well-drained to dry, often rocky or sandy soils in grasslands and roadsides. An indicator of grasslands in good condition.

DESCRIPTION: Native perennial growing from creeping rhizomes, sometimes with a caudex. Stems are erect, somewhat rigid; usually much branched, mostly from base; usually less than 20 inches tall. Lower leaves often shed before flowering; middle leaves narrowly oblong to broadly linear, .5-1 inch long. Upper leaves are reduced in size. The stem and leaves sparsely covered with short, stiff hairs. Flower heads .75-1 inch across; composed of up to 30 pink, red-violet or blue petal-like ray florets surrounding a center of bright yellow disk florets. Flowers are aromatic.

GENERAL INFORMATION: Over 20 asters are found in Nebraska, even more in the Great Plains region. Positive identification is often difficult and hinges on technical details. Furthermore, the asters show much variation in flower color, the flowers of some species ranging from a light pink to deep blue.

Viscid Aster

Machaeranthera linearis

FAMILY: Sunflower (Asteraceae)

FLOWERING PERIOD: Late August, September and into October.

DISTRIBUTION: Panhandle and western Sandhills in Nebraska. Western edge of Great Plains, extending farther east into southwest Kansas, Nebraska and South Dakota.

HABITAT: Dry, often disturbed, particularly sandy soil; grasslands, roadsides.

DESCRIPTION: Native annual or biennial growing from a taproot. Stems are erect, single or branched, often reddish-brown below, 1-2 feet tall. Leaves alternate on stem, linear to narrowly oblong, stalkless, may be slightly sticky; margins often with a few small teeth tipped with a bristle; 1-2 inches long, less than .5 inch wide. Lower leaves often shed before time of flowering. Flower heads, 2 to several, in clusters at top of the stem; .75-1.5 inches across; composed of numerous slender, bright red-violet to blue petal-like ray florets surrounding a center of yellow disk florets. Lower portion of flower head hemispherical, .25-.5 inch tall, covered with *sharp-tipped, reflexed bracts*.

GENERAL INFORMATION: Four members of this genus are found in Nebraska. They differ from plants of the genus *Aster* in growing from taproots (not fibrous roots) and often having dissected leaves which bear bristle-tipped teeth.

AROMATIC ASTER

VISCID ASTER

Willowleaf Aster

Aster praealtus

OTHER COMMON NAMES: Nebraska aster.

FAMILY: Sunflower (Asteraceae)

FLOWERING PERIOD: September and early October.

DISTRIBUTION: Central and eastern Nebraska. Southeastern Great Plains.

HABITAT: Moist soils; margins of lakes, marshes and streams; road ditches.

DESCRIPTION: Native perennial growing from creeping rhizomes, often forming dense colonies. Stems stout, much branched on upper half, 2-4 feet tall. Leaves thick and firm; linear-lanceolate, margins smooth or weakly toothed; 1-3 inches long, less than .5 inch wide. Lower leaves often shed before plant flowers; densely leafy on the upper half. Flower heads numerous; .5-1 inch across; composed of 20-35 narrow, pale red-violet to pale blue petal-like ray florets surrounding a yellow center ot disk florets.

GENERAL INFORMATION: The variety *nebraskensis* is common on lake and stream shores in the Sandhills. Its stems are uniformly pubescent, particularly above. The variety *praealtus*, which is found in southeastern Nebraska and the southeastern Great Plains, is not pubescent on the lower portion of the stem and only sparsely so above.

Blue-Violet to Blue Flowers

BLUE PHLOX

Blue Phlox

Phlox divaricata

OTHER COMMON NAMES: Wood phlox, wild sweet William.
FAMILY: Polemonium (Polemoniaceae)
FLOWERING PERIOD: Late April and May, into early June.
DISTRIBUTION: Principally Missouri Valley counties, farther west in southeast Nebraska. East-central and southeastern Great Plains.
HABITAT: Rich, moist soils in woodlands.
DESCRIPTION: Native perennial growing from tough, fibrous roots; spreading by stolons or rhizomes to form colonies. Stems slender, erect or with bases reclining on ground, usually not branched below inflorescence, sparsely pubescent, up to 16 inches tall. Principal stem leaves opposite, widely spaced, lanceolate to elliptic, on short stalks or lacking stalks with leaf base somewhat clasping the stem, usually somewhat pubescent, 1-2 inches long. Flowers in loose clusters (cymes) of 9-25 at top of the stem. Petals fused into a slender tube spreading to 5 distinct and petal-like lobes which are often notched at the tip; blue to blue-violet; up to .75 inch across. The flowers are often slightly fragrant, particularly when fresh.

Narrow Beardtongue

Penstemon angustifolius

FAMILY: Figwort (Scrophulariaceae)
FLOWERING PERIOD: May and June.
DISTRIBUTION: Central and western Nebraska. Central and western Great Plains.
HABITAT: Dry to moist, particularly sandy and gravelly soils in grasslands.
DESCRIPTION: Native perennial from a woody crown atop a taproot. Stems (1-5) are slender to stout, erect, less than 18 inches tall. Leaves thick; linear, lanceolate or narrowly ovate; bases clasping the stem; up to 4 inches long, less than 1 inch wide. Stems and leaves usually covered with a whitish, waxy bloom. Flowers on short stalks, in clusters of 2-10, from the axils of leaf-like bracts along upper portion of stem (a thyrse); tubular, flaring to a 2-lobed upper lip, 3-lobed lower lip; blue-violet to blue; about .75 inch long; a sterile filament densely bearded with yellow hairs.
GENERAL INFORMATION: A northern variety, found in the Dakotas, south nearly to Nebraska's southern border, has narrow leaves and bracts, and deep blue-violet flowers. A southern variety, found from Nebraska's southwest into Oklahoma, is taller, has broader leaves and pink, light blue or deep blue-violet flowers.

Pasque Flower

Anemone patens

OTHER COMMON NAMES: Windflower, Easter plant, prairie smoke, prairie crocus.

FAMILY: Buttercup (Ranunculaceae)

FLOWERING PERIOD: As early as late March, peaking in April, a few flowering into May.

DISTRIBUTION: Primarily northern Panhandle in Nebraska but also along the Niobrara River and other isolated locations farther east and south. Northern half of the Great Plains.

HABITAT: Dry, often rocky soil, full sun or partial shade; grasslands, pine woodland openings and edge.

DESCRIPTION: Native perennial growing from a stout caudex. Flower stalks emerge before basal leaves; usually several in a cluster from a common crown, 4-12 inches tall. All parts of the plant are densely covered with long, soft hairs. Leaves divided into narrow, linear segments; encircling the stem just below the flower. A single flower at the top of each stem; 1-2 inches long, spreading to as much as 2.5 inches across, composed of 5-8 blue, blue-violet or red-violet, petal-like sepals. Basal leaves with stalks 2-4 inches long; leaf blades wider than long, 2-4 inches across; deeply divided into 3-7 lobes which are in turn divided into narrow, linear segments. Basal leaves persist for much of the summer. Each of many seeds (achenes) tipped with a long, feathery plume; gathered in a fluffy, roughly spherical seed head, hence the plant's common name of prairie smoke.

GENERAL INFORMATION: Pasque flower was an important medicinal plant for Indian tribes of the northern Great Plains. The crushed, fresh leaves were applied over the parts of the body afflicted with rheumatism and neuralgia. Because the plant contains alkaloids which are irritating and cause blisters, it was only used externally. Yet in the early 20th century, it was included on the official list of U.S. Pharmacopeia for use as a diuretic, an expectorant and as a menstrual-inducer. For the Dakota Sioux, the plant had particular significance as it was the first flower of the growing season. They believed each species had its own song, an expression of its life or soul. The song of the pasque flower encouraged the children of other flowering nations to awaken from their winter sleep and come up from the heart of the earth.

NARROW BEARDTONGUE

PASQUE FLOWER

BLUE PRAIRIE VIOLET

Blue Prairie Violet
Viola pratincola

OTHER COMMON NAMES: Meadow violet.
FAMILY: Violet (Violaceae)
FLOWERING PERIOD: Late April through May.
DISTRIBUTION: Eastern third, principally south-east, infrequent farther west into south-central Nebraska. Southeastern Great Plains.
HABITAT: Moist to moderately dry soils; prairie, meadows, floodplains, woodland edge and openings, lawns and parks. *Principally a grass-land violet.*
DESCRIPTION: Native perennial, usually less than 10 inches tall and growing from short, thick rhizomes. Stemless. Leaves on stalks growing from root crown. Leaf blade 1.5-3 inches long and nearly as wide; highly variable in shape—*most often heart-shaped* but may be nearly triangular or nearly circular; margins usually toothed. Leaf underside and leaf stalk *not pubescent* at time of flowering. Flowers are on long stalks from the root crown, at first taller than leaves but are soon equaled or surpassed in height by them; 5 petals, medium to deep blue-violet, white with blue lines, or red-violet. Lower 3 petals with darker veins, only the *two lateral petals bearded* at the base; about .75 inch across. Base of lower petal elongated into a nectar spur.

Downy Blue Violet
Viola sororia

FAMILY: Violet (Violaceae)
FLOWERING PERIOD: Late April into June.
DISTRIBUTION: Eastern third of Nebraska, but reported farther west in northern counties. Eastern fourth of the Great Plains.
HABITAT: Rich, moist soil; *woodlands*, woodland edge, thickets, occasionally in prairie.
DESCRIPTION: Native perennial, usually less than 8 inches tall, growing from thick, short rhizomes. Stemless. Leaves on stalks growing from the root crown. The leaf blade is 1.5 inches long and nearly as wide (after flowering, leaf blades larger, up to 4 inches long); variable in shape but *most often heart-shaped;* margins usually toothed. Underside of leaf and the leaf stalk *may be pubescent* (but not always) at time of flowering; later leaves *conspicuously pubescent.* Flowers on long stalks from root crown, at first taller than the leaves but in time equal to or surpassed by them; 5 medium to dark blue-violet petals, lower 3 petals are white at base with darker veins, only the *two lateral petals are bearded* at the base; about .75 inch across. Base of lower petal elongated into a nectar spur.
GENERAL INFORMATION: The differences between several blue violets found in the Great Plains are slight. Characteristics vary within a species from site to site and many hybridize, producing intermediate forms, particularly downy blue and blue prairie violets.

DOWNY BLUE VIOLET

Prairie Violet

Viola pedatifida

OTHER COMMON NAMES: Crowfoot violet.
FAMILY: Violet (Violaceae)
FLOWERING PERIOD: Late April into June.
DISTRIBUTION: Principally eastern fourth of Nebraska, becoming infrequent farther west. Eastern fourth of Great Plains, infrequent farther west in the northern half.
HABITAT: Moist but well-drained soils; prairies, meadows.
DESCRIPTION: Native perennial, usually less than 8 inches tall, growing from a branched caudex. Stemless. Leaves growing from root crown, on stalks up to 6 inches long but typically shorter; the leaf blade is 3 inches or more wide and nearly as long, *repeatedly divided, ultimately into narrow, linear lobes;* often hairy on the veins and margins. Flowers rise above the foliage on long stalks from root crown, the stalks curving sharply downward at top; 5 deep blue petals, *all lower 3 petals are white at base and bearded;* about .75 inch across. Base of lowest petal elongated into a nectar spur.

GENERAL INFORMATION: Known to hybridize with blue prairie violet and downy blue violet, producing plants with intermediate characteristics. The only other violet in our region with dissected leaves is bird's-foot or pansy violet *(Viola pedata);* in Nebraska known only from Jefferson County but more common in the extreme southeastern Great Plains.

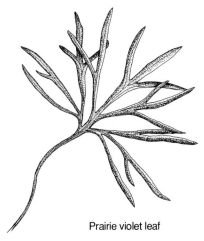

Prairie violet leaf

PRAIRIE VIOLET

VENUS' LOOKING GLASS

BLUE FLAG

Venus' Looking Glass

Triodanis perfoliata

FAMILY: Bellflower (Campanulaceae)

FLOWERING PERIOD: Late May and June.

DISTRIBUTION: Statewide in Nebraska, principally southeast. Most common in southeastern Great Plains, less frequent north and west.

HABITAT: Dry or moist, particularly sandy and gravelly, well-drained soils; disturbed sites, roadsides, along streams, pastures, woodland edge.

DESCRIPTION: Native annual. Stem erect; if branched, usually near the base; angular, leafy; often with a sparse covering of minute hairs; 1-2 feet tall, occasionally taller. Leaves alternate, broadly ovate to nearly circular with coarsely toothed margins, the bases (particularly above) clasping the stem; underside of lower leaves with coarse hairs; 1 inch or less across. Flowers at most leaf nodes, 1-3 per node; usually only one flower at each node opens, the others, and most of those growing low on the stem, remain closed, producing seeds of which few are viable. Flowers tubular, spreading to 5 pointed, petal-like lobes; deep blue-violet or deep blue; up to .5 inch long, .5 inch or slightly more across.

GENERAL INFORMATION: The origin of the name Venus' looking glass is rather obscure. Some say it is a reference to the shiny, mirror-like seeds; others attribute it to a resemblance of the rounded flower on top of its somewhat cylindrical ovary to a round mirror on a handle.

Blue Flag

Iris virginica

OTHER COMMON NAMES: Virginia iris.

FAMILY: Iris (Iridaceae)

FLOWERING PERIOD: Late May and June.

DISTRIBUTION: Extreme southeastern Nebraska, reported only from Missouri Valley counties. Southeastern Great Plains.

HABITAT: Moist to wet soils; ditches, stream and pond margins.

DESCRIPTION: Native perennial from horizontal rhizomes with fibrous roots. Leaves rise directly from the rhizomes, sheathing lower stem; usually 2-3, gray-green and sword-shaped; 16-20 inches long. Stem slender, occasionally branched above, rising above the leaves, up to 3 feet tall. One or 2 flowers above leaf-like bracts at top of stem or branches; composed of 3 petal-like sepals encircling 3 smaller petals. Sepals are spreading and recurved, blue with darker venation lines and yellow near the base; petals are narrower, erect, similarly colored but lacking yellow at base.

GENERAL INFORMATION: Even though the roots are poisonous, they were used in small amounts to induce vomiting and to purge the body of undesirable emotions by North American Indians. The only other native iris found in Nebraska is western blue flag *(Iris missouriensis)*, a wildflower of the western U.S., reported from several locations in Cheyenne and Kimball counties in the southern Panhandle.

Blue-eyed Grass
Sisyrinchium montanum

FAMILY: Iris (Iridaceae)
FLOWERING PERIOD: May and June.
DISTRIBUTION: Statewide in Nebraska except eastern fourth, more common north. Central and northern Great Plains.
HABITAT: Moist, particularly sandy soil; floodplains, meadows, low prairies.
DESCRIPTION: Native perennial growing from fibrous roots, often in tufts. A pair of wings running the full length of the stem, *wings not as broad as stem;* 8-12 inches tall. Leaves erect, basal, grass-like, less than .12 inch wide, half as tall as stem. Flowers (usually several) on slender stalks from a pair of leaf-like bracts near top of stem; 3 petals and 3 virtually identical sepals, each terminating in a sharp point; deep blue-violet or blue with darker nectar guides and bright yellow bases; about .5 inch across. The fruit is a 3-sectioned, globular capsule about .25 inch in diameter.
GENERAL INFORMATION: A similar species of blue-eyed grass, *Sisyrinchium angustifolium*, is found statewide in Nebraska and throughout the Great Plains. It has stem wings broader than the stem, wider leaves (up to .25 inch) and varies in other technical details.

BLUE-EYED GRASS

MARSH SKULLCAP

Marsh Skullcap

Scutellaria galericulata

FAMILY: Mint (Lamiaceae)

FLOWERING PERIOD: June into July.

DISTRIBUTION: Statewide in Nebraska, probably more common north. Northern two-thirds of the Great Plains.

HABITAT: Moist to wet soils; low prairies, meadows, floodplains, shorelines.

DESCRIPTION: Native perennial growing from rhizomes with fibrous roots. Stems are slender, erect or reclining on the ground, often rooting at nodes; not branched or branching above, *8-16 inches tall*, occasionally taller. Leaves on very short stalks or stalkless, opposite on stem; lanceolate with a *few shallow teeth;* 1-2 inches long and half as wide or less. Stem and leaves smooth or minutely and inconspicuously pubescent. Two flowers per leaf node, from axils of upper leaves (axillary racemes); tubular, spreading to a small upper hood and larger lower lip with an undulating margin; deep blue-violet or blue; *.5-.75 inch long.*

186

Small Skullcap
Scutellaria parvula

FAMILY: Mint (Lamiaceae)
FLOWERING PERIOD: May and June.
DISTRIBUTION: Eastern third of Nebraska, extending farther west in northern counties. Eastern third of Great Plains, principally southeast.
HABITAT: Moderately dry (but occasionally in moist soils), particularly sandy or sandy-loam soils; prairies, meadows, woodland edge.
DESCRIPTION: Native perennial growing from rhizomes with fibrous roots. Stems, 1 to several, slender, erect, not branched or branching near the base, *4-10 inches tall.* Leaves opposite on stem; ovate below becoming lanceolate above, *margins smooth, not toothed;* mostly less than .5 inch long and half as wide or less. Stem and leaves smooth or minutely and inconspicuously pubescent. Two flowers per leaf node, from the axils of upper leaves (axillary racemes); tubular, spreading to form a small upper hood and larger lower lip with an undulating margin; deep blue-violet or blue, upper surface of lower lip pale with darker spots; *.25 - .5 inch long.*
GENERAL INFORMATION: Eight skullcaps are found in the Great Plains; 4 in Nebraska, 1 of which is uncommon. A third widespread species, mad-dog skullcap *(Scutellaria lateriflora),* is only found in the eastern and central Great Plains, bears *several to many small flowers on a common stalk* (a raceme) from axils of upper leaves.

Palespike Lobelia
Lobelia spicata

FAMILY: Bellflower (Campanulaceae)
FLOWERING PERIOD: Late May into July.
DISTRIBUTION: Statewide in Nebraska except the southwest, less common west. Principally eastern and northeastern Great Plains, extending west in the Dakotas and Nebraska.
HABITAT: Moist to moderately dry, particularly sandy to sandy loam soils; prairies, meadows, lake and stream margins.
DESCRIPTION: Native perennial growing from fibrous roots. Stems slender, erect, simple or branched near base; usually pubescent, particularly below; 1-2 feet tall. Leaves alternate on the stem. Lower leaves narrowing to short stalks or essentially stalkless, oblong-lanceolate, shallowly toothed or not toothed; .75-3 inches long and less than 1 inch wide. Leaves becoming progressively smaller higher on stem, bases somewhat clasping stem, narrowly elliptic to lanceolate and eventually reduced to inconspicuous bracts on the upper portion of the stem. Flowers arranged along top of the stem or branches (in racemes); on short stalks from axils of small, leaf-like bracts. Flowers small, less than .5 inch long and about as wide; pale blue to white; tubular with two small, erect, ear-like upper lobes and 3 larger, spreading, pointed lower lobes. The flower tube is split along the upper side.

SMALL SKULLCAP

PALESPIKE LOBELIA

Silvery Lupine

Lupinus argenteus

FAMILY: Bean (Fabaceae)
FLOWERING PERIOD: June and July.
DISTRIBUTION: Nebraska Panhandle. North-western and extreme western Great Plains.
HABITAT: Dry soils in grasslands.
DESCRIPTION: Native perennial growing from a short, usually branched caudex. Stems, 1 or several, erect or angling upward; occasionally branched; sparsely to densely covered with stiff hairs; 1-2 feet tall. Leaves are alternate on the stem with 6-9 palmately arranged leaflets; on stalks shorter than leaflets to 2 times as long. Leaflets narrowly lanceolate to broadly oblong-lanceolate, 1-2 inches long; upper surface dark green, smooth or with stiff hairs; lower surface silvery-green with stiff hairs or silky pubescence. Flowers on short stalks, in a spike-like arrangement (racemes) up to 8 inches long at the top of the stem or branches; pea-like, typical of a legume. Individual parts of a flower variously colored; overall, usually blue-violet, but may be red-violet to pink and rarely white. Seeds are produced in a hairy pod .5-1 inch long.
GENERAL INFORMATION: Five lupine species are recognized from western Nebraska and the Great Plains. Small or rusty lupine *(Lupinus pusillus)* is the only annual species, partial to sandy soils and seldom exceeds 8 inches in height. On the average, Platte lupine (*Lupinus plattensis)*, is shorter than silvery lupine, less than 15 inches tall, and its banner usually has a dark purple spot. The remaining two species are considered rare.

Harebell

Campanula rotundifolia

OTHER COMMON NAMES: Fairy or witches' thimbles, bluebells of Scotland.
FAMILY: Bellflower (Campanulaceae)
FLOWERING PERIOD: Principally June.
DISTRIBUTION: Northern Panhandle and ex-treme north-central counties of Nebraska. North-ern Great Plains.
HABITAT: Moderately dry to moist soils, often in gravelly or rocky soils on meadows, stream banks and grassy openings in woodlands.
DESCRIPTION: Native perennial growing from branched rhizomes, spreading by basal shoots to form clumps. Often found in open colonies. Stems slender, 1-2 feet tall. Basal leaves mostly withered prior to time of flowering. Stem leaves stalkless, margins toothed or not, linear or nar-rowly oblong, 1-3 inches long. Flowers nod-ding, at ends of short stalks near top of stem; bell-shaped, 5 triangular lobes, blue-violet, up to .75 inch long. Flower color reported to be deeper at shaded sites.

SILVERY LUPINE

HAREBELL

Erect Dayflower

Commelina erecta

FAMILY: Spiderwort (Commelinaceae)

FLOWERING PERIOD: June, principally July, but into September.

DISTRIBUTION: Principally the Sandhills region in Nebraska. Southern half of the Great Plains.

HABITAT: Dry to moderately moist, particularly sandy soils; disturbed sites, roadsides.

DESCRIPTION: Native perennial growing from a cluster of thickened and fibrous roots. Stems more or less erect, slender, watery, branched, often reclining on other plants; up to 3 feet long but seldom more than 18 inches tall. Leaves alternate, linear, 2-4 inches long, less than .6 inch wide, clasping the stem. Flowers at ends of the branches; emerging from clasping, keel-shaped, pubescent, leaf-like bracts with red-dish-brown margins. Three petals; the upper two large (up to 1 inch across), blue-violet to blue; lower petal smaller and white. Three bright yellow, infertile, lyre-shaped anthers at the center of the flower over a large, yellow stigma; 3 fertile stamens arch downward between the two large petals. Flowers open in the morning and generally last but a few hours.

GENERAL INFORMATION: Another dayflower, *Commelina communis*, a native of Asia, is a common weed in southeastern Nebraska; frequently invading shady, moist sites, particularly in gardens and yards. The genus name *Commelina* was given by Linnaeus and is a reference to the Commeline brothers of the Netherlands, two of whom were productive botanists (represented by the two large, showy petals) and the third who died before he achieved as much as his brothers (the reduced white petal).

189

PRAIRIE-TURNIP

Prairie-turnip
Psoralea esculenta

OTHER COMMON NAMES: Indian breadroot or turnip, prairie apple or potato, *pomme de prairie* (French for "apple of the meadow").
FAMILY: Bean (Fabaceae)
FLOWERING PERIOD: May into July.
DISTRIBUTION: Statewide in Nebraska. Found throughout the Great Plains except southwest.
HABITAT: Dry to moist but well-drained, high-quality grasslands.
DESCRIPTION: Native perennial growing from a deep taproot. Root enlarged to a top-shape 2-4 inches below ground, 1-3 inches in diameter and 2-5 inches long. Stems (1-3) are erect, usually not branched and densely covered with long, white hairs; usually 6-12 inches tall, occasionally taller. Leaves alternate on stem, on hairy stalks 2-4 inches long, with 5 palmately arranged leaflets. Leaflets are elliptic, oblong-lanceolate to obovate; underside and margins sparsely covered with long white hairs, upper surface usually not; 1-2 inches long, .5 inch or less wide. Flowers are on short to long, stout stalks from leaf axils (often so long they appear to be branches from main stem); clustered in dense, hairy spikes 1-3 inches long. Flowers pea-like, deep blue or blue-violet fading to buff brown, about .5 inch long.
GENERAL INFORMATION: Soon after the seeds have ripened, the plant breaks off at ground level and tumbles across the grasslands dispersing its progeny. The starchy, turnip-like roots were a staple in the diet of most Great Plains Indian tribes. They were peeled and eaten raw or cooked, and dug in quantity and braided into strings which were hung to dry for winter use. Prairie-turnip is far less abundant today and they should not be dug.

Silver-leaf Scurf Pea
Psoralea argophylla

FAMILY: Bean (Fabaceae)
FLOWERING PERIOD: June into August.
DISTRIBUTION: Statewide in Nebraska. Found throughout Great Plains except extreme south.
HABITAT: Dry uplands of prairies and plains.
DESCRIPTION: Native perennial growing from a caudex atop a woody taproot, spreading by root buds and rhizomes. Stems usually erect, branched, sometimes zigzag in form, pubescent, 1-2 feet tall. Leaves alternate on stem, on stalks .5-1.25 inches long, with 3 or 5 palmately arranged leaflets. Leaflets lanceolate, elliptic or narrowly obovate ending in a sharp tip; silvery and silky pubescent above, silvery and densely silky pubescent below; .5-2 inches long, up to .75 inch wide. Flowers are on stalks from the axils of upper leaves, each spike with 1-5 whorls of 2-8 pea-like flowers; deep, rich blue in color; small, usually less than .25 inch across.

Wild Alfalfa

Psoralea tenuiflora

OTHER COMMON NAMES: Slender scurf pea, few-flowered psoralea or scurf pea, scurvy-pea.

FAMILY: Bean (Fabaceae)

FLOWERING PERIOD: Late May into July.

DISTRIBUTION: Statewide in Nebraska except northeast. Southern half of the Great Plains.

HABITAT: Dry uplands of prairies and plains, woodland edge and openings, roadsides.

DESCRIPTION: Native perennial growing from a caudex atop a deep taproot. Stems, 1 to several, erect, usually with many upward angling branches, 1-3 feet tall. Leaves are alternate on stem, on stalks up to .75 inch long; leaflets palmately arranged, usually 3 leaflets per leaf (5 per leaf low on stem but they are usually shed by time of flowering). Leaflets narrowly elliptic to oblong-lanceolate, usually ending in a sharp tip; .5-2 inches long and less than .3 inch wide. Upper sides of leaflets with conspicuous glandular pits. Leaves (particularly undersides) and stems with gray hairs lying flat, pressed against the surface. Flowers are in clusters (racemes) on stalks from axils of upper leaves, the stalks longer than the leaves; pea-like; blue-violet to blue; small, usually less than .3 inch long.

GENERAL INFORMATION: Two varieties are recognized. Variety *floribunda* is found in southeastern Nebraska and the southeastern Great Plains. It has more flowers per cluster and slightly larger flowers than does the variety *tenuiflora* found in the central and western portions of Nebraska and the western Great Plains. The variety shown in the photo is *floribunda*. Cultivated alfalfa is introduced from Europe and Asia.

Brooklime Speedwell
Veronica americana

FAMILY: Figwort (Scrophulariaceae)
FLOWERING PERIOD: June and July.
DISTRIBUTION: Throughout Nebraska and the Great Plains.
HABITAT: Saturated soils or in shallow, slow-moving water; sloughs, streamsides, margins of ponds, lakes and marshes.
DESCRIPTION: Native perennial growing from fibrous roots, occasionally forming mats. Lower portion of stem usually reclining on ground, rooting where lower stem nodes touch soil, then erect or angling upward; usually branched; .5-2 feet tall. *Leaves on short stalks*, opposite on stem; leaf blade lanceolate to ovate, margin shallowly toothed; .75-2 inches long, about half as wide. Flowers on stalks from the axils of upper leaves (axillary racemes), each stalk bears 10-25 flowers; 4 rounded, overlapping, petal-like lobes (the large upper lobe is 2 fused petals) spreading from a short tube; blue to light blue with darker markings at base; about .25 inch across.
GENERAL INFORMATION: Apparently the name originated in England where "speedwell" was a parting wish of good luck, similar to "godspeed," a reference to the fragile flowers of this genus which readily detach when touched.

Water Speedwell
Veronica anagallis-aquatica

FAMILY: Figwort (Scrophulariaceae)
FLOWERING PERIOD: Late May through the summer.
DISTRIBUTION: Statewide in Nebraska and throughout most of the Great Plains.
HABITAT: Wet soils or shallow, slow moving or standing water; shorelines, ditches, sandbars.
DESCRIPTION: Naturalized perennial spreading by rhizomes to form colonies. Lower portion of stem may recline on the ground (rooting where lower stem nodes touch soil) then erect or angling upward; fairly stout, not branched or branched only near base, 1-3 feet tall. Leaves opposite on the stem, *stalkless, bases clasping stem;* leaf blade lanceolate, oblong-lanceolate, elliptic or oblong; margin shallowly toothed or smooth; 1-2.5 inches long, 1 inch or less wide. Flowers on stalks from axils of upper leaves (axillary racemes), each stalk bearing 30-60 flowers. Flower is a short tube spreading to 4 petal-like lobes of unequal size; pale blue with darker markings; about .25 inch across.
GENERAL INFORMATION: Native to Europe, now widely established through temperate North America. More common than brooklime speedwell in the Great Plains.

BROOKLIME SPEEDWELL

WATER SPEEDWELL

LARGE-FLOWERED STICKSEED

Large-flowered Stickseed

Hackelia floribunda

OTHER COMMON NAMES: Beggar's lice, tall or many-flowered stickseed, false forget-me-not,
FAMILY: Borage (Boraginaceae)
FLOWERING PERIOD: June and July.
DISTRIBUTION: Nebraska Panhandle. Northwestern Great Plains.
HABITAT: Usually moist soils in partial shade; stream sides, woodland openings, thickets.
DESCRIPTION: Native biennial or perennial. Stems, 1 to several, from the same root, erect, stout, branched above, 2-5 feet tall. Leaves alternate on stem; lower leaves on short stalks, narrowly oblong-lanceolate, 2-6 inches long, less than 1 inch wide; upper leaves becoming stalkless, smaller and linear. Stems and leaves minutely hairy. Flowers in clusters (cymes) on short stalks from axils of upper leaves; tubular, the tube shorter than the 5 spreading, petal-like lobes; pale blue with a yellow ring at the mouth of the tube; about .25 inch across. Each

flower produces 4 small, shield-shaped nutlets with hook-like prickles on the margins, hence the name stickseed.
GENERAL INFORMATION: Virginia stickseed *(Hackelia virginiana)* is found in eastern Nebraska and the eastern Great Plains. Its flowers are usually smaller, about half the size of large-flowered stickseed. The nutlets of both cling to fur or clothing, transporting the seeds to establish new plants far from the parent plant.

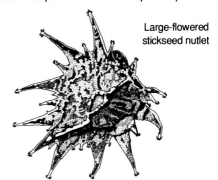

Large-flowered
stickseed nutlet

FRINGELEAF RUELLIA

Fringeleaf Ruellia
Ruellia humilis

OTHER COMMON NAMES: Wild petunia, hairy ruellia.
FAMILY: Acanthus (Acanthaceae)
FLOWERING PERIOD: June into August.
DISTRIBUTION: Southeastern Nebraska. Southeastern Great Plains.
HABITAT: Dry, or moist but well-drained soils; prairie uplands, woodland edge. Occasionally found flourishing on disturbed sites.
DESCRIPTION: Native perennial growing from a fibrous root system. Stems, 1 or more, erect; not branched early in season, branched later; stem bases often reclining on the ground; leafy; up to 2 feet tall but usually less than 1 foot. Leaves on very short stalks or stalkless, opposite on stem, usually ovate; up to 2 inches long, half as wide. Leaves (particularly the margins and the midvein) and stem sparsely covered with long white hairs. Flowers from axils of upper leaves, usually solitary; tubular, flaring widely to 5 wrinkled lobes; pale to medium blue-violet; nearly 3 inches long, up to 2 inches across. Flowers open overnight and last but one day, readily falling from the plant when handled. Late-season flowers are apparently self-fertile, the flower not opening to permit cross-pollination but still producing seeds.

Blue Lettuce
Lactuca oblongifolia

FAMILY: Sunflower (Asteraceae)
FLOWERING PERIOD: From late June through August.
DISTRIBUTION: Statewide in Nebraska. Found throughout the Great Plains, becoming rare or absent south of Kansas.
HABITAT: Rich, moist soil; ditches, low prairies, meadows, thickets, woodland edge and openings, near streams.
DESCRIPTION: Native perennial growing from a caudex atop a taproot and spreading by rhizomes. Stems, 1 to several, erect, rather slender, exuding a white, milky latex, usually not branched below inflorescence; 1-3 feet tall. Leaves alternate on stem, stalkless, variable in size and form. Lower leaves usually narrowly ovate to oblong in overall outline, but deeply incised into a few prominent and pointed lobes (somewhat resembling a dandelion's leaf); up to 5 inches long and seldom more than 1 inch wide. Middle and upper leaves linear to oblong and smaller, incised into pointed lobes like lower leaves, or with smooth margins. Flower heads borne in an open and spreading inflorescence (a panicle) at top of stem; nearly 1 inch across (the showiest native species of wild lettuce); 19-21 light blue (rarely white), strap-shaped florets, each with its own stamens and pistils. Florets on margin of head mature first, center florets last. Fruit an achene with a tuft of hairs which aid dissemination by the wind.
GENERAL INFORMATION: The most common of 3 blue-flowered species of wild lettuce in Nebraska. Positive identification can best be determined by minute differences in the achene.

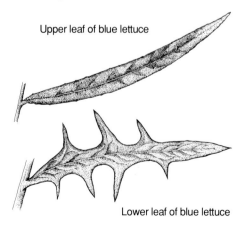

Upper leaf of blue lettuce

Lower leaf of blue lettuce

Chicory

Cichorium intybus

OTHER COMMON NAMES: Blue sailors, coffee-weed, wild succory, wild bachelor-buttons.
FAMILY: Sunflower (Asteraceae)
FLOWERING PERIOD: Flowering peaks during July, less frequent into autumn.
DISTRIBUTION: Statewide in Nebraska, most common east. Principally southeastern Great Plains.
HABITAT: On a variety of soils; disturbed sites, particularly roadsides.
DESCRIPTION: Naturalized perennial growing from a deep and often branching taproot. Stems are erect, branched, 1-3 feet tall. Leaves mostly at the base of plant; oblong-lanceolate tapering to a point, shallowly to deeply lobed and toothed, somewhat like a dandelion's; 3-10 inches long and 1-3 inches wide. Leaves sparse, smaller and reduced to bracts on upper plant. Numerous flower heads are borne singly or in clusters from axils of small leaves; composed entirely of strap-shaped ray florets (no central disk florets), each with 5 teeth on the outer margin; usually blue-violet but occasionally more pinkish, rarely white; 1-1.5 inches across. Flower heads open early in morning and on hot, bright days close before noon.

GENERAL INFORMATION: Introduced from Europe and Asia. Its roots can be roasted and ground for use as a coffee additive or extender. In Europe its leaves are valued as a salad green and potherb. Reportedly used medicinally by the Romans for ailments of the liver, kidneys and stomach, and for jaundice.

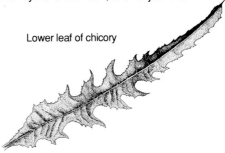

Lower leaf of chicory

Lead Plant

Amorpha canescens

OTHER COMMON NAMES: Prairie or devil's shoestrings, wild tea.

FAMILY: Bean (Fabaceae)

FLOWERING PERIOD: Late June through July.

DISTRIBUTION: Statewide in Nebraska, becoming infrequent in Panhandle. Throughout the Great Plains, infrequent or absent west.

HABITAT: Found on a variety of well-drained soils; prairies, roadsides.

DESCRIPTION: Native perennial shrub growing from extensive, deep (up to 16 feet), tough, woody rootstocks, often spreading by rhizomes. Usually several stems, often branched, 1-3 feet tall; young stems are white with pubescence, the lower stems becoming woody with age. Leaves alternate on stem, odd-pinnately compound, 2-4 inches long. Leaflets oblong to elliptic, 13 to 20 pairs plus an unpaired leaflet at the tip; usually less than .5 inch long; silvery green, densely covered with short, whitish hairs.

Many small, single-petal, dull red-violet to blue flowers with protruding yellow stamens densely clustered on 2-4 inch long, spike-like stalks (racemes) rising from axils of upper leaves. The central flower stalk is the longest and flowers the earliest.

GENERAL INFORMATION: Lead plant is a palatable and nutritious livestock forage which decreases under heavy grazing pressure. Great Plains Indians dried green leaves for smoking and for making tea. The Omaha-Ponca called it "buffalo bellow plant," because buffalo would soon be coming into rut, the bulls bellowing, when it was in flower. Its pioneer name, prairie shoestrings, is a melancholy reminder of the endless miles of grassland which have been plowed under. Its stout roots, which spread extensively just below the soil surface, resisted, stretched and then snapped like a breaking shoestring when they were severed by a sod-breaking plow. The name devil's shoestrings attests to the difficulty the roots caused settlers breaking-out native prairie.

LEAD PLANT

AMERICAN BELLFLOWER

196

Blue Lobelia
Lobelia siphilitica

OTHER COMMON NAMES: Blue cardinal flower, great or big lobelia.
FAMILY: Bellflower (Campanulaceae)
FLOWERING PERIOD: Principally August and September.
DISTRIBUTION: Statewide in Nebraska. Central and eastern Great Plains, becoming less common farther west.
HABITAT: Moist to wet, particularly sandy loam soils; meadows, floodplains, low prairies, margins of streams, ponds and lakes.
DESCRIPTION: Native perennial growing from strong fibrous roots. Stems erect, stiff, simple or branched near the base; sparsely hairy or smooth; 1-2 feet or more tall. Leaves alternate on the stem; stalkless, upper leaves sometimes clasping stem; lanceolate to oblong-lanceolate; margins with small, irregularly spaced teeth; 2-6 inches long and usually less than 1 inch wide. Flowers are arranged along top of the stem or branches (racemes) on short stalks from axils of bracts shorter than the flowers. Flower is tubular, split on upper side, flaring to an erect, divided, 2-lobed upper lip, a spreading 3-lobed lower lip; 1 inch or more long. Flower deep blue to blue-violet; lower portion of tube with white stripes.
GENERAL INFORMATION: Although it contains the toxic compound lobeline, medicines prepared from blue lobelia were believed to be a cure for syphilis, hence the species name.

American Bellflower
Campanula americana

OTHER COMMON NAMES: Tall bellflower, bluebell.
FAMILY: Bellflower (Campanulaceae)
FLOWERING PERIOD: Principally July, less frequently throughout the summer.
DISTRIBUTION: Eastern Nebraska, occasionally farther west, as along the Niobrara River. Southeastern Great Plains.
HABITAT: Moist to wet soils, usually in partial shade; ditches, streamsides, woods, thickets.
DESCRIPTION: Native annual or biennial. A robust, erect, leafy plant with a moderately stout stem, 3-6 feet tall; not branched or sparingly so midstem and higher. Leaves alternate on stem, lanceolate to ovate-oblong, 3-6 inches long with finely toothed margins and bristly with

BLUE LOBELIA

short hairs. Flowers on short stalks and closely hugging the elongating, spike-like upper stem. Each flower about 1 inch across; 5 pointed petals fused at the base and spreading widely at maturity; blue-violet, blue or red-violet with a white center. An unusually long style (the neck of the pistil) protrudes from the flower center, curving gently downward before arching abruptly up. Flowers seem to bloom in random order along the flower stalk.
GENERAL INFORMATION: The genus name *Campanula* is from the Latin *campana*, meaning "little bell," a reference more appropriately describing the flower shape of other species of the genus than the flat-faced, mature flower of American bellflower. Stamens of an individual blossom shed their pollen even before the flower fully opens. After the stamens shrivel and the flower opens, the protruding style elongates and stigma lobes spread to receive pollen brought by insects which have visited less mature flowers bearing pollen, ensuring cross-pollination.

197

Downy Gentian
Gentiana puberulenta

OTHER COMMON NAMES: Prairie gentian.
FAMILY: Gentian (Gentianaceae)
FLOWERING PERIOD: Late August through September.
DISTRIBUTION: North-central and eastern third of Nebraska. Eastern fourth of the Great Plains, found sporadically farther west in Nebraska and the Dakotas.
HABITAT: Dry to moderately moist soils; prairie uplands, woodland edge. An indicator of high-quality grasslands.
DESCRIPTION: Native perennial growing from a taproot with thick lateral roots. Stems, 1 to several, from a common root, erect, stiff, usually not branched and usually less than 1.5 feet tall. Leaves numerous, opposite on stem, stalkless to somewhat clasping the stem, firm to stiff, lanceolate to oblong-lanceolate, less than 2 inches long and half as wide. Flowers erect, crowded in a cluster at top of the stem; funnel-shaped, usually 5 prominent, pointed, reflexed lobes alternating with shorter and ragged-edged lobes; deep blue-violet to blue; up to 1.5 inches long. The flower's stigma does not fully develop until the anthers have shriveled, thus ensuring cross-pollination. Large, yellow anthers on *filaments not fused to petals*. Flowers open mid-morning and close in evening or may not open at all on cloudy days. Each flower opens and closes for several days before withering.
GENERAL INFORMATION: The name gentian refers to Gentius, 2nd century B.C. king of Illyria, who is credited with recommending European yellow gentian as a cure for bubonic plague. The plant was known as "blue-blossom medicine" by the Winnebago, "yellow medicine" by the Dakota (because of the color of the roots). Preparations of the root were used as a general tonic.

Closed Gentian
Gentiana andrewsii

OTHER COMMON NAMES: Bottle, barrel, blind or cloistered gentian.
FAMILY: Gentian (Gentianaceae)
FLOWERING PERIOD: Late August through September.
DISTRIBUTION: Principally north-central and northeastern Nebraska but reported nearly to Kansas border. Northern half of Great Plains.
HABITAT: Moist to wet soils, full sun or partial shade; low prairies, meadows and shorelines.
DESCRIPTION: Native perennial. Stems, usually several from a common root, erect, fairly stout, not branched, 1-2 feet tall. Leaves opposite on stem, stalkless; lanceolate to lance-ovate; 1-4 inches long and 1 inch or less wide. Leaves and stem are usually smooth, at least not noticeably pubescent. Flowers in clusters of 3-5 at top of the stem above a whorl of 4-6 leaves and singly or as pairs from the axils of upper leaves; flower lobes closed, forming a tube which never opens; blue with darker blue, parallel stripes (rarely white); 1-2 inches long.
GENERAL INFORMATION: Bumblebees are strong enough to force their way into the flower tube and accomplish cross-pollination. Some botanists believe the flowers are self-fertile. Apparently, closed gentian was once a fairly common wildflower in Sandhills wet meadows. Annual summer mowing, preventing seed production, has probably contributed to a decline in the abundance of this late-flowering species.

DOWNY GENTIAN

CLOSED GENTIAN

PRAIRIE GENTIAN

Prairie Gentian

Eustoma grandiflorum

OTHER COMMON NAMES: Russell's or catch-fly gentian.

FAMILY: Gentian (Gentianaceae)

FLOWERING PERIOD: Late June into August. Prairie gentian has usually finished flowering before other gentians begin.

DISTRIBUTION: Potentially statewide in Nebraska on appropriate sites. Infrequent northeast and absent southeast. Frequently encountered in the Platte Valley. Southern half of the Great Plains.

HABITAT: Moist, particularly sandy or sandy-loam soils. Floodplains, meadows, low prairies and pastures. Usually not found on heavy clay or loess soils. Not grazed by cattle and so may be conspicuous in pastures.

DESCRIPTION: Native annual or short-lived perennial growing from a taproot. Stems erect, 1 to several from a common root, branched above, 10-16 inches or more tall. Leaves op-posite on stem, stalkless, upper leaves some-what clasping stem; broadly lanceolate to nar-rowly ovate or elliptic; 1-2.5 inches long, up to 1 inch wide. Leaves and stem blue-green with a smooth surface and a *whitish waxy bloom* as found on plums. Flowers are upright, solitary at ends of long, erect stalks from short branches near top of plant; broadly bell-shaped with 5-6 distinct petals which spread widely; color vari-able (white, pink or yellow) but usually blue-violet to red-violet, darker at flower center; up to 2 inches across and long. Large, prominent, yellow anthers on *filaments fused to lower por-tion of petals;* large, 2-lobed yellow stigma. The stigma not fully developed until the flower's an-thers have shriveled, ensuring cross-pollination.

GENERAL INFORMATION: Differentiated from other gentians of the genus *Gentiana* in that its foliage is covered with a white waxy bloom and the lobes of its flower tube are distinctly sepa-rate, not joined by a folded pleat. Cultivars of this genus have recently become available from commercial nurseries.

AZURE ASTER

Azure Aster

Aster oolentangiensis

OTHER COMMON NAMES: Sky-blue aster.

FAMILY: Sunflower (Asteraceae)

FLOWERING PERIOD: September and October.

DISTRIBUTION: Southeastern Nebraska. Southeastern Great Plains.

HABITAT: Dry to moderately moist soils; prairies, woodland openings and edge, bluffs, roadsides.

DESCRIPTION: Native perennial growing from a branching caudex or short rhizome. Stems erect, with ascending, spreading branches on upper half; 2-3 feet or more tall. Leaves thick and firm, hairy, with smooth margins or sometimes with minute serrations; the *lower leaves heart-shaped (cordate) on long stalks*, blades 2-6 inches long, .5-1.5 inches wide, but mostly shed by the time of flowering; upper leaves on short stalks, lanceolate to ovate and becoming smaller, narrower and stalkless higher on the plant. The *inflorescence is open, branched and spreading.* Flower heads .5-.8 inch across; usually composed of 13-18 blue-violet to blue (less commonly pink or red-violet as in photo) petal-like ray florets surrounding a center of yellow disk florets.

Blue Sage

Salvia azurea

OTHER COMMON NAMES: Pitcher sage or salvia.

FAMILY: Mint (Lamiaceae)

FLOWERING PERIOD: Late July and August, into September.

DISTRIBUTION: Principally southeastern Nebraska but at least as far west as Franklin County. Southeastern Great Plains.

HABITAT: Dry to well-drained moist grasslands; roadsides, pastures.

DESCRIPTION: Native perennial growing from a thick caudex with fibrous roots. Stems, 1 to several, erect; if branched at all, principally near the top; 2-5 feet tall. Leaves recurved, on short stalks up to .5 inch long. Lower leaves usually shed before flowering; midstem leaves opposite, narrowly elliptic becoming linear above, margins smooth or toothed; up to 3 inches long, less than .75 inch wide. Stem and leaves finely to sparsely pubescent. Flowers clustered in whorls about the top of the stem and branches in spike-like inflorescences; medium blue-violet to deep blue (rarely white); .5-1 inch long; tubular, spreading into an upper lip forming a small hood and a large, broad, lower lip which appears to be 4-lobed. The style is densely hairy.

New England Aster

Aster novae-angliae

FAMILY: Sunflower (Asteraceae)

FLOWERING PERIOD: Late August through October.

DISTRIBUTION: Eastern and north-central Nebraska. Eastern third of the Great Plains.

HABITAT: Moist, often sandy soil; margins of streams and ponds, ditches, roadsides, woodland edge.

DESCRIPTION: Native perennial growing from a branched caudex or stout rhizome, occasionally spreading to form colonies by creeping rhizomes. Stems stiff, erect, leafy, coarsely hairy; usually in clusters; branching on upper half; 4-5 feet or more tall. Leaves lanceolate to oblong, the *bases clasping the stem*, smooth margins, covered with small, stiff hairs; 1-3.5 inches long, less than half as wide. Lower leaves often shed before flowering. Numerous flower heads, 1-1.5 inches across; composed of 30-50 pink to rose, but most frequently blue-violet or deep blue, petal-like ray florets surrounding a center of yellow to orange disk florets. As in all asters, both the ray and disk florets are fertile and produce achenes.

GENERAL INFORMATION: New England aster is the Great Plains' largest-flowered and showiest native aster. Easily established on appropriate sites by raking the pappus-borne seeds (achenes) into the soil surface in the fall.

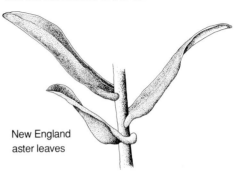

New England aster leaves

BLUE SAGE

NEW ENGLAND ASTER

201

Glossary

Achene: A small, dry, hard, one-seeded fruit; often with hairs or bristles which aid dispersal. See page 158.

Alternate: A single leaf at a stem node. Consecutive leaves at different positions on the stem and typically on opposite sides.

Annual: A plant completing its life cycle in one year. Also see "winter annual."

Anther: The enlarged, terminal part of the stamen which bears pollen.

Ascending: The tip rising, as a branch.

Axil: The upper, inside angle where a leaf joins the stem, from which flower stalks often emerge.

Banner: The upper, often erect petal of a flower in the bean family.

Basal: Rising directly from underground parts, as leaves.

Biennial: A plant completing its life cycle in two years; usually not flowering until the second year.

Blade: The broad portion of a leaf or leaflet, beyond the leaf stalk (petiole) if one is present.

Bract: Small, modified leaf-like structure, green or colored, usually found below a flower.

Bulb: A short, enlarged, underground stem covered with scaly leaves like an onion or with fleshy scales as a lily.

Calyx: The outer circle of sepals on a flower; usually green, sometimes petal-like and colored; may be separate or joined.

Caudex: The tough, persistent, usually enlarged base of a stem at or below ground level.

Clasping: A leaf with a base wrapping at least partially around the stem. See page 201.

Compound leaf: A leaf divided into smaller leaf-like leaflets.

Compound umbel: An inflorescence in which stalks radiate out from the same point, each of those stalks bearing its own umbel of flowers.

Corm: The thick, solid, bulb-like underground stem covered with thin, papery leaves, as in spring beauty. Not layered or scaly like a bulb.

Corolla: The flower structures immediately surrounding the stamens, usually the petals considered collectively.

Corymb: A more or less flat-topped inflorescence with individual flower stalks rising from different points on the central stalk; the *outer flowers blooming first.*

Cyme: An inflorescence terminating in a *single, central flower which blooms before the lateral flowers,* often compoundly branched into a flat-topped or rounded shape.

Disk: The button-like center of a flower head. Found in plants of the sunflower family. Composed of numerous tiny, tubular disk florets, typically surrounded by a circle of ray florets.

Disk florets: Small, tubular, usually fertile flowers clustered on the central disk of flower heads in the sunflower family.

Filament: The stalk of a stamen, usually slender and thread-like.

Flower head: A compact, crowded cluster of stalkless flowers (or with inconspicuous stalks), as found on sunflowers or asters.

Floret: A single, typically small flower, especially as found in the flower head of plants in the sunflower family. Parts of the floret may look like a petal.

Forb: Any non-grass-like herbaceous plant. Most wildflowers in this book are forbs.

Herb: Non-woody plants which die or "die back" to ground level each year. Includes grasses.

Herbage: Stems and leaves considered collectively.

Inflorescence: The flowering part of a plant considered as a whole.

Keel: The two united, boat-shaped, lower petals of flowers of the bean family.

Leaflet: A leaf-like division of a compound leaf.

Legume: A plant belonging to the pea or bean family; producing seeds in two-parted pods; the roots of which often bear nodules containing nitrogen-fixing bacteria.

Lobed: A leaf with indented margins leaving rounded lobes. Particularly one divided more than halfway to the midrib.

Midrib: The central vein of a leaf or leaflet.

Naturalized: Not native to an area but introduced and persisting on its own.

Node: A stem joint, often swollen, from which leaves arise.

Opposite: Two leaves at a stem node, opposite one another.

Ovary: The swollen base of the pistil where seeds develop.

Palmate: Spreading like fingers from the palm of the hand. Used to describe the arrangement of leaflets, leaf lobes or leaf veins.

Panicle: A compound inflorescence in which flower groupings are borne on side branches from a main stalk, the lower branches usually longer.

Pappus: Hairs or bristles attached to an achene which aid in seed dispersal. Found in the sunflower family as on thistles or dandelion. See page 158.

Perennial: A plant with a life cycle of 3 years or more.

Petal: An individual segment of the corolla. Usually colored. May be separate or fused into a tubular funnel or bell shape.

Petiole: The stalk of a leaf.

Pinnate leaf: A compound leaf made up of leaflets arranged in rows along the leaf stalk.

Pistil: The female organ of a flower composed of a swollen ovary at the base, a stalk (the style) and a knobbed tip (the stigma) which receives pollen.

Pubescent: Covered with fine, soft or downy hairs.

Raceme: An elongated inflorescence with a central stalk on which flowers are borne singly, *each on its own stalk*. Flowers low on the stalk generally mature before those at tip.

Ray florets: Small flowers encircling the central disk of flower heads in the sunflower family. Often colored and petal-like. Often infertile.

Rhizome: An underground stem, usually growing parallel to the ground surface and giving rise to roots and new plants from nodes.

Rosette: Basal leaves radiating out in a circle, as a dandelion.

Runner: An above ground, horizontal, creeping stem which occasionally roots and establishes new plants. A stolon.

Sepal: Usually a small, green, modified leaf found on the rim of a flower, outside of the petals. A part of the calyx. May be colored and showy, as in pasque flower.

Spadix: A club-shaped, often fleshy spike on which small flowers are crowded. Characteristic of the arum family to which Jack-in-the-pulpit belongs.

Spathe: A leaf-like hood or sheath enclosing an inflorescence or spadix.

Spike: Slender, elongated inflorescence with central stalk on which *stalkless flowers* are borne singly.

Spur: A horn-shaped, modified petal or sepal which contains nectar, as on prairie larkspur.

Stamen: The male organ of a flower composed of a slender stalk (the filament) and a terminal, knobby anther which bears pollen. Usually several per flower.

Stigma: The tip of the pistil where pollen is received. Often knobby, divided and sticky.

Stipule: Small leaf-like appendages (usually in pairs) at the base of a leaf stalk. See page 79.

Stolon: Stem shoots which recline on the surface of the soil and periodically root. A runner.

Style: The stalk of the pistil. The part of the pistil joining the stigma and ovary.

Taproot: A vertical root, usually thickened; as a carrot.

Tepal: Used to describe petals and sepals when they are similar, as with lilies.

Thyrse: A compact, cylindric to tapering panicle with flowers in distinct clusters around the stem, each flower on its own stalk. The typical flower arrangement of penstemons and mints.

Tuber: The enlarged end of an underground stem, usually rounded and fleshy, in which food is stored. As in Jerusalem artichoke.

Umbel: An inflorescence in which each flower stalk radiates out from the same point, like the ribs of an umbrella. May be compound.

Whorl: Three or more leaves arising from the same stem node.

Wing: A thin, membranous flap extending along a seed, leaf stalk or stem. See page 159.

Wings: The side petals of a flower in the bean family.

Winter annual: A small plant produced from seed in late summer or fall and overwintering underground; flowering and dying during the next growing season.

Illustrated Glossary

Leaf Shape

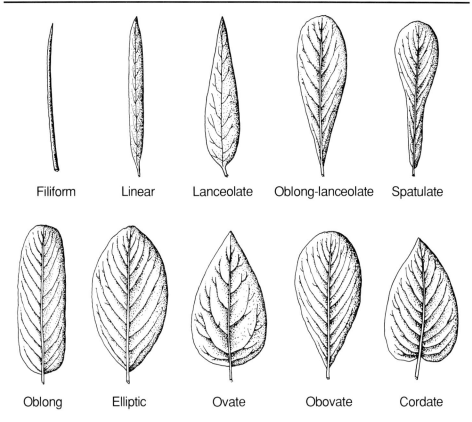

Filiform   Linear   Lanceolate   Oblong-lanceolate   Spatulate

Oblong   Elliptic   Ovate   Obovate   Cordate

Leaf Margins

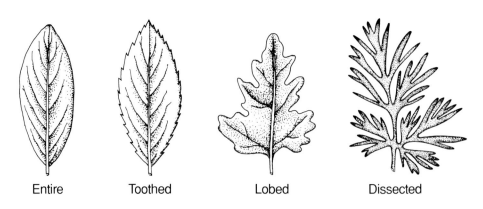

Entire   Toothed   Lobed   Dissected

Leaf Types

Simple leaf (feather venation) Simple leaf (parallel venation) Palmate

Even-pinnately compound Odd-pinnately compound Bipinnately compound

Leaf Arrangements

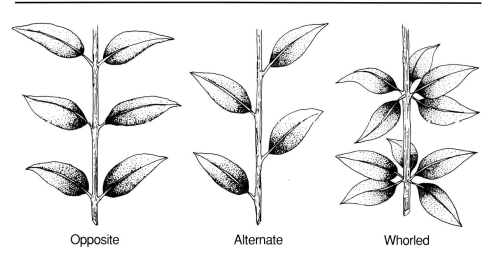

Opposite Alternate Whorled

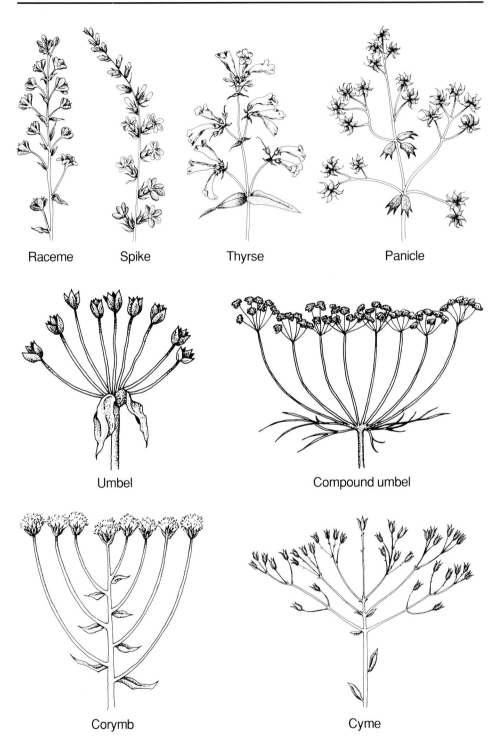

Raceme   Spike   Thyrse   Panicle

Umbel   Compound umbel

Corymb   Cyme

Flower Types

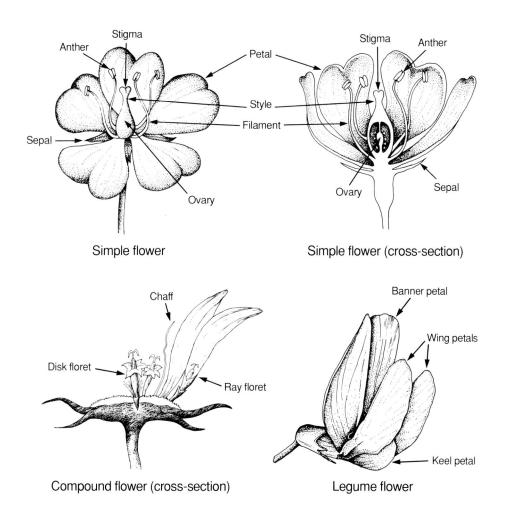

Simple flower

Simple flower (cross-section)

Compound flower (cross-section)

Legume flower

Modified Stems

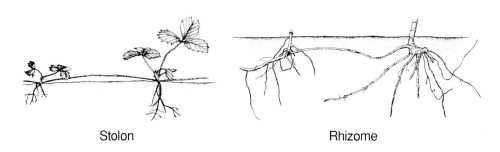

Stolon

Rhizome

Underground Parts

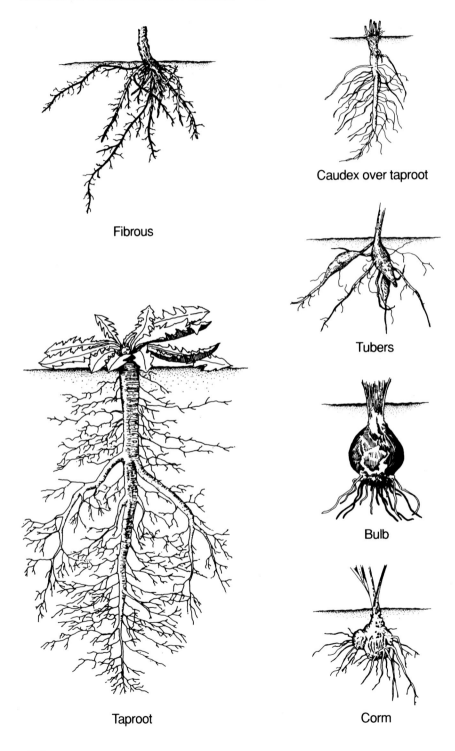

Fibrous

Caudex over taproot

Tubers

Bulb

Taproot

Corm

Additional References

Bare, J.E. 1979. **Wildflowers and Weeds of Kansas**. Regents Press of Kansas, Lawrence, Kansas.

Barr, Claude A. 1983. **Jewels of the Plains**. University of Minnesota Press, Minneapolis, Minnesota.

Craighead, John J., Frank C. Craighead and Ray J. Davis. 1963. **A Field Guide to Rocky Mountain Wildflowers**. Houghton Mifflin Co., Boston, Massachusetts.

Gilmore, Melvin R. 1977. **Uses of Plants by the Indians of the Missouri River Region**. University of Nebraska Press, Lincoln, Nebraska.

Kindscher, Kelly. 1987. **Edible Wild Plants of the Prairie**. University Press of Kansas, Lawrence, Kansas.

Lommasson, R.C. 1973. **Nebraska Wild Flowers**. University of Nebraska Press, Lincoln, Nebraska.

McGregor, R.L. and T.M. Barkley (Eds.). 1986. **Flora of the Great Plains**. University Press of Kansas, Lawrence, Kansas.

Moyle, John B. and Evelyn W. Moyle. 1977. **Northland Wild Flowers, A Guide for the Minnesota Region**. University of Minnesota Press, Minneapolis.

Peterson, Roger Tory and McKenny, Margaret. 1968. **A Field Guide to Wildflowers of Northeastern and North-central North America**. Houghton Mifflin Co., Boston, Massachusetts.

Rock, Harold W. 1981. **Prairie Propagation Handbook**. 6th edition. Hales Corners, Wisconsin: Wehr Nature Center.

Runkel, Sylvan and Alvin F. Bull. 1987. **Wildflowers of Iowa Woodlands**. Iowa State University Press, Ames, Iowa.

Runkel, Sylvan and Dean M. Roosa. 1989. **Wildflowers of the Tallgrass Prairie: the Upper Midwest**. Iowa State University Press, Ames, Iowa.

Smith, J. Robert and Beatrice Smith. 1980. **The Prairie Garden — 70 Native Plants You Can Grow in Town or Country**. The University of Wisconsin Press, Madison Wisconsin.

Stubbendieck, J., Elverne C. Conard. 1989. **Common Legumes of the Great Plains**. University of Nebraska Press, Lincoln, Nebraska.

Stubbendieck, J., Stephan L. Hatch and Kathie J. Hirsch. 1986. **North American Range Plants**. University of Nebraska Press, Lincoln, Nebraska.

Stubbendieck, J., James T. Nichols and Charles H. Butterfield. 1989. **Nebraska Range and Pasture Forbs and Shrubs**. University of Nebraska, Institute of Agriculture and Natural Resources.

Van Bruggen, Theodore. 1983. **Wildflowers, Grasses and Other Plants of the Northern Plains and Black Hills**. Badlands Natural History Association, Interior, South Dakota.

Vance, F.R., J.R. Jowsey and J.S. McLean. 1984. **Wildflowers of the Northern Great Plains**. University of Minnesota Press, Minneapolis, Minnesota.

Weaver, J.E. 1965. **Native Vegetation of Nebraska**. University of Nebraska Press, Lincoln, Nebraska. (out of print)

Weaver, J.E. and T.J. Fitzpatrick. 1934. **The Prairie**. Reissued by Prairie/Plains Resource Institute, Aurora, Nebraska. 1980.

Photo Credits

Unless otherwise credited below, photos by Jon Farrar.
Greg Beaumont: 21 left; Ken Bouc: 72 bottom, 143 left; Don Cunningham: 24 left, 153 left.
Mike Fritz: 184 right; Bob Grier: 47, 178 right; Rocky Hoffmann: 17 right, 113 right, 146 top.
Chris Mercer: 25.

Index